The General Who Never Was

The Armorial Bearings on the title page are the author's. They are composed of the Arms of Carmichael, Earls of Hyndford, and of Galloway, Barons Dunkeld, confirmed to the descendants of George Galloway, by his wife Janet, daughter of Andrew Carmichael (married November 26, 1763) by Letters Patent from Her Majesty's Court of the Lord Lyon, Edinburgh, and matriculated in the Public Register of All Arms and Bearings in Scotland with congruent differences according to the Laws of Arms.

THE GENERAL
Who Never Was

by
Strome Galloway

Mika Publishing Company
Belleville, Ontario
1981

To
My Grandson
Robert William Andrew Blackburn

ISBN 0-919303-54-4

Printed and bound in Canada

The Author, Ortona, Italy, January, 1944.

Contents

CHAPTER I

THE GENERAL SPEAKS OUT

In June 1970, about a year after my retirement from the Regular Army, having reached the age limit for my rank, there arrived by morning post one day an official looking piece of mail addressed to Brigadier-General A.S.A. Galloway, ED, CD. It was a reminder that it was my "duty to report any change of address to Canadian Forces Headquarters."

This was no particular surprise. I knew that my name was on the Supplementary Reserve of Officers List and would remain there until either I died or reached the prescribed age of removal — whichever event took place first. In those days Supplementary Reserve officers were — and perhaps still are — considered available for recall to active duty in a national emergency, such as an outbreak of war, when an immediate increase in the nation's military forces is needed.

By 1970 Canada's army was in a sorry state. For the previous six years its organization, administration and training had been chaotic. This had been brought about by the defense policy initiated by Prime Minister Lester B. Pearson, a singularly misguided Liberal politician aided and abetted by an overly ambitious and militarily ignorant Minister of National Defense named Paul Hellyer. Between them they produced the shambles in which the Canadian Army found itself by the time I retired from professional soldiering.

As it happened, I was to devote another ten years to the military cause. I was offered and I accepted the appointment of Honorary Lieutenant-Colonel of the Governor General's Foot Guards, a militia unit concerned not only with normal training for war, but with certain ceremonial duties in connection with the Vice-regal Household in Ottawa. This kept me in fairly close touch with the military establishment, such as it had become, and meant that I did not have to hang up my sword for all time until 1979. And this allows me to lay claim to more than 47 years of continuous military service, both pensionable and non-pensionable.

The background to the army's sad condition in 1970 was a syndrome of two hundred years of Canadian history. But it was crystallized by the British *débâcle* at Suez in 1956. With Suez went the old idea of imperial commitments for Canada's soldiers, sailors and airmen. With Suez their role as "empire troops" finally disappeared. It had been the British tradition which had sent thousands of Canadians hurrying across the Atlantic in two world wars, and to serve under British command in the Boer War; to join the Commonwealth Division at the time of the United Nations' action in Korea fifty years later, and even to serve as part of Britain's Rhine Army during the first nineteen years of NATO. Indeed, it was really the British tradition which saw Canadian troops proposed as peacekeepers between Britain and Egypt at Suez. It was a brash offer to help the Motherland out of a mess.

But the Suez brought personal humiliation to Lester B. Pearson, Canada's Secretary of State for External Affairs. When he became Prime Minister some six years later, he initiated a defense policy designed to give the armed forces a new Canadian role, and a new Canadian look. Unification of the three fighting services was the method by which he chose to do this. In the years between Suez and Pearson's rise to power the Royal Canadian Navy, the Canadian Army with its units steeped in British lore, and the Royal Canadian Air Force survived. But their British configuration and attitudes spelled eventual doom. By 1970 none of them existed.

The Pearson policy was put into effect under Paul Hellyer. In eighteen days he wrote in longhand a *White Paper* which set forth an entirely new defense philosophy and devised an entirely new defense organization to support it. The role of global peacekeeping would be accepted by Canada, and to carry it out there would be one Service only.

There were other things which stimulated his facile pen. There was the mounting tide of French-Canadian aspirations; there was the post-war Americanization of Canadian life; there was a tendency to disenchantment with the British way of doing things. Everywhere the new-found consciousness of French Canada pricked and nudged those in authority. Everywhere the gigantic American presence dominated Canadian thinking — especially among the nation's youth. Britain no longer held the same appeal or affection as it had in the past. Hellyer decided to capitalize on all of these things.

Unification would make it easy to jettison British uniforms, British titles, British attitudes. In this surreptitious manner the Royal Canadian Navy, and the Royal Canadian Air Force would disappear. This in itself would be a move toward a truly North American environment. Both the French-speaking and the American-oriented English-speaking members of the Forces would be pleased. Those who were not pleased could leave their Service if they wished. Many did. To have any future in the new green-uniformed amalgam, the individual had to "get with it". There were rewards for those who did. Double promotions were not unknown. For "personal reasons" admirals, generals and air marshals began to retire before their time. So did numerous colonels, majors and lesser ranks. No one was hindered in this exodus. It made way for Hellyer's followers.

Canada had become a British colony in 1763 when some seventy thousand French colonists became unwilling subjects of King George III. Two centuries later, by natural increase, their population reached the staggering figure of five and a half million. This compared with eight million Canadians of British descent and five million more of other ethnic origins. Wartime industrialization of French Canada in the 1940s had resulted in urbanization and rising educational standards. A once largely localized race of *habitants* gained new vigour and broader horizons. With this came new ambitions, a demand for language recognition, cultural acceptance and equality of opportunity with the English-speaking establishment. The "revenge of the cradle" had finally arrived.

Meanwhile, two centuries of British tradition had saved Canada's English-speaking population from cultural and political absorption by the swelling millions in the adjacent United States. Having always managed to maintain a numerical superiority of ten-to-one over Canada, this populous neighbour poured its literature, its motion pictures and its radio programmes into the narrow strip of inhabited Canada for successive generations. By the mid-1950s television cascaded the American way of life and a sense of American values into every Canadian home. Because of this situation and the fact that well over half the population were now of non-British origin, resistance by the old order began to crumble.

Canada was at the crossroads. Having ceased to be British, it was in immediate danger of becoming American. In desperation it decided to try its best to become *Canadian*. Only in the armed forces, always guilty of some degree of anachronism, did the British myth continue and the old commandments stand. But they could not stand for long. And Suez provided the moment in time which was necessary to end them.

When Britain and France became entangled in Egypt, Canada offered the United Nations the use of Canadian troops to help restore the international equilibrium, and also, it was said, with the idea that such action might stay the disintegration of the Commonwealth. By a twist of fate the unit alerted for immediate dispatch was a battalion of the Queen's Own Rifles of Canada. The unit was readied. Aircraft and shipping were assembled to transport Canada's peacekeeping troops to the scene of their proposed triumph. But it was not to be. In Cairo, the long nose of President Nasser smelled a rat. It occurred to the President that the name of the would-be peacekeepers seemed uncommonly like the names borne by the very troops he wanted ejected from Egyptian soil. How could the Queen's men from Canada be unbiased in their dealings with the Queen's men from England? That they would come to his country bearing the U.N. flag meant little. It appeared to be just another imperialistic trick. Lester Pearson's offer was rejected, and in this rejection was born the idea of the need for a Canadian military machine which must be unmistakably *Canadian*.

The Suez peacekeeping proposal had also shown that the three Services could not have combined their skills with enough speed and accord to mount the operation in the time required by its concept. Clearly, thought some, if Canada's future military role was to be that of a global peacekeeper, then a unified, distinctively uniformed force was needed. As the Suez episode was studied, the outline for Paul Hellyer's 1964 *White Paper* began to take shape.

It was eight years before the effects of Suez were felt by Canada's three Services. As a first step, the Chiefs of Staff Committee was abolished and a single Chief of Defense Staff was appointed. Then the three Services were abolished and the Canadian Armed Forces were set up on a functional basis with a Mobile Command, a Training Command, a Material Command, a Maritime Command, an Air Transport Command and an Air Defense Command. For several years the mammoth upheaval continued. Confusion boiled like a witch's brew, but eventually four banners floated above the bubbling surface. These were the defense priorities of a "clear statement of policy" which the defense authority had written about. They were Peacekeeping, NATO, North American Air Defense and Canada itself, in that order. Four years later these priorities were reversed. The reason was obvious. Although Paul Hellyer's *White Paper* had also promised that unification would mean immense savings in defense dollars, it now developed that this was a pipe-dream. Instead of saving money, unification devoured it. There was no possible way that the defense budget could look after the sophisticated equipment for the imaginative peacekeeping role of the Pearson government. Neither would there be enough money to keep the NATO brigade in Germany in fighting condition. There were other needs for the nation's taxpayers to take care of, such as the huge bilingualism programme and its subsidiary expenses. There was money needed to be pumped into underdeveloped countries, including Canada's own province of Quebec, bursting at the seams with people plagued by unemployment.

Following the Suez rebuff, some Canadian administrative troops had been accepted as part of the United Nations Emergency Force in the Gaza Strip. After ten years in situ this force was ejected by Nasser, causing them to depart in a most unceremonious way. Later, Canadian peacekeepers went to Cyprus, a commitment still being fulfilled in 1981. At the moment, it takes Canada some thirteen days of trooping to relieve one battalion with another in that unhappy Mediterranean island. The Pearson vision of a highly mobile group of Canadian peacekeepers cracking about the globe like Superman has never been realized.

For nineteen years Canada maintained a British-oriented mechanized brigade group of 6000 men in Europe. Another 6000 men made up an air division, also under NATO command. Then these 12,000 were cut to some 5000, of whom only 2800 were land troops. This tiny land force was moved into Southern Germany, out of the British zone of influence and into that of the Americans. Canada's European defense stance became a pitiful one, especially since Hellyer's *White Paper* foresaw "bolstering our contribution" to NATO as one of the results of his bizarre unification programme.

In 1962 Canada had 120,000 regular soldiers, sailors and airmen, which constituted a peacetime peak for the three Services. By 1970 this had shrunk to less than 90,000. In a like period the militia fell from around the 50,000 mark to less than half that and continued downward. In fact, the militia was less than half what it was in 1939, despite the fact that Canada's population had doubled since that fateful year! Such realities as these sickened many of the officers and senior warrant and non-commissioned officers. Many of the former resigned, while droves of the latter left the army instead of re-engaging when their current enlistments were up.

Such was the state of affairs in the Canadian Army

when I received instructions to report my whereabouts, if they had changed since the date of my retirement.

I acknowledged the notice in the prescribed manner. Then I dashed off a note to my solicitor instructing him to write on my behalf to the Hon. Leo Cadieux, by then Hellyer's successor as Minister of National Defense. He was to ask two questions. One was to determine the date of my seniority as a Brigadier-General, the other, whether I could expect to be employed in that paid rank if I were to be called out on active service.

That this action may strike the reader as strange is understandable. However, the reason for these questions to the Minister stemmed from the fact that the previous August I had been released from the Armed Forces with the rank of Colonel! Although it was indeed a pleasant enough thing to learn that I had been promoted in the interim (until then an unheard of retirement bonus), I wanted confirmation of my good fortune from the highest authority. Such things cannot be left to chance messages from office underlings.

The Defense Minister was quick to reply to my solicitor's letter, though he appeared hazy as to answers to the questions asked. His letter read:

"I have for acknowledgment your letter of June 22 concerning your client, Brigadier-General A.S.A. Galloway, ED, CD of the Canadian Armed Forces Supplementary Reserve. I shall be pleased to look into the questions which you have raised and will write to you again as soon as I have the necessary information. Yours sincerely, Leo Cadieux."

Cadieux then went off to Europe to preside over the required transplant of the shriveling Canadian Land Forces from the British Army of the Rhine to the U.S. area of operations in Baden. He turned the matter of the inquisitive General over to a subordinate, and while that worthy went into the matter Cadieux stood under a canopy in a Westphalian downpour and reviewed the soaking wet rump of Canada's once proud NATO contribution. Then he watched them as they bade farewell to the Soest area, where they had served in the frontline of Freedom for nineteen years.

Cut from a viable fighting force to one of doubtful combat value, and placed in the obscurity of South Germany, Canada's NATO force had become emasculated and Americanized out of all recognition. With its obsolescent equipment and U.S. look it had become a sorry spectacle compared with then Defense Minister Paul Hellyer's 1965 version of a "bolstered NATO contribution" — one of the key phrases in his pitifully inept *White Paper* on unification of the Forces.

Meantime, back at Canadian Forces Headquarters in Ottawa, General Frederick Sharp, the former air force officer who had, as a result of the unification program, become the Chief of the Defense Staff, launched a mammoth questionnaire to see what youth in the Forces thought of the life they had chosen. This questionnaire was just one more way of dispersing the dwindling defense dollar, and would tell General Sharp and his fellow desk-warriors in their 'unification green' uniforms no more than any good commanding officer or any experienced recruiting sergeant could tell them in a five-minute interview. The latter dialogue, however, would not be fit to print.

Had Canadian Forces Headquarters known in those days what was going on in the Forces, it is reasonable to assume that they would not have had to resort to question-and-answer games to find out. One good question, I thought at the time, might be: "Who are the Generals in the Armed Forces these days? Name any 50, 15 or five. Send a reasonable facsimile of their identity discs and await our early reply." The trouble with this would have been, in my opinion, that Canadian Forces Headquarters wouldn't have known the answer themselves. This sounds quite incredible, and of course it is. I had noted that a new fad had entered the dress regulations and that members of the Forces were wearing name tags on their uniforms so that officers would know who their men were, and senior officers would know who their juniors were. Before this jet-age approach to the matter, the military tradition was "know your men" — that was an officer's first duty. Now, I decided, the Minister of Defense didn't even know who his Generals were!

What a sorry pass our army, navy and air force had come to, now that they were all lumped together into an amorphous mass in green uniforms which made them look like a cross between gasoline station attendants and South American policemen.

As I reflected on what, in my view, was wrong with the Forces, work was going on to produce an answer to my solicitor's letter. Six days later it was revealed that Brigadier-General Galloway was the General Who Never Was. His solicitor received a lengthy epistle over a signature which appeared to be 'H.E.T. Douche', and in keeping with the unusual name of the signatory, the contents poured cold water onto the warmth conveyed earlier by the Supplementary Reserve notice and the use of the presumed rank by the Minister himself. The letter read in part:

"Information now available to me indicates that the Supplementary List Reporting Card received by *Colonel* (the italics are the author's) A.S.A. Galloway, ED, CD, was in error by showing his rank as Brigadier-General. Reporting cards are sent to Supplementary List personnel through a computer print-out and it is apparent that the information held by the computer is in error regarding the rank of Colonel Galloway. As the recent despatch of these cards was the first by this system, it is not possible to correct errors on the file before their despatch. However, corrective action is being taken as errors are revealed."

The letter, in typical government gobbledygook, waffled on as Mr. Douche explained several other irrelevant matters pertaining to the inadequacy of the record system at Canadian Forces Headquarters, winding up with the conclusive information that "Colonel Galloway was released from the Regular Force in the substantive rank of Colonel and he has not been promoted during his service on the Supplementary List."

Finally, Mr. Douche added a pithy last paragraph: "I trust," he wrote, "that this information will enable you to advise Colonel Galloway on his status as a member of the Supplementary List and that the error of our information system has not caused him any personal or social discomfiture."

The word 'discomfiture' selected by Mr. Douche bothered me. The *Concise Oxford Dictionary* gives its meaning as 'defeat in battle' from the Old French, *desconfit*. I presumed from this choice of words that Mr. Douche was probably a Francophone. In any event, I took it as a good omen that personnel in the Defense Department were still using warlike terms, in their written work at least.

My 'discomfiture', so ably penned by Mr. Douche, was of concern only to myself as a soldier. But as a taxpayer I became quite disquieted contemplating a situation in which the Armed Forces found themselves in such a state of chaos that the Defense Minister didn't even know who his Generals were! I wondered how those more junior heirs of the Forces' unification were faring as they struggled on amid their piles of brand-new green uniforms and stacks of aging warlike stores — all those captains and corporals with their astronomical SIN numbers, their names sewn over their breast pockets. I wondered at the time if, as they read of the Minister of Defense flying here and there, from the Arctic wastes to the soggy plains of Northern Germany, they considered whether he knew who *any* of them were — or even cared.

CHAPTER II

AMATEUR SOLDIER BETWEEN THE WARS

I can almost remember the Great War. When I was two and a half years old I fell through an open door into a basement four feet deep in polluted Saskatchewan flood water. Thanks to the presence of mind of a man named John H. Hilton to whom my father gave a gold watch in appreciation of his saving my life— I was rescued just in time and the water was pumped from my young lungs. Rushed home to a hot bath and other aids to recovery, I have a sharp recollection of my mother chastising me for not looking where I was going. The whole episode remains so vivid in my memory that, had some similar excitement taken place in the war zone, such as a shelling or some other frightening experience of warfare, I certainly would have remembered that too. For my near drowning took place in the Spring of 1918, at the very time when the great German offensive had put the British Army in France and Flanders with their backs to the wall. As it is, I have a less vivid memory of myself following a column of khaki-clad troops marching behind a military band, and of my mother coming after me and deterring me from my first attempt at following the drum. This was during a visit to my maternal grandparents in Brandon, Manitoba, in the late summer of 1918. In fact, it was at the very time when the Canadian Corps was leading the Allied Armies into the Hindenburg Line for the 'Last Hundred Days' which were to end the war on November 11th.

But it is my uncle's homecoming in May, 1919 that has provided me with the most detailed memory of the Great War, or at least of its immediate aftermath. His uniform, his Sam Browne belt, his walking stick and that other kind of 'stick', the brass buttonstick used in the process of shining the brass buttons on his tunic, have remained in my mind's eye over the decades. It must have been this early close personal 'hero worship' of my uncle — I was constantly in his company during his demobilization leave at our house — that made me decide to be a soldier too. Certainly, nothing in my family backgrounds, paternal or maternal, put soldiering into my blood.

My uncle, a Sapper subaltern, mesmerized me as I watched him shining his brass buttons and his Sam Browne, as he awaited his CEF discharge papers. Wide-eyed, I watched him and knew I wanted to be a soldier too. His leather gleamed like dark mahogany. His buttons got so bright! He must have been a good soldier, because years later when I finally donned khaki myself I was told, "A good soldier obeys orders without question — and keeps his buttons bright." I always did both — until I gradually found out that some orders are criminal nonsense. I still believe in polishing brass. It is not done in the Canadian Army any more, which is a pity and will probably prove a battle-losing factor in the next war, if there is one.

I have one vivid childhood memory of what I later found out to be a sidelight on the Chanak crisis. This was in September 1922 when the British almost went to war against Turkey in support of the Greeks, the Turks and Greeks being in a border conflict. History records that Lloyd George's government appealed to the wartime Allies and the British dominions to rally round for a war against the Turks. Canada's prime minister, Mackenzie King, turned the proposal down flat. However, I remember very well going down to the railway station with my parents to see a troop train. The soldiers were mounted troops, either cavalry or artillery, as they wore riding britches and leather bandoliers. They also wore khaki Wolseley helmets and I was quite thrilled at being in proximity to such people, as they stretched their legs on the platform. They may have been Permanent Force on their way between Sarcee and Winnipeg, or they may have been some militia unit coming back from summer camp. As we drove away from the station in our McLaughlin Master-Six with the yellow spoked wheels, I remember my mother saying, "If there is going to be another war, those poor young fellows will soon be on their way." As we drove into the fiery setting sun, across the wheatlands of Southern Saskatchewan, my seven-year-old yearnings to be a soldier and go to 'another war' welled in my heart.

In Saskatchewan at the end of the Great War, May 1919.

About nine years later I joined the militia as a Boy Soldier. That meant I was ranked lower than a Private, but then I had just turned sixteen and weighed 110 pounds! My Attestation Card also reveals that I was five foot four inches tall. However, I was a willing fellow and they were lucky to get me.

I remember the night I came home with my khaki uniform and my webb equipment all piled into a rubber ground sheet. "What is all that?" my mother asked. When I told her I had joined the militia she was not at all amused. She still saw me in terms of the Boy Scouts. A week later, on my first parade night, the fellow who had taken me to join up arrived to accompany me to the armoury. I was all ready; puttees well rolled, buttons, badges and brasses shining like mirrors. I was every inch the soldier except that my uniform was much too big. Boots were not supplied to the militia in those days, and I had bought a pair and polished them diligently every day for the previous week. My friend was a young Irishman, fresh out from Ulster. "How d'you like your soldier boy?" he asked my parents in his rich brogue, before bearing me away to my first lessons in forming fours.

A couple of months later the garrison church parade was held to St. Paul's Cathedral in London, Ontario. After the service there was a march-past of all Western Ontario's militia units. Brigadier-General Charlie Armstrong, a dapper and diminutive man, took the salute. The band of the RCR played each unit past to its regimental march. Ours was *I'm Ninety Five*. Just as we passed the base, the last of the militia units — and I was in the last file feeling very proud of myself — the band changed its tune to *The RCR March*. Behind us came Regimental Headquarters and "C" Company of that regiment. They were dressed in summer khaki drill, and wore beautiful whipcord caps and white buff belts. They marched with that ease that is acquired after years of soldiering. My pride was somewhat deflated when I heard a little old woman with a decided cockney accent say to her companion, "Oh, 'ere they are Nellie, 'ere's the *real* soldiers now".

The term "Boy Soldier" is now archaic. In the days

when a Private was paid one dollar a day and ten cents for cleaning materials, a Boy Soldier got fifty cents. In the militia this was mere theory, as we got no pay at all, and only a two dollar bill on General's Inspection at the end of the annual training period. When we enlisted we signed an agreement that all our pay would be turned over to the Regimental Fund. This didn't mean much, as we were only credited with some thirty days paid service per year anyway. However, fifteen years later, on being accepted for the Regular Army in the rank of major my back pension contributions were computed on about two years of paid Boy Service and I was officially shown as having enlisted in His Majesty's Service as a Boy Soldier. This was a bit of paper nonsense also, as before my eighteenth birthday I had qualified as a Sergeant and been promoted Lance-Corporal and then Corporal. I was made a Sergeant just after my eighteenth birthday, at which time my Company Commander approached my father and asked him if he would put up the money necessary to outfit me if I were commissioned as a Second Lieutenant.

Fortunately, my father agreed. I didn't have a cent, was just out of high school, unemployed and spending most of my time at the local armoury, or writing poetry! I didn't really want a job anyway. I wanted to get into the Permanent Force and I hoped that with a militia commission I might get in through the 'back door' by way of what was called the Long Course. This was an amazing misnomer. The 'Long Course' was really the short course. The proper way to get a commission in the Permanent Force (as the Regular Army was called in those days) was to go through Royal Military College at Kingston. This took four years and graduates emerged as Lieutenants. If one were not academically capable of that he could get a military qualification in two years. Then, *mq* instead of *rmc* was put after his name in the Defense Forces List and he commissioned in the rank of Second Lieutenant.

A militia officer got his qualifications for a Permanent Force commission by an immediate attachment to a Permanent Force regiment. In the case of the infantry this would be The Royal Canadian Regiment, Princess Patricia's

Canadian Light Infantry or the Royal 22e Régiment. During this period of attachment he would attend a few weeks at RMC taking purely military subjects and would emerge a Second Lieutenant. What was 'long' about this course I never quite understood. Originally, I had wanted to try for RMC, but I flunked Grade XIII and the year required to complete my Senior Matriculation put me over the age limit to try the competitive examinations for entry to the College.

Second Lieutenant, The Elgin Regiment, in scarlet and gold, November, 1935.

When I joined the militia, actually The Elgin Regiment, a county regiment with Regimental Headquarters at St. Thomas, Ontario, the Commanding Officer was a Boer War veteran who had served with the RCR at the time of its famed participation in the Battle of Paardeberg with Lord Kitchener in command. His name was George Stanbury and one of the Company-Sergeants-Major, Neville by name, was also a Boer War veteran of the British Army. In my own company the CSM and a walrus-moustached corporal in the stores both wore the 1914 Star with clasp for taking part in the historic Retreat from Mons. These men had lived with history as I saw it, and I admired them very much. They seemed so much more exciting than the rather drab bankers, clergymen, doctors and lawyers I met in my father's house.

Our military training was pretty much of an amateur performance. Some of the chaps were in the regiment only for the shooting, others for the bar privileges found in the messes, or for the free issues of beer on our occasional outings. Among the officers the social aspect — mess dinners, dances, ceremonial parades and garden parties — seemed to be the main appeal. But many were keen on all aspects of soldiering and this became apparent in June 1940 when the regiment was mobilized. All ranks volunteered, almost to a man. Among the officers only one among the thirty to forty on strength failed to answer the Call to Arms. Strangely enough, he had carried the King's Colour quite proudly on the last church parade before war broke out.

The unit was very democratic, as is often the case in those militia units scattered about the small centres of population. The CO, the senior company commander, the adjutant and the Regimental-Sergeant-Major were all linotype operators in local printing offices. The Second-in-Command and my own company commander were lawyers; one company commander was an accountant and another was a coal merchant. Most of the junior officers served behind the counter in some sort of shop, the more swanky among them being bond salesmen or bank clerks. One was a farmer and another a hotel manager. However, I was not about to complain, as I had no job at all. Some of the senior

NCOs had better jobs in civilian life than had their superior officers. Of course, in the 1930's people were lucky to have employment of any kind and young-men-about-town without a profession had to take what they could get. In better times they probably would have had better positions. One officer who actually had money drove a big, cream-coloured convertible and had a uniform that must have cost a fortune by the standards of those days. Most of us wore $35 Tip Top khaki, but he wore beautiful stuff which apparently came from England. He was a handsome fellow with curly black hair, a dashing black sabre-moustache and a real Hollywood smile. He was the complete playboy but he eventually left the regiment. The reason given was that his family had two maids and he had got both of them pregnant at the same time. His father had outfitted him and when he appeared on parade for the first time wearing his sword, he pointed to the Royal cipher "GR" on the hilt and in all innocence said to his incredulous brother-officers, "My father got this sword made especially for me, with my own initials on it." Indeed they were the same as his own initials, and like the King his name was also George!

We always had a full complement of officers, but it was difficult to keep the unit up to authorized strength. To produce enough men on parade at the General's Inspection, to qualify for the annual financial grant which was needed to keep the regiment going, was difficult. The solution to this problem was to get a few old-timers from the Legion and some local high school boys, or pool parlour denizens to dress up in khaki and stand in the ranks. When the General's staff officer called the muster roll these fellows answered to the names of people long since gone, sometimes dead. They got two dollars for this. Nobody checked very closely. It all seems rather amateurishly dishonest now, but it worked back in 1932. Once, when one man answered to two different names he got four dollars, not a bad wage for a couple of hours 'work', by the economic standards of the Hungry Thirties.

Early in 1933 during the winter months, a so-called Provisional School was run at our local headquarters to qualify young militiamen for NCO rank. Lectures were three nights a week as I recall it, with outdoor exercises on Saturday and Sunday. Capt. Charles Foulkes, of The Royal Canadian Regiment, stationed at Wolseley Barracks in nearby London, Ontario, conducted the training. Little did I think, as a seventeen-year-old militia Lance-jack, that less than twelve years later in far-off Italy I, as the Second-in-Command of the RCR, would argue the finer points of committing infantry into battle with my Corps Commander, and that that Corps Commander would be Lieutenant-General Charles Foulkes. Certainly, as the years go by, we are inclined to see more clearly the feet of clay so often encased in a good pair of riding boots!

When I was a young soldier, army trousers didn't have pockets, for two reasons: First, we didn't have any money to put in them, and Second, we couldn't put our hands in them and slouch about like a sloppy civvy.

To help us march around in a "smart and soldierly manner", there was the swagger stick, more officially called "canes, short, soldiers for the use of, one."

Lack of pockets caused one difficult situation for the most fastidious of the King's men, the officers and those young soldiers who aped them: There was no place to put a handkerchief. Well, we tucked them up our sleeves, although this gave us a somewhat sissy appearance in the eyes of some. Many soldiers simply did without.

I was not an officer but I was fastidious. One day I stood in the front rank of a guard of honour for the Earl of Bessborough, Canada's Governor-General. His Excellency stepped imperially from the vice-regal railway coach and paused to receive the honours. The command was given: "Royal Salute, present-*hipe*!"

Slap, slap, *wumph* went the movement. Butt, sling — and then the instep of the right boot wrapped itself around the heel of the left as the rifle dropped into its final position with the *wumph*. The band struck up the national anthem. The G.G. doffed his silk topper and stood elegantly at attention, a slight smile on his lips.

And no wonder! On the second slap my left sleeve

had thrown out a white handkerchief that sailed in a graceful curve, across the front of the guard like a dove in flight, landing just in front of His Excellency's polished toes. Fortunately, it didn't drop into his upturned silk hat. That would have been a hole-in-one to remember.

His Excellency inspected us with the city mayor beside him. Then he left for civic ceremonies and we marched away. Behind, on the cinders beside the vice-regal railway coach, lay my snowy linen handkerchief — a victim of the no-pocket system.

Swagger sticks were also troublesome. Stick drill was supposed to clarify how to carry them, but always the argument persisted whether they should be placed under the left armpit with ferrule to the front or ferrule to the rear. This was a big decision in the days before panzer divisions began to occupy the military mind.

I saw my swagger stick stolen in 1935, but because the thief, Willis Moogk, was one rank above me I decided not to complain. I bought another for 35 cents, a relatively high financial outlay when a Second Lieutenant's pay was $3.00 a day.

Sixteen years later, however, when Moogk and I were for a time the same rank, I complained over a drink that the wretch had stolen my stick.

My complaint sank in after 17 more years. Both of us had grown old in the service and wore red tabs. As I sat behind my desk one morning in far-off Germany, a long cardboard tube postmarked Camp Borden arrived. I opened it up and there lay my slender, highly polished swagger stick. My thieving friend had attached a note saying he was retiring the next day and would not need the stick anymore. Neither did I. By that time, swagger sticks had gone the way of Brown Bess muskets, khaki blanco and hoof picks.

Whether it was the actual stick he had so brazenly purloined in Wolseley Barracks 33 years before, I suppose I will never know. But then, one can hardly call a brother-officer a liar. Today, both sticks are among my souvenirs.

I remember once in England during the 'long wait' when our CO decided that some stick drill would smarten up the subalterns. Perhaps he had seen them idling about with their thumbs in their pockets, which were now in vogue. An order came from the adjutant giving the date, time and place all subalterns would parade. The message stated that it would be the responsibility of each young officer to provide himself with a stick or "a reasonable facsimile". In 1942, swagger sticks were in rather short supply. There were more facsimilies than real ones, some less "reasonable" than others, at the drill.

I have often wondered if the stick I believe to be my old one is no more than its facsimile. Perhaps it is a substitute, like the false moustaches some Life Guardsmen had to wear in the 1930's because they were too young to grow them and an uncompromising King George V had ordered that moustaches be worn.

To get back to The Elgin Regiment: It was a 'rural' regiment, which meant that it was split up within the County of Elgin. The company I belonged to was in the Town of Aylmer and the local company commander was the Crown Attorney. In St. Thomas, where the headquarters were, a lot of the officers, as I have already stated, were in the printing and publishing business. In 1935 when the King George V Jubilee Medal was awarded it went to the CO, the Second-in-Command, the Adjutant and the RSM, all of whom were normally afflicted with inky fingers. Perhaps their military appointments rather than their civilian occupations accounted for their good fortune. But, when the one Jubilee Medal awarded to the detached company in Aylmer was bestowed on the CSM, who was a linotype operator for the local weekly, it seemed as if some sort of trades unionism had got into the Honours and Awards business!

As a Second Lieutenant I had two years within which to qualify as a Lieutenant. Although one might get an extension if conditions warranted it, the normal pattern was that if you did not qualify within that period you were required to resign your commission. So, having no civilian job anyway, I was delighted when in March 1935 I was selected to attend the junior officers' qualifying course on attachment to The Royal Canadian Regiment at Wolseley Barracks in London, Ontario.

For six weeks about a dozen junior officers from the militia of Western Ontario studied Military Law, map reading, tactics, organization and administration in the classroom under Permanent Force officers or Small Arms training, and company, platoon and arms drill under non-commissioned officers in chill drill halls, or on the wind-swept barrack square. It was exactly the life I wanted. It was, in those days, a gentleman's life. We dined-in three nights a week in scarlet mess jackets, wing-collared and black bow-tied. On other evenings the meal was buffet style and civilian clothes were worn. Mess servants wore white jackets. There was none of the vulgarity of the modern bar. One rang a wall bell, "pressing the tit" we called it, and a waiter appeared and took our order. When he served the drink it was from a silver tray. On Guest Nights things were even better. The Band played a stirring *"The Roast Beef of Old England"* as we quit the ante-room to enter the dining room. The band was stuck in a rather crowded manner into the billiard room at the head of the stairs. During the meal it played popular music and such old favourites as selections from Gilbert and Sullivan.

One night the Director of Military Training visited us. He was Major and Brevet Lieut.-Colonel George Randolph Pearkes, VC, DSO, MC. To an eighteen-year-old subaltern, to meet him was better than meeting God Himself. When the great mahogany table was cleared and the port was passed, the Loyal Toast was drunk and then the cigars were brought round by the Mess Sergeant, who wore a civilian evening tail suit with a black tie. His name was Boddy and his wife was the Officers' Mess cook. Her baked Alaska, brought in looking like a sleeping tiger undergoing suttee within all the blue flame, was her pièce de résistance. The Wine Steward, who eventually became a well-known regimental character and member of the Army Show in World War II, was called "Pop" Morton. His music hall song on Hitler, *"He'll Never do the Goose Step Down the Mall"* brought him a certain amount of fame in the 1940s. But my first memory of him was in his brass-buttoned blue livery with dark red lapels, a waistcoat with horizontal blue and white stripes and a dignified air, standing immobile beside the wine bottles until someone's glass needed topping up.

The names of the regimental officers travel down these almost fifty years. The CO was Lieut.-Col. Murray Kirk Greene, whom I served under again in England on his second tour of regimental command some five or six years later. The adjutant was Capt. Arthur Roy and the OC of the company to which we "attached officers" were attached was Major Hugo Poston. The subalterns were Neel Hodson and Willis Moogk and a miserable "Long Course" candidate who was overbearing and eventually found wanting. He never got his hoped-for appointment to The Regiment and nine years later when I was the acting Commanding Officer of the RCR in Italy I saw him on the street at Ortona, a reinforcement lieutenant to some unfortunate infantry battalion.

My attachment to The Royal Canadian Regiment came, like all things do, to an end. I went back home to evening and weekend soldiering and writing poetry.

I think it was in the early summer of 1935 that our regimental fund reached the level where the purchase of full dress uniforms was possible. These were scarlet tunics, blue trousers, white pith helmets and white buff belts. They had survived from before the Great War, but were in mint condition. Our first parade in our gala gear was to be on Dominion Day, when we 250 scarlet-coated heroes would Troop the Colour in the local arena at Pinafore Park in St. Thomas. Unfortunately, one item of the helmet fittings, the brass spikes, had not arrived and had to be ordered from England. As a result the helmets were topped by the mushroom-shaped air vent worn on non-ceremonial occasions.

As the battalion was forming up to march the eight or ten city blocks to the park, the Mess Sergeant ran out of the Armoury and signalled to an officer standing nearby. After a few words this officer marched smartly across the parade ground to where the CO was giving the command for the battalion to move off. A flurry of salutes and muffled words took place and the adjutant and the officer ran to a car and drove off toward downtown. Fifteen minutes or so later the reason for all this activity was apparent. As we neared the park, up drove an open truck. In the back stood the adjutant and the other officer with several large cardboard boxes. From these they were taking tiny, tissue paper wrapped objects which they tossed to the marching troops. The brass spikes had arrived at the railway station in the nick of time! Without halting, all ranks unscrewed the air vents, stuck them inside their tunics (there were no pockets in the trousers) and screwed on the spikes. I was in the last file of the last company as a supernumerary officer. Just as we entered the park gates I caught my spike from the slowly moving truck and screwed it into place. The battalion marched before the grandstand crowd properly dressed. Behind it, like leaves in the autumn wind, some two hundred squares of tissue paper danced in the summer breeze.

In 1936 I published my slim volume of verse under the title of *The Yew Tree Ballad and Other Poems*. It was rather rotten poetry, I am inclined to think now, but the financial gain was enormous for those times. After paying the printer and mailing costs I cleared between ninety and a hundred dollars. In the spring of 1937 King George VI was to be crowned and I decided that I would go to England to be among the thousands of people who were to converge on London for the event. I managed to get a berth on a cattleboat for $25, and after sixteen days of being tossed about the Atlantic in the hold of a foul-smelling ship with 250 head of cattle bawling for food and water, I arrived in London. I bought a bowler hat and an umbrella and eight hours after being paid off by the SS *Dakotian* at Cardiff, I was being presented to the one-time Victorian beauty, Violet, Duchess of Rutland, now a fragile relic of countless summers, by a Mrs. Arnoldi from Toronto, whose social position I don't recall.

The Coronation festivities, particularly the military processions, thrilled me, but I was somewhat appalled when General Sir Walter Kirke, the Director General of the

Territorial Army, fell from his horse coming down Constitution Hill.

Another memorable moment was when the carriages and coaches occupied by the foreign dignitaries passed by and the eyes of the crowd focussed on Hitler's representative, the grim-jawed, steel-helmeted *Generalfeldmarschall* Werner von Blomberg and his equally grim-faced, similarly steel-helmeted carriage companions. "Look! it's the bloody Nazis," I heard someone shout as they wheeled by in front of Drummond's Bank at Trafalgar Square. This remark was followed by a prolonged, unmistakably British "Boo-oo-oo". I scanned the London papers next day, but the incident had not been reported. At the time, Lord Rothermere who controlled a large segment of the British press, and other press lords, were quite pro-Nazi, believing Hitler was no threat to Britain, but rather its best bulwark against Communism. The incident could hardly have gone unobserved, so it must have been censored. By my surface mail dispatch to the St. Thomas *Times-Journal* next day I got my mini-scoop into print a week or so later.

Three years later, as I walked past Drummond's Bank, at the exact spot on the pavement where I had stood on Coronation Day, a sandbagged, barbed wire emplacement sat four-square. Hitler's invading troops were expected and Churchill's statement, "We will fight in the streets . . . we will never surrender", looked like becoming a reality. No longer a 'colonial sightseer', but now a uniformed officer of the King, I received the perfect salute from the Scots Guards sergeant in charge of the post. But the times never tire of change. In 1958, a mere eighteen years later, a Metropolitan Police band stood across the road from Drummond's Bank playing *"Deutschland Uber Alles"*. Indeed, military and civic bands were stationed at intervals along the Mall from Buckingham Palace and up the Strand to Temple Bar, playing that once odious tune. For, in a procession of carriages, escorted by a detachment of the Household Cavalry in all their glory of scarlet and gold, their steel breastplates gleaming, their horsehair plumes dancing and their accoutrements jingling, rode the President of the Federal German Republic, Herr Theodor Heuss, on his way from an audience with the Queen to luncheon with the Lord Mayor of London!

Behind the President in another landau sat grey-clad, rock-jawed German army attachés staring straight ahead. Only this time the gruesome Hun helmets were missing. They wore the ornately peaked cloth caps of the new *Bundeswehr* — less horrible than the barbarian headgear of two German wars of aggression — more in keeping for our German allies in the newly constituted NATO force.

It was the first visit of a German Head of State to England since Kaiser Wilhelm II's last visit before the outbreak of the first World War. Since then two German wars had intervened. London still showed the scars of the second war's 1940-41 blitz and of its 1944 V-bombs. Noon-hour crowds lined the streets as they always do when bands blare and a mounted cavalcade trots by. But these crowds were dumb. No one cheered. No one waved a kerchief or a hat. From where I stood, across the street from Charing Cross station, I could still see unrepaired bomb damage behind the rooftops. Beside me an undersized Cockney, gaunt and grey, wearing a shabby overcoat and a grimy cloth cap, shoved his hands deeper into his pockets and said what everyone probably thought. "Bloody b*aw*stards", he murmured. Then he turned and walked away.

But to return to my Coronation trip twenty-one years before.

Having run out of money and used up the hastily requested funds sent me by my father, I shipped aboard a cargo vessel at Glasgow. I was assigned as pot-walloper to the cook, a rugged fellow who mixed his bread dough with hands and forearms covered with coal dust from stoking his stoves. A letter sent to me from my militia regiment's headquarters, care of Canada House in London had been forwarded, reaching me just before we sailed. The adjutant had addressed it to "Lieut. A.S.A. Galloway". When the cook saw it he said: "You oughn't to tell people you're a leftenant, you know. You can go to jail for passing yourself off as an officer." I didn't reply. Down on my knees scrubbing out an

34

iron porridge dixie was no time to try to convince my rough-cut boss that I actually was His Majesty's *'Trusty and well beloved Andrew Strome Ayers Galloway'*.

The ship was the *S.S. Sularia* and the voyage was to provide me with one of the greatest frights of my life. One foggy night in mid-Atlantic I was almost tossed out of my berth by a tremendous shuddering which ran through the ship, ending with the awesome sound of the engines stopping, their noise giving way to a grinding, rasping sound. Then there was a series of loud crashings and breakings. The lights went out and the porthole about a foot from my face was shattered. My blanket was littered with broken glass and slivers of ice. For a few seconds I lay in terror. Then the muted engines started up and the ship moved slowly astern. By now the lights were on again. I jumped down from my berth, glimpsing through the broken porthole an awesome wall of ice. In the companionway seamen were running back and forth. From out on deck orders were being shouted. Since we slept fully clothed, I quickly climbed up a steel stairway and onto the deck, which was strewn with jagged chunks of ice. Apparently we had sailed above a projecting ice shelf, close enough to the main berg to allow for smaller pinnacles to project out of the water. One of these pinnacles had grazed along our superstructure, shearing away a few railings and fixtures, breaking at least one porthole, mine, and then falling in shattered bits and pieces all over our decks. The reversed engines took us off the shelf without damage to the hull and when dawn broke we were seen to be in the middle of a large ice field. Until we got clear of the area things were tense. My memories of reading about the *Titanic* disaster as a child returned most vividly when I glimpsed the iceberg through my porthole and I am sure it was the most terrifying moment of my life. I am no sailor. The vastness of the ocean, its depths and the secrets they hold have always overawed me. I am by nature a landlubber and of that there is no doubt.

An anticlimax to all this was that the second cook, who had sickened the day we left the Clyde and had remained in his berth the whole time, suddenly died on the eighth day out. As we sailed up the St. Lawrence with our flag at half-mast the merchantmen and lesser craft saluted the corpse aboard our ship with blasts from their fog horns. We docked in Montreal just as I was supposed to wash up the first shift's breakfast vessels — the big iron porridge pot and the crew's greasy divided mess tins. Under my coveralls I wore my suit. My luggage had been quietly hidden beside a hatch on deck. My bowler hat and umbrella were wrapped up in my Burberry all ready for a hurried getaway. When I told the cook I had to go to the 'heads' he believed me. I never saw him again, nor did he see me. For, without the usual 'signing off', I was over the rail and doubling up the street to the nearest taxi stand, my ship's dungarees left in a greasy heap inside a coil of rope.

The summer of 1938 saw me qualify as a captain at a Camp School at Wolseley Barracks. Once again I was attached to the RCR, whose CO was the much-loved Lieut.-Col. 'Beak' Holloway and my company commander was Major Billy (sometimes called 'Ducky') Home, MC. This was pretty well an outdoor course and many of the young NCOs I met there I would later meet as senior NCOs with the RCR overseas, or in quite a number of cases, as officers. We militia officers were much impressed by how well they knew not only their own jobs, but the jobs of the ranks several notches above their own. I remember we were given company drill by Pte. (Acting Lance-Corporal without pay) Murray MacDonald, who later fought beside me in Italy and reached the rank of Lieutenant-Colonel in the post-war army. The fact that several of the candidates on the course were over forty years of age, wearing medals and even decorations from the Great War, did not bother the young professionals one bit. That, of course, was typical of the calibre of many of those young regular soldiers who had either been born to be soldiers, or who had been driven into the barrack room by the Great Depression and the Hungry 'Thirties which followed. During the Second World War, of the fifty-six Warrant Officers and Sergeants on the RCR Instructional Cadre, three became Lieutenant-Colonels, twenty became Majors and fifteen became Captains. Of the youngsters at regimental duty, like the young Pte. Mac-

Donald who handled some twenty militia officers qualifying for certificates as militia captains and majors, I am sure several score were commissioned, some like Sandy Mitchell and Ted Littleford being among the best fighting company commanders we had.

Shortly after the Royal Visit of June 1939, when I was detailed for street lining duty and had the rare privilege of personally saluting King George VI with my drawn sword, it became apparent that we were on the brink of war. By this time I was scraping a living as a sub-editor on a weekly newspaper and as a district correspondent for a city daily. One sunny afternoon in late August, as the flies buzzed lazily on the warm window pane beside my desk, I saw a silvery-haired cyclist approach the office, lean his bike up against the wall and enter the office. He was our local telegraph agent, an elderly man, somewhat out of breath. Clutched in his skinny hand was a buff-coloured envelope.

"I guess this is for you", he wheezed.

It was addressed to the 'Officer-in-Charge, The Armoury, Aylmer'. It was a call-out order from Ottawa instructing me to post a twenty-four hour guard over the local post office, since our 'armoury' was a group of rooms on the second floor. Here we kept our fifty-or-so rifles, our three or four Lewis Guns, our uniforms and equipment and whatever other warlike stores we possessed.

"I think we're going to have a war, Jim", I said. I thanked him for his delivery and then, making the first military decision of the many I would make during the course of the next six years, I went out onto the hot sun-drenched pavement. Past the movie house, past the butcher shop, past the Royal Bank and into the pool room I went, the Call to Arms order held firmly in my hand. I knew where my local soldiery could be found!

When I emerged from the smokey interior of the pool room I was followed by three good men and true. I had persuaded them to exchange their cues for Lee-Enfield rifles. Before nightfall their khaki-clad figures and those of several others, summoned by party-line and farm boy messengers, the barnyard still clinging to their boots, were posted with fixed bayonets on sentry-go under the town clock. The local people were astonished. The war had come to their town.

Along the Polish frontier with Germany, Hitler's panzer divisions were massing. Stuka dive-bombers were tuning up their motors a few miles behind. And in the Baltic swastika flags were flapping in the salty air as naval gunners readied to shell the Polish port of Gdynia — the opening shots of the world-wide catastrophe. The World was moving swiftly toward the greatest war in its history. It was then that I received my second message from the General Staff at Defense Headquarters in Ottawa.

"Bayonets will be sharpened", it read.

And that was the first time I decided to forget to carry out a foolish order. Sharpened bayonets on my home town's streets would be more dangerous to our local security than any *saboteurs* who might be in the offing.

War was declared a few days later. Poland was soon destroyed and the Empire mobilized lazily. Canada began recruiting an Active Service Force. My dutiful militiamen and I wanted to join up. Indeed, the local citizenry rather wondered why we stayed in town guarding the post office when hitherto unmilitary young locals had hastened up to Wolseley Barracks to enlist in The Royal Canadian Regiment, presumably to go overseas.

By December we were pretty well fed up with our hometown guard duties. But there was no release. The men "called out" were on the payroll. I was not, but my militia CO had forbidden any of his officers to try for a transfer. "Our time will come soon enough", he told us and so we joined in the war by singing *We're Going to Hang Out the Washing on the Siegfried Line*, until we suddenly realized that our fellow townspeople didn't believe us.

At Christmas the town council erected the usual huge tree outside the post office, almost in the line of march of my sentries. Strings of coloured lights were hung on its branches, and although it was rumoured that Canada's 1st

Division, containing quite a number of local men, was on the high seas bound for the war, the war fever had pretty well died down since the German victory in Poland. It was the time of the Phoney War. Then, one night just before Christmas, all the lights were stolen from the municipal Christmas tree. The local laughs were hard to take. I decided to defy my militia CO and one morning I took the bus to the Canadian National Exhibition grounds in Toronto where reinforcements, both officers and men, were being trained for The Royal Canadian Regiment.

I knew that Col. Holloway was in charge at the CNE Barracks, in the Exhibition's Automotive Building, and I went directly to his office. Like Caesar in Egypt — I came, I saw, I conquered.

In my English-bought bowler, a white scarf and an oxford grey raglan I passed muster of the adjutant, Capt. Billy Pope, and asked to see the Commanding Officer. Col. Holloway recognized me at once.

"What can I do for you, Galloway?", he queried.

"I want to join your Regiment", I said.

"Of course you do", he replied.

Then he told me to go back to my home and wait for a call from Major Neilson, OC the RCR Depot at Wolseley Barracks in London. The call came in less than a week, and almost before I knew it, I had been ordered to Wolseley Barracks, much to the consternation of my militia CO, who, when he was informed that I was to be taken on strength of the Active Service Force, phoned me directly and gave me a ticking off, the gist of which was that he wished me no luck in my new-found military home! Six months later The Elgin Regiment was mobilized, but by then my eight years militia service seemed only the beating of a very distant drum.

CHAPTER III

WHEN ENGLAND STOOD ALONE

For a few short weeks Camp Borden was my training area. Then the Inspector General, Major-General Ashton, visited us. The whole of No. 1 Infantry Training Centre was lined up, the officers out in front, and our Commanding Officer, Lieut.-Col. Archie Campbell, RCR, accompanied Ashton down our lines. I noticed that the ancient warrior, if one could call him that — he had never been beyond the Canadian training camps in England during the Great War — stopped at each subaltern and asked a question. In front of the platoon on my right was Len Carling. When the General spoke to him I cocked my ear and heard him say to Len, "How much service have you got?" Len replied something like, "About sixteen weeks, Sir!" and I immediately did some mental arithmetic. Sure enough, the General asked me the same question. I knew that Len's service was even longer than some of the others and I had noticed that the General had looked a little perturbed at his answer. So, when I had the question put to me I set him back on his heels.

"Eight years, four months and twenty-two days, Sir!" I barked out in a parade ground voice.

Ashton turned to the CO and without a moment's hesitation said, "Put this officer on the next draft." It was exactly what I wanted.

A few days later I was preparing for embarkation leave when a runner arrived at my tent and told me I was 'up for interview' with the company commander — immediately! This scared me a bit, and I wondered if I were going to be removed from the draft. Such things had happened before.

I duly reported and stood before the major, seated behind the unpainted table that served as his field desk. He was a World War I type and in my eyes seemed quite an old man. I suppose he was about 45, possibly even younger. His name was Pat Haire and he belonged to the PPCLI, a regiment which seemed to attract some oddballs both in war and peace.

"Galloway", he said, pursing his mouth and closing his eyes. "Galloway, I have some advice for you."

I wondered what I had done wrong.

"Yes sir," I answered, trembling a bit and pushing my thumbs more stiffly down the seams of my trousers.

"You are going to England," he said, "and as my memory serves me, the grass there is very lush. I suggest you provide yourself with a pair of gum boots. You will find them most useful, especially on your early-morning rounds when the dew is heavy. That is all. Good luck."

I saluted and left the tent, relieved that I was still on draft. Dunkirk was in the headlines. To have been kept in Canada would have been heart-breaking.

So, with that advice I went off to war, prepared to meet Hitler's victorious armies, possibly on the beaches, on the landing grounds, in the fields, streets and hills of England — even if they were heavy with dew.

Soon I was on a ship in Halifax harbour. Four of us were assigned to a tiny cabin where we had to step out into the companionway to find enough elbow room to button up our trousers. Originally a single, it had been fitted with three extra berths when overhauled and made into a troopship.

"This set-up is ridiculous", said the older of our quartet, a former Toronto stockbroker named Booie Garfunkel. "We don't have to put up with this sort of accommodation. I know how to fix things. All we have to do is tip the purser and ask him to put us in that stateroom we passed one deck up. There is nobody in it and I know how these chaps operate."

One of our foursome was skeptical, but two of us, Freddie Crich and myself, decided to give it a try. In those days five dollars was a princely tip. I had a five dollar bill, so we put it in an envelope, addressed it to the purser and sent it to his office with an accompanying note which the three of us signed. Then we went out on deck and waited to have our wishes acceded to.

As a cattleman on an Atlantic crossing off Fastnet Rock, Cork, April, 1937.

We didn't have long to wait, but our wishes had nothing to do with the message which the loud hailer system began blaring throughout the length and breadth of His Majesty's Troopship *Oronsay*. Lieuts. Garfunkel, Galloway and Crich were to report to the OC Troops immediately!

When we entered the OC Troops' cabin, accompanied by the Ship's Adjutant, we were met by the flashing eyes of Brigadier Pete Leclerc, a World War I ranker who had won the MM. In his hand was a five dollar bill.

"Well, gentlemen", he began almost before we had a chance to salute, "Well, gentlemen. Whose money is this?"

As a trio we were singularly silent. He repeated his question. "Whose money is this?"

Somebody had to answer. I was standing closest to him.

"Sir," I murmured, "it belongs to all of us."

"Nonsense," he retorted. "How can you divide five dollars three ways?" He was a French-Canadian and spoke with a heavy accent. He pronounced the words '*dol-LARS*', and '*t'reeWAYS*'. It made our apparent crime seem all the worse. "Is it yours?" he queried, looking directly at me.

"Yes, Sir," I answered softly.

"Take it then, it is dirty money. It is bribery money. . . ." and with that he thrust it forward and I accepted it weakly.

There was a pregnant pause. We breathed hard. The brigadier stared at us, reducing our self-confidence to zero. Finally, he spoke.

"I shall send you back. . . ." There was a pause which seemed endless. We all had visions of being returned to our depot in disgrace, losing our chance to go to the wars. Then he repeated himself.

"I shall send you back — to your *miserable* little cabin, where you belong. That is all, gentlemen."

We left with sighs of relief, but exceedingly humbled.

Next day at a ship's cocktail party the brigadier asked me to bring him a sherry and when I did he smiled kindly. He had taught us all a good lesson.

That evening we weighed anchor for Britain's beleaguered isle. Despite our having strayed from the paths of righteousness we were safely off to the wars — Booie, Freddie and I. Only a U-boat might stop us now!

It was an 'amazing summer', and that was the title that novelist Sir Philip Gibbs chose for his romance of the summer of 1940. From the Clydeside dockyards we had arrived by train at the Canadian Holding Unit in Bordon Camp, Hampshire. The next day I was posted on detached duty to RAF Station Odiham. The Battle of Britain was on. The Few, as Prime Minister Churchill called the fighter pilots of the Royal Air Force, were shooting the *Luftwaffe* out of the skies and being shot down themselves. And every day those skies were robin's egg blue, shimmering with sunshine. There was no rain and the grain stood tall and golden in the fields.

There were no vacancies in my Regiment, so I was sent off to serve with an *ad hoc* ground defense unit at the Odiham airfield north of Portsmouth.

Two years before, General Erhard Milch, Inspector-General of the *Luftwaffe*, had officially opened the modern Hore-Belisha luxury air station at Odiham as the RAF's special guest. To commemorate the event a life-sized oil portrait of the Nazi air chief had been hung over the mantelpiece in the main ante-room of the officers' mess. In August 1940, with the war almost a year in progress, the portrait still hung in its place of honour. Meanwhile, Milch, who had been appointed Director of Aircraft Production in Germany and was soon to be promoted Field-Marshal, was doing everything in his power to destroy the RAF and thus help in the conquest of Britain.

One incident in the Battle of Britain occurred during a heavy raid on the Odiham area. The village was hit, incurring some loss of life. The airfield also received a few bombs. The raid was brief, taking place shortly after dusk.

44

The power went off, windows were shattered, and the blackouts in the mess were knocked out of their frames, but it only took a few minutes to get things in order once the raiders had passed.

When the lights came on again, and the spilled whiskies, scattered newspapers and magazines had been replenished or retrieved, a young RAF pilot suddenly noticed that the portrait of General Milch had been knocked askew by the force of the blasts. I watched this slim youngster, wearing the up to then rarely seen DFC ribbon, rise out of a deep leather chair and cross the thick blue carpet to the fireplace. There, with gentle hands he straightened the crooked picture and returned to his seat. A faint crackling of applause condoned his action. Then English heads bent down again deep into *The Times*, or *Country Life*, or *Flight* magazine.

Twenty-five years later I discussed this incident with Lieutenant-General Adolf Galland, then a Bonn businessman, and formerly Hitler's chief of fighter aircraft during the Battle of Britain. Galland was one of Germany's greatest aces, totalling 70 "kills" before being promoted to the job of directing all fighter activity over Britain in that fateful summer. Galland was responsible only to Hermann Goering, and *in extremis* to Der Fuehrer himself. No other warlords interposed themselves.

When the Nazi air armada began to disappear under the British aerial counterattack, Goering stood on the coast of occupied France gazing across the English Channel. Watching his vaunted *Luftwaffe* being knocked out of the skies, he turned to Galland, suggesting with sarcasm that he must need something more to win the battle. "What do you want, Galland?" he queried.

"Perhaps a squadron of Spitfires, Herr Reichsmarschall", replied Galland in biting tones.

Despite his saucy answer, which undoubtedly wounded Goering's pride in his beloved Messerschmitts, Galland remained at his post. He soon became the first officer of the entire Wehrmacht to receive from Hitler's own hands the Oak Leaves with Swords badge to augment his already rare Knight's Cross of the Iron Cross.

Galland survived the war. In its very last days he left his desk and took to the air again as a fighter pilot, personally shooting it out once more with his country's aerial opponents as he had done in Poland and in the West five to six years before. His war memoirs, *The First and the Last* proved a best-seller during the 1950s. Today an aircraft sales executive, he flies from appointment to appointment in a light aircraft through the same skies where he once fought so gaily, then so desperately, many years ago.

When I recounted the incident of General Milch's portrait to "Dolfo" Galland, to use the nickname he gained during his days with the Condor Legion in the Spanish Civil War, he smiled and, in his best English said, "Only in England, of course, is such chivalry possible."

One night I was on duty in one of the sandbagged Lewis Gun emplacements which served as anti-aircraft protection for the airfield. Ours was not a fighter station, but was full of Free French airmen for whom, at the moment, there were apparently no planes and therefore no employment. A Canadian Army/Air Co-op squadron was also languishing at Odiham since there was no army to co-op with, the British units still licking their wounds from Dunkirk and the Canadian division filling in time as spectators of the dog-fights over Surrey, Sussex and Kent. With me was another Canadian officer named Smeltzer from the West Nova Scotia Regiment. On his shoulder straps were the brass letters W.N.S.R., which, he told me, meant 'we never shall return'. I thought that was a good philosophy for those times.

The sandbagged walls reeked of creosote, pungent and irritating to the nostrils. A strong odour, equally unpleasant, pressed down on us from the heavy tarp which sagged above in the form of a roof. Inside our stinking airfield dugout the air was blue with cigarette smoke. It stung our eyes as we squinted at a map spread out under the hissing lamp.

"That must be the woods," suggested Sgt. Frank

46

Lloyd, poking his finger at a pale green blur. I agreed.

We pulled on our equipment, tightened the strings holding our respirators in the "Alert" position, stuffed tousled heads into heavy tin hats and went out into the night. Outside, the cool air chilled the sweat on face and neck into a cold, greasy film.

"Okay, driver?" Lloyd asked Pte. Frank Ball, who was draped over the steering wheel of the 15-cwt. truck. The motor was running and half a dozen men in fighting order, one clutching a Bren gun, sat in the box. It was pitch dark. Forty miles away the sky over London glowed red. Its east end had been under constant air attack since mid-morning. It was now around 10 p.m. on September 7th, 1940. At 8 p.m. the code word, "Cromwell" — meaning "invasion imminent" — had been passed by Home Forces. Church bells, the signal that Hitler's army was on its way to invade England, rang from ancient towers in little villages scattered across that green and pleasant land.

"Okay!" answered the driver. I clambered into the seat beside him, the map folded in one hand and a masked flashlight in the other.

I was not very happy. An hour before I had made a fool of myself. Besides, we were getting into a soft-skinned vehicle and driving off in the dark into unknown country, to look for German paratroopers reported to have dropped into a woods north of RAF Station Odiham in Hampshire.

The field phone had jingled shortly after 8 o'clock. The voice of Major Ed Matthews had squawked over the line, "Do you hear the bells?" I replied that I did — and that they sounded nice.

"Well, do you know what they mean?" he shouted.

"No sir," I answered truthfully.

"Good God," was his retort. "You'd damn well better know. It means the invasion has started!"

Across the Channel the German Army, fresh from victories over Poland, Norway, the Low Countries and

France was singing, *Wir Fahren gegen England* — "We are on our way against England." Overhead the skies of England had been flecked with German aircraft for weeks. Many civilian dead already lay buried in the folding cardboard coffins which a farsighted British government had stockpiled in thousands the year before. Falling bombs had become routine. Church bells, muted by order until the time would come when they must announce this fearful moment, were clanging wildly. It was to be the army's turn now.

We weren't much of a unit — the Odiham Guard Detachment. Our commander was Major Matthews, of the Hastings and Prince Edward Regiment and we were made up of men from every infantry regiment in the 1st Division. Mostly we came from the holding units, a hodge-podge of half-trained recruits, or men who had been returned from their field units for physical or other defects, or were buckshee for some reason.

We took off for the woods marked on my map. When Matthews had recovered from my ignorance and I from the shock of his interrogation, he had told me that German parachute troops had come to ground under silk in a woods a couple of miles from the airfield we were protecting. We were to intercept them, the nine of us with our Bren gun, and shoot them up before they reached our airfield.

As we were leaving, the phone rang again. It was Matthews. "One more thing," he said, "it is reported that a web-like substance is falling from the sky. Warn your men on no account to touch it. It could prove fatal."

Off we drove, to attack the Nazi paratroopers — and to avoid a deadly, web-like substance falling from the sky!

As all the world knows, the invasion never took place. And that is why we never saw any paratroopers that night — or any web-like substance either.

Thank God, those church bells were wrong.

People often speak of the Battle of Britain as though it were a non-stop affair from 3 September 1939 until 8 May 1945. This, of course, is nonsense. The Battle of Britain began on 8 August 1940 and ended eighty-four days later on

31 October of *the same year*. During that period 2,375 German aircraft were known to have been destroyed in daylight. This slaughter of Hitler's war birds cost the Royal Air Force 375 pilots killed and 358 wounded, 47 of them Canadians. Most of the Canadians killed were serving with the RAF, but some were with No. 1 Fighter Squadron RCAF.

The Battle of Britain was won, but the aerial war went on for a bit. The period of harassment by night raiders and by lone daylight coastal raiders was at hand. But there was no further attempt by the German Air Force to destroy the RAF. Such an attempt would have been impossible. It was the *Luftwaffe* which had been destroyed. An invasion of Britain was now highly unlikely. We who were in Britain with the Canadian Army in those days numbered no more than 40,000, compared to the total of 370,000 Canadian troops who eventually served in Britain during the build-up period for the invasions of the Continent.

There is no doubt we ground troops played our part in winning that battle. If England had been without adequate ground defenses, invasion might well have been attempted under cover of the desperate combats in the sky above. If British fighter stations such as Tangmere, Lympe, Hawkings, Deal, Manston, Biggin Hill, Middle Wallop and so on had been seized by seaborne assault troops, or parachutists, during August or early September, the RAF could have been grounded. It was the fighter pilots of the RAF who won the Battle of Britain, but without the army, including Canada's forty thousand, it might not have been possible.

I have a remarkable receipt from the Park Lane Hotel, Piccadilly, showing that my private room with bath cost only 13 shillings and sixpence (about $3.70) at this first-class hotel on October 24, 1940, the height of the London blitz. A paperback describing Britain's "finest hour" said that about 50 bombers were over London that night. At the time I thought there must be 500.

Bombers or no bombers, blitz or no blitz, life went on in London. The streets were empty after dark, except for fire engines, ambulances, anti-aircraft gunners and the police. But indoors the people of London and khaki-clad visitors from overseas made the best of it.

I was just getting out of my tub when the sirens sounded. By the time I was dressed the cracking and crashing were becoming alarming. The heavy drone of enemy aircraft generated its own particular feeling of doom.

On the back of the door a notice told guests what to do during an air raid: Go to the basement with steel helmets and respirators; it was mandatory that all troops carry both.

My helmet was there, but the respirator case contained only my pyjamas, a change of socks and undershorts. I grabbed a towel to square it out and made for the basement. When I arrived six floors down I found splendid air raid accommodation. But there were only three people taking advantage of it: two elderly ladies and me! Hoping they wouldn't notice, I withdrew hastily, took the lift to my room, dumped my protective paraphernalia and decided to try the American bar, which was crowded and friendly. After an hour several of us went out into Piccadilly and watched the show.

The next morning, walking down Whitehall, I drew opposite the Admiralty. The great stone blocks that had formed one of the gates were lying in disarray on the sidewalk and a huge hole in the street necessitated a pedestrian detour. Rather foolishly, I spoke to one of the workmen resting on his shovel.

"I say, what happened here?" I babbled in my friendliest tone.

"Bloody chap was over again last night, wot does yer fink?" he replied with disgust, spitting out of the corner of his mouth.

Outside London, too, people faced up to the dangers, almost ignoring them at times. Whenever the alert sounded, the Odeon cinema at Redhill in Surrey flashed a message on the screen: "An air raid is in progress. If you wish to go to the shelter, please do so QUIETLY so as not to disturb our other patrons." Few people went. How could you, in the face of such an admonition?

I was on leave in Penzance in the West Country the night of their first raid of the war. Next morning the locals were jubilant; they were finally in the war! Luckily there were no serious casualties, although some real estate was damaged. At opening time my host and I went into the local and had just taken our places on stools at the bar when a well-known regular came in. He had been a brigadier in the first war. A fire-eater, apparently.

"The Hun tried to do me in last night," he confided.

"Is that so, Sir?" answered my companion, attempting to show interest.

"Yes, the *baw*stard did his best. Blew in my window, glass everywhere. As a matter of fact, he missed me by inches. A piece of brick flew across the room, right under the bed where I was lying and smashed the chamber pot to smithereens. Just like old times. *H-rr-rr-umph!*"

He called for his usual gin and tonic, a glow of pride on his ancient, lined face. He was in the front line again, damn it! Not only those pesky Londoners and people around the Thames Estuary would have their blitz stories now. He, too, had been the object of an attack by the King's enemies.

Forty thousand Britons were killed by enemy air action and probably five times as many were wounded. Whole streets went up in dust and flame. The administrative organization that co-ordinated clean-up after each raid was the work of geniuses.

In some instances the rubble of bombed out streets was trucked into the country, dumped in orderly fashion along rural roads and then examined to salvage valuables, restore them to their rightful owners where possible, and identify the dead by bits and pieces of bodies and personal effects. Each convoy represented a street, each vehicle a separate house, so if a gold watch or a severed finger with a

51

ring on it were found in a certain heap of broken brick and crumbled mortar, the fate of a loved one who had disappeared might be determined. Perhaps this was better than knowing nothing, but it was one of those tasks that made you lose your appetite.

Saluting is one of those things servicemen have to live with. Old soldiers used to say that if things in barracks didn't move you whitewashed them, but if something moved, you had better salute it. This simple philosophy could, and often did, create awkward situations.

Back in the 1930s a famous Permanent Force RSM was drilling the troops on the barrack square when his eagle eye discerned officer-like movement in the distance. Quick as a flash he turned smartly to his left, raised his hand in the perfect salute and bellowed, "Permission to carry on, Sah!" To his horror he then saw that in full view of an RSM's parade, he was saluting the driver of a laundry delivery truck. This fellow was dressed in a fawn-coloured suit with a facsimile Sam Browne belt to hold his leather change purse. The poor RSM was never quite the same.

Some wartime servicemen thought saluting an antiquated and undemocratic practice. Yet the worth of a unit, indeed its alleged fighting efficiency, was often rated by the saluting standard of its men. And many methods were introduced to raise the standard. In 1942 one bloody-minded Canadian brigadier used to drive about his brigade's UK area in his flagged car followed by two provost chaps on motor-bikes. These goggled riders had the job of laying charges against any officer or man who failed to salute their wheel-borne superior as he passed by.

A celebrated American soldier of World War I, General John J. Pershing, said: "Give me soldiers who can shoot well and salute well and I'll lick the enemy." He meant that good training and good discipline won battles, that both were necessary.

"To the front, salute. Up, one-two-three, down." That was the drill. "Longest way up, shortest way down", shouted the sergeant. Then, "Fingers together, palm to the front . . .

and keep those bloody elbows back!"

It's not that way any more. All Canadian servicemen salute sailor-style nowadays. Unification of the Forces has brought in the palms down salute. Today's would-be warriors sweep their right arms up as if they were about to scan the seascape for the sight of a Russian periscope or the scaly hips of a willing mermaid. Canada's airmen adapted easily to the faraway-look salute. The RCAF always had their own twist, saluting as though they were staring up at the wide, blue yonder. Sometimes the RCAF salute was almost a palms up effort, with the thumb placed just a little bit too close to the nose to suit sensitive Army brass.

In the early autumn of 1940, with Hitler's aerial navy shooting up the skies above England's green and pleasant land and Hitler's invasion fleet gathering on the coast of France, a 48th Highlander friend named Erskine Johnstone and I happened to be in Windsor. We were making our way down the winding High Street along the castle wall to the railway station when a black Daimler moved slowly up the slope toward us. Neither of us really noticed the vehicle until all of a sudden we saw an arm in Air Force blue come to the salute against the RAF wedge cap of the figure in the rear seat. A familiar face smiled through the window at us. Erskine came to life first. "My God," he blurted out, "It's the King!"

Our heads swivelled to the left in unison and both our right hands snapped tardily to the salute as the King's car passed. The King had saluted us. We had merely returned his salute. Like stupid tourists we stood gawking, unbelieving. The car disappeared through the castle gate. Immediately the Royal Standard broke from the castle masthead — a signal to the whole world, the enemy included, that the King was in his castle.

There was a lump in each of our throats. Our eyes were misty. "Christ Almighty," Johnstone gasped. "Imagine that, *he* saluted *us*!"

It is difficult, four decades later, to even understand the emotions of other far-off days, let alone explain them to another generation. But that day, had a regiment of German paratroopers landed nearby, the two of us would have attacked the whole ruddy lot with our bare hands.

It's amazing what the right kind of a salute can do to change a man's attitudes toward life — and death.

In 1940, when gas capes were carried rolled up on top of the small pack, as worn in fighting order, each brigade in the 1st Canadian Division had a different colored pull-tape to release the cape down over the shoulders in the event of a shower of mustard gas. One brigade had a red tape, a second a green tape, and a third a blue tape. If they had been khaki, as they should have been, they would have been just as awkward to use. They didn't work very well, but they certainly looked pretty. They gave a natty look to our rather dull khaki shapes.

Colour used to play such a big part in war. I remember the red tabs worn on the collars of the Brass hats, the white chalked stripes of the more fastidious NCOs; the multi-colored forage caps — scarlet, emerald, yellow and purple topped; and the brightly hued lanyards of royal blue or rifle green; or the variegated ropelets worn by REME. Then there were the regimental shoulder flashes, divisional patches, and finally, in 1945, that rainbow effect over the left pocket of many of the uniforms.

'Sober and properly dressed' is a well-remembered military phrase. I recall one company commander who refused to interview a soldier, telling the company-sergeant-major, "This man is improperly dressed. When he is properly dressed bring him back."

The CSM marched the man in and out three times, inspecting him each time from boot laces to cap badge. Finally exasperated, he went back in by himself. "Sir," he said, "I can find nothing wrong with the man's dress."

"Well, I can," answered the officer. "This man is entitled to the General Service and Victory Medals. He is not wearing them. When the ribbons are correctly sewed above his left breast pocket, as they should be, bring him back."

Some regiments had particularly colourful dress items. The 48th Highlanders wore blue puttees. In the British

Army the Royal Welch Fusiliers retained on the back of their tunic collars the bunch of black ribbons originally designed to keep the pigtail grease off their scarlet jackets. Powdered wigs and greasy pigtails were the hallmarks of British military beauty at one time. Both were abolished in the late 18th century, but the Royal Welch kept their pretty black 'flash' of ribbons.

One military item, which was not designed to enhance human beauty, but which eventually did so, was the bright yellow cellulose silk triangle that was to be pulled out of a soldier's respirator pocket and hung over his back like a Boy Scout scarf to indicate to friendly aircraft that the wearer was on the same side. Two of these triangles, when sewn together made cute panties for English girl friends. Losing these triangles was a serious offense, punishable by a pay stoppage and sometimes more. However, lots of the chaps thought they looked better when used sewn together, despite the punishment.

Ultimately it was decided that as ground to aircraft signals these triangles were not such a good idea anyway. They had proved to be just another communication failure from an army/air standpoint. From a boy/girl standpoint they were a wow! The postwar bikini wasn't nearly as fetching and not nearly as much fun to wear — or so I've been told.

On Christmas Day, 1940, our battalion was on coast defense duty in Brighton. The company I belonged to had its headquarters in the aquarium, with responsibility for the Palace Pier and stretches of the barbed wire along the beach on either side. My own platoon had a section on the pier. One Bren gun was set up in a neat little sandbagged nest, the grey waves of the channel lapping the sandy shore below. The pier had been cut in two by the engineers and the Bren covered the gap between the shoreside box-office and the fun houses and dance hall at the far end.

Came the dawn on this grim Yuletide and I made my bleary-eyed way down the Esplanade for 'stand to'. After gazing across the winter sea toward the coast of France, my binoculars tugging at my eyeballs, I decided that there wasn't much chance of an invasion that morning. 'Stand down' arrived and my platoon sergeant, 'Sly Sam' Mackness, whispered in my ear that he had a Christmas present that he would like to share with me. Off we went to his billet, on an upper floor of a vacant seafront hotel.

He began to unwrap his mysterious gift.

It became evident to my nostrils what the gift might be. After the outer wrappings were removed a familiar scent was wafted toward me, as my companion's eyes took on a worried look. The smell got stronger as layer after layer of damp comic papers was unrolled. Finally, there emerged a loaf of bread, soggy and thoroughly soaked in Scotch whisky! Inside the hollowed-out loaf was a bottle of a familiar brand, smashed into a dozen pieces. Christmas looked bleaker than ever, and it didn't improve much as the day wore on. That evening we had our Christmas dinner in the Brighton aquarium while a single, forgotten fish swam sluggishly around in the huge tank which formed one wall of our dining chamber. All the other fish, like the residents of the deserted hotels, had been evacuated inland.

Across the channel the Germans were no doubt having a similarly bleak Christmas away from their homeland. Worse Christmasses were to follow for both sides.

In the spring of '41 in England our battalion was assembled on a football field to be paraded before John G. Winant, the U.S. ambassador to Great Britain. When the Yankee diplomat arrived we were drawn up in threes, the proper formation since the drill book had been rewritten before the war. Despite this, the Second-in-Command shouted out, "Battalion, form fours!" No Canadian soldier had formed fours for the previous five years and, since most of our men had less than two years service, the results of this stupid order were appalling.

NCOs bawled out, "As you were! Stand fast! Don't move!" Some old-timers, forgetting that life had moved on since first they pounded the barrack square, attempted to obey the impossible order. The young ones swung their idle heads right and left to see what the next fellow was doing.

That most beautiful sight, a battalion at the slope with bayonets fixed, became a jumble of misdirected mass soldiery. But as a whole, the men stood solid as rocks and the battalion retained its shape.

The Commanding Officer almost melted to a grease spot; the U.S. envoy, the brigade, divisional and corps commanders were all viewing the shambles. Then the regimental-sergeant-major dashed across the field and whispered the awful truth into the dazed major's ear. Soon the mistake was corrected and in threes the unit swung past the saluting base in proud array, bugles blaring and drums beating.

Although the CO made the major's life hell on earth, it was he who was fired, for always the top man gets the axe as well as the accolade. The major survived, his mistake forgiven. In war, the unexpected always happens.

I remember an acting company commander whose platoons were doing their turn on 'stand to' at Bognor Regis during the invasion scare. He was eager to make his temporary authority felt. The evening that his troops were to be on call to move at a moment's notice, into anti-invasion positions, as the brigade's first 'punch at the enemy', should any landings take place, he looked out to sea and made his tactical appraisal. It was a stormy night, dark as pitch, with breakers pounding the shoreline. He concluded that not even Hitler's generals would be mad enough to risk sending the toughest raiders ashore on a night like this. So he decided to keep his troops confined to barracks, busy. He ordered all their webbing to be disassembled, scrubbed and blancoed.

Then the unexpected happened!

The brigadier decided it was a good night to test his defenses. Out went the code word. With the men's webbing in bits and pieces, dripping with wet blanco and laid out on tables and benches, the response was a good half an hour later than the brigadier required. Needless to say, the men's morale was not improved by the experience; nor was the colonel's happiness, nor the brigadier's temper, nor the acting commander's prospect for confirmation.

In the spring of 1941 I went on leave to Scotland, staying for a few days with the Earl and Countess of Elgin at Broomhall in Fife. Lord Elgin's estate included the two villages of Limekilns and Charlestown on the north bank of the Forth, not far from the Rosyth naval base. One day Lady Elgin invited me to accompany her and one of her daughters to afternoon tea on a huge battleship moored off one of their villages. The ship was commissioning, having never been to sea, and all was bustle on deck and below. We were piped aboard in deference to Lady Elgin's status as the wife of the King's Lord Lieutenant of Fife and greeted by the captain, a telescope under his arm in true Nelson style. We went to the admiral's quarters for tea prior to a tour of the ship. The admiral had not come aboard and the captain, Leach by name, was living in the beautifully panelled and furnished quarters of his superior. A few weeks later the ship made the headlines of the world as it joined in the chase that eventually ended with the sinking of the *Bismarck*. Before the year was out she, too, was at the bottom of the sea. My host, Captain John Leach, went down with his ship; so did the admiral who flew his flag aboard her and so did almost one thousand of her crew of three thousand. The ship was H.M.S. *Prince of Wales*. Considering her short life and the secrecy which surrounded her building, few people other than her crew ever saw the magnificent sea monster. But I was one who did.

The worst air raid on London took place the night of May 10-11, 1941, while our company was on guard duty at Chartwell Manor, Prime Minister Winston Churchill's country home near Westerham in Kent, about 25 miles as the crow flies from the heart of London. Our tour of duty had been going on for about a week, but we hadn't seen Churchill. He wasn't there that night either. According to his postwar book, *The Grand Alliance*, he was spending that weekend with friends at Ditchley.

Our tents were pitched under the spreading trees some 50 yards from the house. Through the window, on a chintz-covered window seat could be seen two of the war leader's famous flat-topped bowlers — the 'plug' hats he wore on most public appearances in those days when the stolid, John Bull image was needed. And no doubt Churchill ensured that a supply of plug hats, like his big cigars, was readily at hand at 10 Downing Street, or Chequers or Chartwell Manor, so that no matter when or where he turned up, his props were available for any morale-building purposes that might be required.

There was great air activity over Chartwell that night. RAF night interceptors usually managed to engage the Nazi raiders in that area, turning them — or at least some of them — back from their London targets. Ted Price and I stood beside Churchill's goldfish pool and watched a number of dogfights above us. The sound of aerial machine-gunning was like someone ripping taut canvas with a sharp knife. The black sky was alive with tracer, as if some unseen hands were throwing rubies, topazes and balls of fire into the void above. Suburban and central London were in agony. Half a dozen flamers screamed and twisted downward to become smouldering heaps on the green fields of England. Tiring of the show above, we crawled into our blankets, knowing that next day we were to march back to our billets in the Chipstead Valley to allow another company the honour of guarding the home of democracy's champion.

While all this was going on Churchill was watching a Marx Brothers' film at his friend's house near Ditchley. He wrote in his war memoirs that, although he inquired about the air raid from time to time, there was nothing that he could do about it, so he continued to amuse himself with the American movie madcaps. Suddenly, a messenger brought him some amazing news. We heard it next morning as we formed up outside the walls of Chartwell Manor for the return march to our regular billets.

"Hess has landed in Scotland!" This astounding information came from one of the troops who had heard the BBC morning newscast. He told us it had said Hitler's deputy, Rudolf Hess, had piloted his own fighter plane from Germany to crash land somewhere near Glasgow while parachuting down with peace proposals.

"Well, I guess the war is over," remarked somebody down the line of tinhatted, pack-laden troops. Most of us thought he was not far wrong. We didn't know that Hess had become mentally unbalanced, that he had flown to Britain with hare-brained schemes of his own. We were sure he was a peace envoy sent by *Der Fuehrer* himself. How wrong we were!

"If it ain't over, it soon will be," ventured another voice.

Then another thought struck one of the chaps. "Jeezuz!" he ripped out. "Just think, this effing war is over and we haven't even seen a German."

"Yeah, what a hell of a rotten war this turned out to be," muttered a juvenile soldier.

"Guess it's back to mom for you, son," answered an oldster. "Just think, no more Piccadilly, no more Soho, no more . . ." His voice trailed off.

But they were all wrong. Even Deputy *Fuehrer* Hess was wrong. He bore no mandate from Hitler to seek peace. He had no plan worth considering. He was only a madman, fleeing from a madhouse. He became a prisoner of war and remained one for years, still locked up in Berlin's Spandau Prison 40 years later, a shell of a human being, well over mankind's allotted span.

And what of the young soldiers who thought the war was over? For many of them it was a much shorter life than that allowed Hess. Some died in Sicily, some in Italy and some in Holland. For the war was not over. Not even Piccadilly and Soho were over. Things dragged on in Britain for two or three years — then eventually for all of us, in different ways, the war was over. By then, most of us had seen a German — too many of them.

Digging slit trenches was one of the main occupations of the infantry during the 'Long Wait' in England, while Churchill and Hitler glared at one another across the Channel. Slit trenches were usually dug in three phases. The first phase was their siting by a junior officer. The wrong site was usually chosen. Nevertheless, the second or shoveling phase would then begin. The third phase was when some visiting senior officer arrived. This fellow always shifted the location of the trenches. This resiting was only a temporary measure. A still more senior officer was bound to arrive later, with his idea of where the soil should be violated.

Captain with 2nd London Irish Rifles, in a trench in Tunisia, February, 1943.

Thus it can be seen that the original three-phased operation was really only one phase of a bigger two, three or even four-phased effort. The only way to avoid such a succession of abortive field works was to get the Corps Commander or at least the GOC of the Division to plot the ruddy slits himself before anyone got their fingernails dirty.

Sometimes, the local farmers became a bit miffed at the way their asparagus beds or other valuable footage of their native land was being abused, dug up and filled in, dug up somewhere else and so on. These farmers weren't straw-sucking rubes, either. They were veritable John Bulls. Like as not they were booted and spurred, with riding crops to emphasize their gestures of displeasure. Most of them stalked about in prickly plus-fours with shotguns under the crooks of their arms, their Savile Row, suiting in bold houndstooth or checks. It was obvious that most of them had at one time in their lives been majors or even colonels in the Yeomanry, probably in Mesopotamia, or possibly at Mafeking. Anyway, they did not like slit trenches, especially if they were being dug on their property.

Came the morning when I was blasted by one of these gentry with, "For God's sake, why don't you chaps make up your bloody minds as to where you want these bloody holes, and stop digging up the entire bloody farm?"

I replied in kind.

"The trouble with you Englishmen," I said, "is that you don't know there's a war on. Now buzz off!" Strangely enough, he did.

In the early afternoon a farm youth appeared and handed me a neat little note written in a feminine hand. Would the lieutenant be kind enough to join the farmer and his wife at four o'clock for tea? It seemed like an olive branch was being extended. I accepted, but at the appointed hour I approached the Jacobean farmhouse somewhat apprehensively.

Their tea service was genuine Queen Anne. On the walls family portraits revealed bemedalled ancestors and spoke not only of service to the Empire, but of sacrifices for the Empire as well.

Finally, after friendly chit-chat, my host steered the conversation into channels which allowed him to show me around the house. By the time we got upstairs he suggested I might like to use the bathroom and more or less pushed me into the place. About a foot above the rim of the bathtub were two gaping holes in the plaster. My host then pointed to the top of the window frame, where the wood was splintered and gouged.

"Messerschmitt cannon," he mouthed quietly. "My wife was taking a bath at the time. Quite lucky, really. However, makes one realize there's a war on."

It was a nice lesson. It was also a nice cup of tea.

The sowing of mines is done not only on land, by engineers, but also at sea by mine-laying craft and from the air. Sometimes these devices washed ashore and had to be disposed of. In the autumn of 1941 our battalion was on coast defense at Selsey Bill. One afternoon, just as I was ripping the guts out of my respirator haversack and stuffing it with pyjamas and my shaving kit for a 'forty-eight' in London, I was summoned to HQ and told to take a sniper with me and go down to the beach where a small sea mine had washed up on the sand. We were to stand off and the sniper was to try to detonate it with a well-placed round.

After the sniper put five holes in the mine with no explosion, I decided the thing was safe enough. I picked it up and took it back to the adjutant's office to report my mission accomplished. The adjutant, Frank Klenavic, was out, so, not wanting to miss the bus to Chichester where I was to catch the train to London, the Park Lane Hotel and other attractions, I placed the perforated mine on his desk and prepared to go.

Just then Klenavic came in the other door. "What's that?" he screamed. Then, focussing on the object, he half queried, half identified it: "Mine?" he mumbled.

"All yours," I answered over my shoulder and bolted for the door.

When I returned from leave two days later I was met with a stony glare. Klenavic had not been as unconcerned about the mechanism as I had been. The local police had been summoned, the offensive item taken down to the beach in their bomb-disposal truck and the sappers called in. With their superior skill they exploded the device.

Treacherous things, mines.

The English people were very friendly during those years of waiting it out, while Hitler glared across the Channel, or turned his greedy eyes toward Russia. Invited to small house parties, or afforded the hospitality of the great homes, we frequently ran into people whose names were known around the English-speaking world, but who lived in some village near London, in a small villa perhaps, or even a castle. The novelist Sir Philip Gibbs, the actress Beatrice Lillie, the Orientalist St. John Philby (whose son became a Communist spy some years later); A.P. Herbert, the poet and politician; were among the people I met over a whisky and soda, a sherry, or a cup of tea.

While we were under canvas in Arundel Park, Capt. Tom Lawson returned to camp one afternoon on the train from London. He had shared a compartment with a quiet-spoken man and when they arrived at the Arundel station this chap asked him if he could take him anywhere, as he had a car. Tom said that he was in a tent in Arundel Park, which was probably out of the way. "Not at all", replied the car owner, "I'd be glad to take you there." They were met by a chauffeur and when they drove in through the great gates of Arundel Castle and the gatekeeper *salaamed* with style, Tom realized that he was being escorted home by the Duke of Norfolk, the first subject of the Realm.

The Duke invited him to come to the Castle for a drink the next evening and asked him to bring a friend. Tom took me and we had a pleasant couple of hours chatting about farming, of which Tom and I knew practically nothing. The Duke, however, who owned many thousands of acres and told us that he was paying 19 shillings and sixpence income tax on the pound, appeared to know a great deal. Wounded at Dunkirk while serving with The Blues, he had been boarded out of the Service and held a post in the Ministry of Agriculture.

We saw more of the Duchess. Every morning she would gallop past the officers' tent lines on her early morning ride. Like as not we would be standing stark naked having a sponge bath in our canvas basins after morning P.T., or shaving, with everything swinging free. Her Grace always waved gaily as she rode by.

The only trouble we had while in Arundel Park was when some of the Mortar Platoon blew the hind legs off a deer during a practice shoot. They dined on venison for a while, but the Duke's gamekeeper could count and later on the buried carcass was discovered and there was a bit of hell to pay. Apparently there is nothing more sacrosanct than a ducal deer.

I had my own family connections in lovely Sussex. About twelve miles away lived Major James Galloway, whose home was called Murrayfield House. It lay right next to Tangmere airfield, a fighter base which had not suffered during the August, 1940 attacks, but which received a fair bit of damage in 1941. I had spent several days there as my aged cousin's guest during the late autumn of '40. In the early summer of '42 the CO laid on a series of exercises in which each company commander was to take his company off on its own to conduct platoon tactical exercises, administer itself away from camp and generally rough it in the open. The CO drew circles on the map and designated these the areas we were to make for. He planned to visit us unexpectedly during the outing to see what we were doing. I was surprised to see my cousin's home circled on my map. This was where I was to bivouac my company the first night!

I kept my secret as we set off on foot. Several hours later the troops were surprised, as we marched down a driveway and into a building complex to see a huge canvas sign over the stable door announcing in large black letters, MAJOR GALLOWAY'S PRIZE SHORTHORN HERD. They were more surprised when my cousin's bailiff, a Mr. Alexander, greeted me with recognition. The Major was away but Alexander let the officers into the house, bedded down the more than a hundred men on clean straw in some vacant stables and put the sergeants up in a stone building by themselves.

There were many more humorous incidents. I remember one Sunday morning when Col. Greene was commanding. At the time, the officers of Battalion HQ messed in a small country house called Merstham Lodge. This was a hideaway belonging to Her Royal Highness the Princess Arthur of Connaught. She was 'really royal' as one chap said, for her father was the late King Edward VII and her late husband was HRH Prince Arthur, son of HRH the Duke of Connaught, Edward VII's brother. In other words both were grandchildren of Queen Victoria and were first cousins.

The Princess had dropped in with her equerry to see how her place was weathering the storm of military occupation. The colonel asked her to stay for a sherry, which she did. As they were sipping, in came one of our junior officers, well over thirty years of age, but junior nevertheless. He noticed that the colonel had a lady with him, nodded politely and quietly went off to a corner. However, the CO hailed him, and asked the Princess if he might introduce one of his officers. Knowing the CO had an eye for the ladies and recalling that an ENSA show had been staged in the camp area the night before, the poor bloody officer suspected she was one of the ENSA 'girls'. When she was introduced as 'Princess' he thought it was a joke and replied, "Well, how-dee-do, Princess, you gals certainly put on a wow of a performance last night. I hope you got a good night's sleep, you sure deserved it."

What actually happened next is a bit hazy in the minds of those who observed things from afar. The officer left for a job at the Holding Unit the next day and the Regiment didn't see him again for well over a year, by which time the mortified CO was long gone and Merstham Lodge a vague memory.

Once before going to Scotland on leave, I had the misfortune to bump into my CO., Murray Kirk Greene, in the lobby of the Park Lane Hotel in London. Contrary to regulations I was carrying a walking stick.

"What are you doing in *this* hotel?" he asked me.

"I'm staying here, Sir", I replied politely.

"Then don't", he barked back at me, adding, "When I was a subaltern we did not stay at the same hotel as our Commanding Officer. You should be at the Strand Palace—and without that walking stick."

I took part of his advice. I checked out and left for Scotland. I certainly wasn't going to stay at the Strand Palace, nor throw away my walking stick.

Another hotel encounter took place one noon when I was lunching in the Buttery at the Berkeley. A young Scots Guards captain was sitting at the table beside me. He finished his lunch and left. A few minutes later I went to the washroom. When I returned a waiter came up to me and said,"I believe you dropped your wallet, Sir." I knew it wasn't mine, but curiosity prompted me to open it. The identity card showed that it belonged to Captain the Lord Lyell. The name meant nothing to me, so I gave the wallet back to the waiter, showing him the identity card. Two years later Lyell's name was on the front page of every London newspaper. He had been killed in action, earning the Victoria Cross. Seventeen years later, while visiting the Scots Guards at Windsor, the CO., Lord Cathcart, laid on a program for me which included a visit to the guard room in the Castle. There I met the guard commander, a very young ensign, who turned out to be the current Lord Lyell, son of the VC winner. I recalled the wallet incident. He had been three years old when his father had sailed for North Africa.

While stationed in the Chipstead area south of London it was sometimes possible to borrow a vehicle and drive up to town for a night out. After duty one winter evening, a fellow officer named Tommy Cantley and I wangled a 5-cwt truck and drove to London, a distance of about twenty miles. We decided to go to the Regent Palace Hotel, a somewhat low-brow hostelry to see if any of our friends were 'out on the town' as well. Our driver was not too sure of the route. London was blacked out and we ran into a dense peasoup fog as soon as we entered the built-up area. We got completely lost and ordered the driver to stop. Getting out of the back of the vehicle, where we had been sitting on the floor boards under the canvas top, we began shouting '*Halloo! Halloo!*' to see if we could raise a reply. We did. Out of the fog came a Bobby. "Where are we?" we queried the constable. "Well, Canada," rejoined the policeman, "You're in the 'eart of the British Hempire. This 'ere is Parl'ment Square. If you wyte ten minutes you'll 'ear Big Ben strike nine o'clock." We didn't wait. We thanked him and went off up Whitehall, a veritable void of pitch black and eventually ended up in the dazzling lobby of the Regent Palace.

The Regent Palace was not looked upon as *the* place to go, but it did have some attractions. The Grosvenor House was popular for Sunday *thés dansant*; the Park Lane was much used by the 1940 influx of Canadian officers, but gradually, when the 2nd Canadian Division, later the growing Canadian Army, and finally the Americans, began to use the place, it lost its appeal. The big spenders went to the Savoy or the Dorchester—and we went off to the war zones.

CHAPTER IV

LOW POINT AT DIEPPE

Veterans of the first war and those of us who got our training between the wars were very familiar with the Lewis Gun, that flanged, fluted and ferocious looking weapon with its 47-round drum. In the early days of the Second World War, the British still used it as a subsidiary anti-aircraft weapon on airfields, on Channel patrol craft and in their pitifully inadequate shore defenses.

Driving along the esplanade at Bognor Regis in a 15-cwt truck one afternoon, our Transport Officer, an unafraid young gentleman with fond memories of the Lewis gun and his pre-war militia ability at stripping and assembling it in a matter of minutes (or was it seconds?), saw a group of British sailors unloading boxes of this historic weapon onto the pavement. He saw himself once again stripping a Lewis gun down piece by piece, laying the pieces on a rubberized groundsheet, then re-assembling the gun, cocking it, clearing it, then jumping up to shout, "No. 1 gun ready, Sir!" His eager mind concocted a daring deed.

Driving past the toiling tars, he removed the tactical number plate from his vehicle to ensure anonymity, then drove back to the Bluejacket working party. Leaping from the cab with an authoritative manner, he approached the sailors.

"Are you the chaps detailed to unload these Lewis guns?" he queried, though their task could not have been more obvious. The Petty Officer replied in the affirmative with a jaunty palm-down salute.

"Right", barked our hero, "now put one of them into

this vehicle. As you know, one is all I need."

"Aye, aye, Sir!" Two seamen humped the long box into the Canadian officer's truck. The bell-bottomed boys were a disciplined lot. Nelson would have been proud of them.

Driving a distance away, the Lewis gun lover replaced the tactical number plate. Arriving in his own area, he lugged his new-found treasure up to his room in the seafront hotel, which we occupied as an officers' mess and billet. He practised his stripping and assembling act every night until he saw his old skill return, and possibly improve. The time for his triumph was now at hand. In the mess, when only his subaltern buddies were present, he openly boasted of his illegal possession and wagered he could strip it and assemble it faster than anyone else there. For a while he had no takers. Then one evening, after a few drinks in the hotel lounge, which served as the mess ante-room, he laid his bet again. The bet was accepted, raised and raised again. Apparently a few people were willing to admit they knew something about the obsolete Lewis gun too. Finally, a little group followed the expert up the stairs to the bedroom where the test could be conducted. The box was pulled out from under the bed. The gun was put on its bipod in the centre of the room. Off came the demonstrator's tunic and a watch was produced. The word "Go" was uttered and the champion Lewis gun stripper began to move. But he was the only thing that did move. Not one single piece of the glistening Lewis gun could be budged.

Somebody had varnished the moveable parts to the point where the stripping act turned out to be an exercise in futility.

By February 12, 1942, the war had become a real bore for Canadian troops in England. The 'phoney war', Dunkirk and the Battle of Britain were now memories. Even enemy air raids were rare. The V-1s and V-2s hadn't made their appearance yet. The word 'buzz-bomb' was still unknown.

Summoned by a company runner from the warmth of my winter billet, I shivered my way down the deserted coastal streets of Bognor Regis to a designated assembly point. Winter gales lashed the seashore. What was up? It couldn't be an invasion scare, the Germans were too busy in Russia. It couldn't even be a smash-and-grab raid. No assault craft could survive in such seas. No paratroops could hope to land safely on their DZs in the kind of winds stinging my cheeks as I hurried along.

I soon found out what was up! Three German battleships were loose in the Channel. For months the *Gneisenau*, the *Scharnhorst* and the *Prinz Eugen* had been bottled up in the French harbor of Brest. But under cover of darkness and stormy winter weather they obeyed a daring order from Hitler to make a break for home and were running up the Channel toward their base at Kiel.

We were to man all shore lookouts in the hope of spotting the elusive enemy ships if they zigged or zagged in our direction to avoid the forces attempting to intercept them. Our post was on top of a high gasometer. With lamps and wireless sets strapped to our shoulders, we made our way up the precarious iron stairway, with rubber in our knees and butterflies in our bellies. The strong winds helped to unnerve us. Suddenly, one man became rigid with fear. The height was too much for him. He refused to move up or down. Someone managed to tear his petrified grasp from the railing and we made a fearful descent. Then, minus our comrade, we began the upward climb for the second time.

Safe at the top we set up shop — telescope, wireless set, heliograph. For several miserable hours we scanned the misty horizon for signs of enemy ships. In our imaginations great hulks loomed out of the distant fog. The action, however, was to the east of us, where the Dover batteries, the Dover MTB patrol and antiquated Swordfish aircraft did their best. Their best wasn't good enough, as the three ships escaped to their haven. But it was six months before *Scharnhorst* was sufficiently repaired to get back into the war, and *Gneisenau* never again appeared on the high seas.

The British public was stunned and angered. How could three enemy warships have an almost free run up the English Channel? Churchill cabled embarrassed explanations to Britain's new ally, Franklin Roosevelt. But the worst was yet to come. Three days later, while still shocked by the Channel episode, the British public was informed that Singapore had fallen and the Japanese had captured 100,000 British troops.

As Shakespeare had written 350 years earlier, it was "the winter of our discontent".

Off to the wars! Lieuts. Galloway, Crich and Garfunkel, H.M.T. Oronsay, Halifax, August, 1940.

Early in '42 the Canadian Army in England went Battle Drill mad. Assault courses, live ammunition exercises and speed marches dominated the lives of all infantrymen and impinged on those in other corps. Training had become boring. For two years, in the case of some of us, barrack square routine and large scale manoeuvres, which nobody below the Commander Home Forces seemed to really understand, had started to turn us into a fed-up, browned-off, disillusioned band of volunteer warriors. We were getting to the point where we couldn't have fought our way out of a paper bag. Something had to be done, and Battle Drill was the answer. Selected officers and NCOs were sent on qualifying courses and, after four weeks of running, wading through, or climbing over obstacles, swinging from ropes and being fired on at close range with live ammunition, they came back proud of themselves and bent on making their comrades suffer twice as much as they had!

It was the best thing that could have happened. For most of us, that is. The strong excelled and it did their egos good. The weak grew strong. Or, if this did not happen, they were weeded out. As a result our "fighting efficiency" increased by leaps and bounds. We got hard. We got lean and mean. Without Battle Drill the 1st Canadian Division could not have done the job it did in Sicily a year later. It didn't pay off for the 2nd Division. But that was because they were dumped ashore at Dieppe, where the restrictions of the deadly beaches didn't allow them to put Battle Drill to the test.

One day our company was being put through its paces. The chief taskmaster was Mickey Austin, a sergeant who was very young and as hard as nails. He had a heart, but he always left it with his surplus kit. He was merciless in the manner in which he led, directed, pushed and pursued the successive sections and platoons over the toughest obstacles. He would get them into difficult places, then dash off and seize a pre-placed Bren gun with which he would fire bursts "up their tails" to get them moving. Meantime, assistant instructors fired weapons on fixed lines. Safety was 90 percent certain.

Our troops did well. Everyone was too proud to falter. Then one day Mickey saw red. Five men were crossing the Arun River, a stream about thirty feet wide, on ropes, and were taking far too long. The lead man was actually dawdling across the ropes as if he didn't intend to hurry. Furiously the sergeant shouted, "Get going, you bloody bastard, you!" The man's two hands continued to grasp the upper rope. His feet only inched along the lower one. He was causing the men behind him to bunch, a battlefield crime. "Get going", roared the sergeant, "or you'll bloody well get shot!" The man continued his snail's pace; the bunching caused the rope to sag in the middle. "Hurry,

hurry, hurry!" admonished the sergeant, leaping and gesticulating on the river bank, "or you bloody well *will* get shot."

The man's hands slipped from the rope and he toppled into the stream. As he fell he called out, "Hell, sergeant, I've been shot twice already."

He had. One bullet had drilled through the soft flesh under his rib cage, another had bored through his left foot from toe to heel. Blood stained the water as we hauled him out.

"I'm sorry", he said as we lifted him onto the grass. "I was okay after I got hit the first time, but the one in the foot really slowed me down".

His name was Private Hood. I have often wondered what we could have done later on with a battalion of Private Hoods — or an army of them.

As for Sergeant Austin, a year later he went to another regiment to become its RSM. In Northwest Europe he won the Military Cross (an almost unique decoration for a Warrant Officer) and two Mentions in Despatches. Gad, they were men!

Cover from view is not cover from fire. But, if the enemy can't see you, he is less likely to hit you. That's one reason personal camouflage is a good thing. You also camouflage other things to deceive the enemy. In the Great War where the 'line' was static for long periods, camouflage became an art. One idea was to construct dummy trees with trunks large enough to contain a sniper. But it had to be situated so the enemy wouldn't say, "*Mein Gott!* Where was that tree yesterday?" Then blast it — and the sniper inside — with a few well-placed shells. Trees big enough to hide a man and his rifle don't grow overnight.

I remember attending a camouflage school at Tunbridge Wells where a drawly British instructor told us: "Now, remember chaps. When you camouflage yourselves don't become more obvious. Don't camouflage yourself as a telephone kiosk if you are in the middle of the Western Desert."

74

Camouflage can become a fetish, then it eventually becomes boring and everybody forgets about it. In England during the big training exercises of 1941-42 every infantryman seemed to become a moving bush. Our tin hats were covered with hessian sacking with loops. Later we were issued camouflage nets. Into these loops and holes we stuffed leaves, branches of trees and local foliage of all kinds. We also stuck branches in our webbing. Of course, the hides of vehicles were also heavily camouflaged.

When the fighting started, camouflage was often forgotten. We had aerial superiority and vehicular camouflage was seldom necessary. Why the troops got careless about 'garnishing' their helmets and equipment is another matter and perhaps some died needlessly as a result. The camouflage net dulled the glint of the steel and the custom of shoving a first field dressing inside the net transformed the telltale shape of the helmet into a lump of earth. Still, soldiers were often seen advancing toward the enemy with shiny steel domes. Certainly, concealment by clever camouflage or just taking advantage of natural cover is one way to evade the effects of machine-gun or rifle fire. And probably gun-fire too.

But I remember one soldier who wanted to be seen by the enemy.

While advancing against the foe one hot day in Sicily, one of the men felt conspicuous. We all wore the 1st Canadian Division's bright red patches on our upper sleeves. We looked like a moving field of poppies. Just before we moved off, one of the men shouted out to his section corporal, "Say, Corp, don't you think we should tear off these red patches? They show up like hell."

"Look you," replied the NCO. "I wore these patches for two years in England to show who I was. Now I want the Jerries to know who I am and who we all are. I'm not taking them off and neither are you." Sad to relate, the corporal was dead within the hour, drilled through the stomach by a sniper's bullet.

During the long wait in England one of our companies was camped in four Nissen huts in the park of a stately home. A friend who was keen on camouflage was wandering around the grounds when he came upon a cluster of unusual trees. "Hah!" he said to himself, "just the thing." He had been a bit worried that the huts would be a visible target during a sneak coastal raid by a marauding Messerschmitt. Soon a fatigue party was digging up and replanting the trees around the huts, shielding them from any German pilot who might be strafing about.

Within 24 hours something worse occurred. My friend got a phone call from a pal at army HQ. "What the hell is going on?" this fellow asked. "The War Office just phoned that some mucky-muck has complained that some Canadian vandals have dug up a cluster of exceedingly valuable cedars of Lebanon, which he had imported from the Holy Land. They claim they are planted around your hutments."

He said that a War Office investigation party would be arriving via army HQ where it would pick up a Canadian staff officer, and added: "This could cost our government plenty and get you court-martialled."

My friend got the message. "Hold them at your office as long as you can," he implored his informant. "I'll take care of everything."

When the War Office Johnnies arrived there were no trees in sight. They had all been dug up a second time and trucked away in a three-tonner. Even the scarred earth was hidden under gravelled paths and flower beds!

"Trees, what trees?" my friend queried the posse from Whitehall. He got away with it. If you can't camouflage some things you can at least conceal others.

Although I am getting ahead of my story, I must say that in war you feel a hell of a lot safer when you're not sticking out of the landscape like the proverbial sore thumb. Bullets might go through a hedgerow or shells might crash through a tile roof, but most of us spent more time creeping about behind foliage and sheltering under rickety roofs than we did parading around in front of our slit trenches with rifles at the slope. The only people I ever saw who really flaunted their lack of love for 'concealment from view' was a bunch of redtabbed generals and brigadiers who arrived at our cleverly concealed brigade headquarters in North Africa one day to watch the start of an attack.

During the night, our HQ was dug in the bank of a gravel pit, or I should say, in the side of a *wadi*. We were right at the infantry start line. Clumps of cactus, camouflage nets and canvas sheets daubed with special shades of paint made us invisible. Leaving our vehicles in an olive grove, we had walked the half mile forward under cover of darkness.

Then, our invisibility burst into full colour! Up roared a motorcycle followed by three jeep-loads of scarlet-collared warriors. Several had sand-colored trench coats over their arms. One wore a gleaming Sam Browne over his coat, the brasses twinkling in the rays of the rising sun.

They all had binoculars and wanted to watch the 'show'. Up the little slope they strode, positioned themselves on the high spot and began to sweep the enemy's lines with their glasses. Having seen enough, they marched back down, and got into their jeeps. Off they went in clouds of dust.

Their 'recce' took about five minutes. One minute later: Swish! The 88s began screaming in and all was pandemonium. Of course, the high-priced help had gone and we were left to hug the dirt, crowd the sides of our trenches and quake in mortal terror.

Luckily, none of us was hurt, but all our camouflage efforts had been for naught. For the rest of the day, as we strove to direct the battle, we were harassed by shell-fire and could not go about our business with efficiency and ease. Fortunately, the attack went well anyway; by evening the Germans had pulled back and we were out of range of their 88s at last. But no thanks to the red-tabbed Johnnies.

Blaming the other fellow is always fun. But few of us are lily-white and free from sin. Some weeks later we were out of the line and I took a company on a route march. After an hour or so we came upon a sign that indicated our corps HQ was hidden in a grove of olive trees, and I decided to march my troops right through the area to show the caravan commandos what fighting troops looked like.

Being an Irish regiment, we had a company piper and I told him to give us *The Wearin' o' the Green*. We hadn't proceeded more than 50 yards when a purple-faced major came roaring out from a camouflaged marquee shouting, "Who the bloody hell are you? What the hell are you doing coming through here? Don't you know this is corps headquarters? Get your blasted people out of here."

In like manner he enlightened me that corps was in hiding, completely camouflaged, with a minimum-movement order. It was all part of a great deception plan that I and my confounded soldiery were in danger of exposing. "If enemy aircraft spot troops in this locality we're in for it. You could be compromising our whole scheme."

Victory Bond parade, Bognor Regis 1942, CSM Bert Hovey and Lieut. Len Carling follow me past "The Drums".

78

Crestfallen, I turned my column about and moved off, the pipes silent. My sergeant-major cheered me up. "Sir", he said, "when that major said we were at corps headquarters you should have said: 'Jeez, major, I didn't know we were that far back.'"

Deception can also be given away by sheer subconscious stupidity. In the spring of '43 Arabs moved about between the lines, going from abandoned farm to abandoned farm, unhindered by either our troops or the enemy. We believed they were local farmers gathering their seed for the spring planting behind the German lines. We did not hinder them — until a clever observer noticed they always walked in step. No shuffling Arabs ever did that, but the well-trained young soldiers of the *Afrikakorps* did. They were actually camouflaged Germans organizing forward machine-gun and mortar ammunition dumps in cellars and root houses to support a smash attack a few days hence.

In August, 1942, I was on a battledrill course in the south of England. One dark night we took part in a mock commando raid on Tangmere airdrome, a fighter station that had been heavily attacked by the *Luftwaffe* during the Battle of Britain two years earlier. Crawling through the wet grass I eventually found myself in a village churchyard, and, deciding to check my map, I noticed I was lying beside three wooden crosses. Turning my thin beam on the first cross I was startled to read the words, Unteroffizier Schmidt, German Air Force, 15.8.40. On the other crosses the inscriptions, in black lettering on raw wood, read, Hauptmann Straucher and Unknown German Airman. Their dates of death were the same as Schmidt's. They were the first war graves I had ever seen and I marvelled that three members of Goering's vaunted air armada would be tucked away in this English country churchyard.

How such scenes jar the sensibilities! A veteran of the Somme told me that he once marched into the attack, passing a sawmill on the way. The saws were buzzing merrily as they turned out hundreds of wooden crosses that were being stacked in full view of the troops, ready to mark their places — perhaps in a few short hours.

In Italy one Christmas Eve, we plodded on in single file to mount an attack and came unexpectedly upon our padre with half a dozen freshly painted crosses under his arm. He was going to plant them a few yards away, where our pioneers could be seen lifting the stiffened corpses into their newly dug graves. The reaction of the troops was a series of ribaldries and awkward jokes. I often wonder how youth can be so brave on its way to oblivion.

As the mist of early morning began to lift one summer day, I walked along a leafy Sussex lane to our company headquarters, located in a large, camouflaged tent. The skies were very noisy. For some hours aircraft had been screaming overhead, flying to and from the coast of France. Some, returning, seemed to limp along. Their motors hummed raggedly. Their wings and fuselages showed evidence of enemy fire.

Suddenly Sergeant Austin emerged from a bell tent. He called excitedly to me "It's begun. And we're not in it!" He looked crestfallen indeed.

"What's begun?" I asked.

"The Second Front," he almost shouted back. "And 2nd Div is over there now."

I began to realize what all the aircraft of the past few hours meant. But he didn't give me a chance to say anything before he blurted out. "I was in Portsmouth last night, 2nd Div was all on ships . . . dozens of 'em . . ."

The sergeant was very disappointed. He wasn't the only one.

Shortly before noon I went to the mess which was in a farmhouse down the road. Several chaps were standing around a mantel radio, listening to a news release. "Why couldn't it have been us?" the CO was asking nobody in particular as I entered the room.

How we began to hate 2nd Division. They were getting all the glory in what was apparently a full scale raid on Dieppe.

By lunch time the country road, on either side of

which our billets and our bivouacs lay, became a stream of ambulances and lorries heading for southern ports. They travelled at higher than convoy speeds.

Then the message came. Company 2nds-in-command and Company-Quartermaster-Sergeants were to leave for an undisclosed destination within the hour. Fighting order was to be worn. We climbed into 15-cwt. trucks and off we went. We were exultant.

"We're going over there, too!" we told ourselves as our wheels spun along the Sussex lanes. "Sure thing. Our division is the follow-up. We'll push through the 2nd Div's beachhead. Sure thing. We're the recce parties. Tonight we'll be staking out areas for our chaps in France." And so the prattle went on as we raced southward, checking our equipment and wondering whether we would be brave enough to do our job.

We didn't know much about amphibious landings in 1942. Neither, apparently, did Combined Operations headquarters.

Finally, we arrived at Newhaven's outskirts and drove straight to the harbour. Large tents had been erected. Vehicles were starting to load a few wounded who came off returning landing craft. We stood around until we were told why we were there. We were not going across the Channel. It was not to be a second front. We were to assist in checking-in those returning from a short, commando-type raid made that morning on Dieppe. The force was now withdrawing.

We stood on the docks and waited. A few craft straggled in. Across the water the sound of battle, 65 miles away, was faintly audible. Wisps of smoke could be seen afar off, blowing high above the sea.

A commando unit arrived back. The men looked tough but exhausted. Their faces were still smeared with blacking. I saw a tall hatless officer with thick, curly hair. He looked confident and calm, as if he had done his job well. He had. It was Lord Lovat and the hardy fellows in the khaki knitted caps surrounding him were the survivors of No. 4

Commando, who only a few hours before had attacked an enemy battery with the bayonet!

A tank landing craft came in and sixteen German prisoners emerged with their captors, their hands up. A few other craft appeared on the horizon and eventually docked. Their interiors were a shambles, containing dead and wounded. Someone who had been closer than I was claimed that the bodies in one craft had RHLI shoulder flashes on their battledress jackets.

It was obvious that the raid had been a disaster.

Later, as we drove back to our camp, having done nothing but watch the wreckage of 2nd Division's hopes arriving in a tired stream from France, someone said, "Well, I guess the CO is glad now that it wasn't us." We were glad too. The war had been going on for thirty-five months. It had thirty-four months more to run. For Canada it had its low point at Dieppe.

Soldiers, sailors and airmen saw very little of one another during the war, except perhaps in Piccadilly Circus. One reason was that they had very little in common. War at sea, war in the air and war on land aren't very much alike. Life on a corvette, or in a Wellington bomber, or in a water-soaked slit trench is not easy to describe to the uninitiated. There's really nothing they can share with you. It's like talking a different language. Sailors drown, airmen crash (perhaps in flames) and soldiers get smashed up with bullets or bits of flying steel. So, like cunning animals they keep to their own breed — on most occasions. It's better that way. Otherwise they might have to call the Red Caps or the Shore Patrol.

Once I did sit next to a sailor in a pub. While I was enjoying my pint he set his own glass down and said, "Are you sober?"

I replied in the affirmative, somewhat miffed, as it was only about ten minutes since opening time.

"Can you prove it?" this audacious naval type rudely answered.

Before I could open my mouth in reply, he shot out his next question, "Can you prove that you were *ever* sober?"

Again, I hesitated. Then this sailorman, some twenty years older than I was, continued his diatribe with, "Well, Pongo, I can prove that I was sober *once* in my life."

With this, he pushed out a mean nautical jaw to indicate that he believed he had achieved some sort of superiority over me. He then yanked a folded, somewhat creased and grubby paper from his wallet. Unfolding it and laying it on the bar he grinned a boozy grin and said, "See, I was sober *once* and I can prove it."

If my memory serves me, the document was entitled 'Hurt and Wounded Certificate'. It had a facsimile signature of Winston Churchill on it, and it stated that my new friend had been hurt on April 23rd, 1915, and further certified that "he was sober at the time."

"There," mumbled my drinking companion, "at least I know that I was sober once in my life." With that he picked up his almost thirty-year-old document and more or less hornpiped his way out into the street.

With Sgt. Frank Lloyd, RAF Station Odiham, during Battle of Britain, Sept. 1940.

RCR guard at Chartwell Manor, home of Prime Minister Winston Churchill, May, 1941. Pte. Talbot with the Bren gun, Pte. Whitcroft standing hatless and Cpl. Prysky with helmet slung. Note the gascapes rolled above packs.

When we weren't training, busy on fatigues, swinging the lead or proceeding on leave, most wartime soldiers seemed to be occupied with interviews. That is, when not facing the enemy.

These interviews were on a variety of subjects. I remember a red-faced, red-haired Irishman who went before his company commander and asked for permission to change his religion. He was a Roman Catholic, but he wanted to become a Hebrew.

"Good God," exclaimed the officer, "why would you ever want to do that?"

"Sir," the man replied, "these bloody padres are driving me crazy. My wife is a Protestant and I have both the Chaplain P and the Chaplain RC chasing me all the time, because my wife knows I have a lady friend over here. Since there is only one Jewish padre in this whole division, I figure he won't have enough time to bother me.

"Permission to change my religion to Hebrew, sir?"

"Not granted," said the one with the crown on his shoulder.

One man told me that he was a member of an interviewing board set up to select candidates for an officer-cadet training course. Each member of the board had a specific type of question to ask the candidates. One queried the aspiring leaders on matters of a military nature. Another tried to find out what their academic capacity was. The third member asked more personal questions to assess the applicant's character. This interviewer was rather on the gruff side. He looked at the candidates through bushy eyebrows and growled out his questions.

"Well, my boy," he asked the smart young candidate standing nervously across the table, "do you drink?"

"No, sir," replied the youth.

"Do you smoke?"

Again the reply was negative.

"For God's sake," continued the officer, "then tell me what you do to make yourself smell like a man."

"I use Lifebuoy soap, sir," was the candidate's reply.

Of all the horrors I experienced during the war, the motorcycle was the worst. Obviously, I wasn't like a lot of young men; the snorting beast had no appeal for me. It didn't matter whether it was the bulky Harley-Davidson or the light English Norton, I loathed the mechanical animal. I would rather have charged with the Light Brigade at Balaclava astride a galloping war horse than cross Salisbury

Plain or splutter down Aldershot's streets astride the saddle of the bloody thing.

Two brief courses — one in the sand dunes at the bottom of Toronto's Cherry Street, the other on the great paved driveway of Gatton Park, mustard king Sir Jeremiah Colman's Surrey estate — failed to turn me into a competent rider.

When I had to ride the damn thing that was on my platoon establishment I very gingerly stuck to the paved roads, hoping we would either fight our war on a sound concrete footing, or wait until I got back to a rifle company. If I had to die I preferred to walk to my death, not die a thousand deaths before it actually happened.

Once, one of Gen. Alexander's great movement exercises took us all over the southeast of England. Dozing in the back seat of the CO's dimly-lit and blacked-out station wagon I was warm, dry and comparatively comfortable.

Suddenly the colonel poked me in the ribs.

"The adjutant has been riding convoy for hours. He needs a rest. Get out of this vehicle and change places with him."

"Yes, Sir," I replied. What else could I say?

It was dark as pitch, the convoy had halted momentarily. So out I got in the chilling atmosphere of pre-dawn. Reluctantly I threw my weary limbs over the saddle as the adjutant mumbled, "It's all yours," and scrambled into the warm, foggy interior to light up and drink a cup of coffee.

Off went the column, while I kicked my starter like mad on a rutted country lane. Finally it worked. Off I shot like the proverbial bat out of hell, twisting the handles to feed the gas and make up for lost time. Actually, all went rather well and my mastery of the two-wheeled terror was sufficient to do my job, but riding convoy without lights on muddy English lanes was not my choice of nocturnal occupations.

The next time I found motorcycling unavoidable was in the wilds of Tunisia. I was doing liaison between 38th

Irish Brigade HQ and a Hampshire battalion. The night was moonless, the location of the Hamps was vague. My task was to find their forward defended localities (FDLs). The brigade major told me to "hop a bike" and "keep going until you find the Hamps."

After passing countless cactus patches — several of which I stopped to question, thinking they were carrying parties or stragglers — I eventually spluttered into the Hampshire area. In fact, almost through it!

"Where the bloody hell do you think you're going?" shouted a cultured public school voice in a rather uncultured manner. Stopping at his 'challenge', I found that I had accomplished my mission. He was the forward platoon commander of the forward Hamps company. Had I continued on my way I would have ended up full of bullet holes or a prisoner of the German Army!

RCR Officers' Mess, Aug. '42: Clark, Burdett, Hungerford, Gregg, Dare, Bindman, Shuter, Liddell and Rory Egan.

My final cycling adventure was a daylight affair. My brigadier told me to mount my iron steed. He straddled the pillion and ordered me to make haste for the place where he was scheduled to attend a divisional orders group. He was late, he said.

We sped along a dusty, rutted trail, the gent clinging to my shoulders. At last the orders group hove into view. Its members were in a semi-circle around the general officer commanding, all nicely camouflaged by a clump of olive trees. As we whizzed up all eyes turned toward the noisy arrivals.

I guess I stopped too fast. The brigadier went arse over teakettle into the centre of the orders group, ending up like a dust-covered, red-tabbed sack of potatoes.

In December, 1942, familiar faces began disappearing in ones and twos from every Canadian officers' and sergeants' mess in the United Kingdom. Only those who packed their kitbags and disappeared knew why, or where they were going.

It was four months after the disastrous Dieppe raid. Canadian soldiers had been slaughtered by the score in that half-day battle. They had fought bravely, but they lacked battle experience and paid the price for this deficiency.

Every few weeks until March, 1943, the mini-drafts moved off. By then 201 officers and 147 senior NCOs had silently departed from the Canadian hutted camps in southern England. They had been posted to Q List. Their immediate destination was the Non-Effective Transit Depot (NETD) on Thursley Common; their final destination, a secret.

NETD was the purgatory of the Canadian Army Overseas. People were usually posted to NETD for return to Canada with blots on their escutcheons. Drunks, black marketeers, chronic offenders against military discipline, misfits and crooks made up the main population of NETD.

That is why one Q List officer was greeted by an acquaintance with: "Good God, Harry. You here? What did you do?" NETD was a cesspool of lost hopes and broken men, a stopping place on the way to perhaps dishonorable discharge, cashiering or, at very least, 'adjutant-general's disposal' — an ominous and uncertain fate.

But Q List did not contain those who had fallen foul of military or civil authority. It was a select list, supposedly the best of the bunch. It just happened, so far as the Canadian Army Overseas was concerned that they were temporarily 'non-effectives'. Hence, NETD was the only place they could be borne on ration strength and administered.

In their case, it was a stepping-stone to high adventure. They had been chosen to join the British 1st Army in North Africa to learn the trade of war by leading and commanding men in the heat of battle against Rommel and his *Afrikakorps*, then to return to lead their own men later in the war.

Who were these chosen men? One was Maj. Frankie White, a curly-haired extrovert from Canada's Strathcona Horse. He became acting second-in-command of the swanky 17th/21st Lancers; their battle honors included Balaclava where they led the Charge of the Light Brigade, and Omdurman where Winston Churchill galloped against the Fuzzy-Wuzzies at the head of one of their troops.

Then there was Sgt. G.A. Hickson of the Royal Canadian Engineers. Only four months before, he had won the rare DCM at Dieppe. Soon he was to receive the Military Medal for bravery in the deadly minefields of Tunisia.

Another was George Corkett, a Princess Patricia's captain. Posted to the Coldstream Guards, he was severely wounded in the head by enemy air action while in a vehicle convoy on the way to join that regiment.

For some weeks, the 2nd London Irish Rifles, a battalion of civilian soldiers from Knightsbridge and Chelsea, had a Canadian second-in-command, three Canadian company commanders, a Canadian platoon commander and a Canadian company-sergeant-major. I was one of the company commanders.

With the famous Buffs was Eddie Dunlop of Toronto's Queen's Own Rifles. Wounded slightly in the eye, he returned to Britain to ready his own men for battle. But he was to fight no more. He was totally blinded while saving the life of a man who mishandled a live hand grenade in training. Dunlop received the George Medal, but Canada lost a brave and efficient officer.

One Q List Canadian, a tank lieutenant from Winnipeg, believed his CO had nominated him for the three-month attachment to the British 1st Army in the hope that he would never come back. Perhaps it was the same with some of the others, although none ever admitted it so readily.

In any case, none of them failed. A few, like Hickson, were decorated. Others received temporary promotion in the British Army. Fourteen officers and eleven NCOs were battle casualties; four officers and four NCOs lost their lives. Total casualties were about 10 per cent of the group. All, the quick and the dead alike, were awarded the Africa Star with 1st Army clasp. But despite all this, they were the forgotten Canadians of World War II. Most of them fought again, in Sicily, in Italy or in Northwest Europe. A few fought in all three places. Their record was a good one. Some, like Alec Ballachey, the dapper Calgarian in the black beret of the Armoured Corps, died heroically in France.

Yet their contribution to the achievement of the first Allied victory in World War II — the driving of the enemy from the African continent — has never really been recognized. In their limited capacity these Canadians helped win such battle honours as Bou Arada, Oued Zarga, Stuka Farm and Djebel Bir el Mahdi, but these are emblazoned on British colours, not Canadian ones. Except for the few aging Canadians who wear the Africa Star in Remembrance Day parades, there is little evidence that some Canadians fought bloody actions long before the vast majority of the Canadian Army became involved.

For one of this gallant band the end of the North African adventure was farcical. He was an Engineers captain and his services were so vital that his British CO refused to let him return to the United Kingdom with his proper draft. Finally, with the Germans driven out of Africa, he was released. The Canadian found a seat on an aircraft bound for the United Kingdom. It was now high summer in Africa and his battledress was packed away. He emplaned in bare knees, shorts and an open-necked bush shirt, all regulation for the desert. A few hours later, he reported to Canadian HQ in London. It was a weekend and no one could solve his baggage or other problems. Annoyed, he went out into Trafalgar Square to look for a bite to eat — only to be arrested by a Canadian provost major for being improperly dressed!

What price glory, one might say!

With Alec Ballachey on the way to the Front. Algeria, February, 1943.

CHAPTER V

DRINKING THE KING'S RED RUM

By the fall of '42 I was a company commander, having been promoted to Captain the previous spring. Many things had happened. We had become professional warriors in every respect except that we had not had our baptism by fire. The Dieppe Raid had been a shock, but the Allies were on the offensive. In October the General Montgomery who had driven us so hard the previous year of training suddenly appeared in the news as the winner of a great battle at El Alamein in the Western Desert. Then we heard of an Anglo-American landing in North Africa with a quick advance across Algeria and halfway across Tunisia. Victory was in the air! A long way off, perhaps, but now almost certain. Britain was filling up with American soldiers and airmen. Canada had five divisions, two of them armoured, and thousands of backup troops on this once beleaguered island, and the RCAF was building up on British soil as well! Despite the continuous battles it had been fighting in Greece, Crete, the Western Desert and in far-off Burma — not to forget the terrible losses at Singapore and Hong Kong in December, 1941, the British Army was stronger than ever.

For the first time since "invasion night" in 1940 the church bells of England rang. That was on November 15, 1942, and I remember it well.

On November 2, General Alexander had sent a message to Winston Churchill from Africa which read: "Ring out the Bells! Prisoners estimated now 20,000, tanks 350, guns 400, M.T. several thousand. Our advanced mobile forces are south of Mersa Matruh. Eighth Army is advancing."

Churchill did not want to be premature with his announcement of what only looked like the beginning of a great victory. To have rung the bells, then found that Rommel's forces had stopped Montgomery's advance, or worse still, counterattacked and repulsed him, would have been too much for the British public to stand. They had seen nothing but defeat since the Dunkirk evacuation two and a half years before. Churchill waited until Rommel's retreat became an absolute rout and the Anglo-American landings had succeeded at Algiers. Then he made his famous statement:

"Now this is not the end. It is not even the beginning of the end. But it is, perhaps, the end of the beginning."

There were strong men sitting in pubs across the land or at their own firesides who, when they heard those words coming over the "wireless", clenched their fists just that much tighter, felt a lump in their throats and a wetness in their eyes and said to themselves, "By God! We'll beat the bastards yet."

Then on November 15, the prime minister gave the order to ring out the bells of victory, for Monty's victory at El Alamein.

We were in Nissen huts at a place called Possingworth Park. As I heard the bells in the crisp night air I grabbed a pencil and scribbled a few verses, the first of which were:

> I heard the bells of Britain
> Ring out across the Weald;
> The clanging notes of victory,
> O'er forest and o'er field.
> From Sussex up to Sutherland
> The bells of victory pealed.

> I heard far bells in Hampshire,
> My memory two years turned,
> To midnight at an aerodrome
> When the skies of Britain burned.
> Those bells rang out dread warnings—
> But wrongly, as we learned.

Late in November we were warned for a secret move to an undisclosed destination. The rumour was that it was Scotland and the rumour was correct. Early in December I left with a platoon of the Hastings and Prince Edward Regiment, a platoon of the 48th Highlanders and a platoon of my own Regiment, with a composite Company Headquarters, for Victoria Station, London. We wore full marching order, with kitbags and with our platoon weapons, including the awkward Boys anti-tank guns. At Victoria we were met by an RTO sergeant who told me that I was to take my men across London to Euston-St. Pancras where we would entrain for our ultimate destination. There were no army vehicles. I was to move my 126 men across town by underground! It was the five o'clock rush when we entered the Victoria tube station and pushed our way into the already crowded coaches. We made few friends among the Londoners hurrying home from office and shop. Time was short and we could not politely take our turn. I told the CSM there was only one way to do it. "Right turn, Left wheel, Quick march!" And that is how we loaded ourselves, our packs, kitbags and weapons into the coaches.

The overnight trip ended by midday a few miles from Inverary in mountainous Argyllshire on the west coast of Scotland. TCV's took us the last few miles to a Nissen-hutted camp on the castle grounds of the Duke of Argyll's estate. For a week or so we took long hours of instruction from the English Combined Operations instructional staff on how to load landing craft, how to off-load them, how to use scrambling nets on the sides of Landing Ships Infantry and all the tricks of the Commando trade. We practised our new-found skills and by the time our three battalions arrived a few days before Christmas we were able to act as their instructors.

The training was rough, tough and nasty and in very uncomfortable weather. Snow lay deep on the mountain sides, but on the shores of Loch Fyne, where our camp was, the rain came down in a steady drizzle. After a period of rugged cross-country and obstacle training, successive practices in embarkation and disembarkation and getting in and out of assault landing craft, the first big exercise took place. This was called "Noel I" and was held on Christmas Eve. It entailed an assault landing from Loch Fyne and a rapid pursuit inland, culminating in the seizure of high, mountainous features. The whole affair was carried out in a downpour of rain, but as we got near the top of the mountains the snow was, in some places, knee-deep. The Regiment's performance did not please the Brigade Commander, Brigadier Guy Simonds, and this resulted in a repeat of the exercise as "Noel II" several days later. On New Year's Eve the training ended and entrainment for the sunny south took place. On the afternoon of January 1, 1943 we arrived back at our Sussex camp in Possingworth Park to find it under a blanket of snow. A week later my Commanding Officer, Lieut.-Col. Eric Snow, told me I was going to one of two places. I could make the choice, to go on the company commanders' course at Shillinglee Park, or on attachment to the British First Army fighting in North Africa. I chose the latter. Smiling, the colonel said he knew that that was what I would choose!

I went off to the Non-Effective Transit Depot as described in the previous chapter and after a few days sailed from Liverpool on HMT *Duchess of York* for Algiers. Our passage was uneventful. We were part of a huge convoy of battleships, liners and destroyers, most of which peeled off a few days later, sailing south around the Cape to the Far East, destined for Burma to fight the 'Japs'. We turned sharp left to enter the Straits of Gibraltar. Twice during our course through the Mediterranean we received U-boat alarms. It was most unpleasant, sitting below decks where we could see nothing and only hear the thud, thud, thud of our depth charges, while we visualized the bulkheads suddenly bursting with a German torpedo explosion and the sea rushing in to drown us all like the proverbial rats in a trap!

The *Duchess* brought us safely into harbour at Algiers at the end of January on a cloudless afternoon. The sun beat down on a shimmering city that looked like a collection of shiny, white shoeboxes piled high on a broad staircase. This vision of loveliness soon faded when we went ashore and saw and smelled the Oriental squalor. The first touch of local culture was revealed when a scrawny Arab hoisted his tattered robes around his waist and proceeded to urinate in the gutter as we marched by.

We were kept at No. 1 Infantry Base Depot in Fort de L'eau, within walking distance of Algiers, for the next five days. This gave us a chance to sample the novelty of life in a North African city, but the novelty soon wore off. We were glad when, on the 6th of February, we set off in a convoy of nineteen vehicles for Souk el Arba. The trip took four days. Each night we bivouacked in the open, our vehicles forming a circle like the covered wagon trains of the American Wild West. This form of leaguer, with sentries posted, saved us from the catlike thievery of the Arabs who swarmed from the *wadis* and mountainsides every time we halted for the night.

Souk el Arba was the site of a forward reinforcement unit for the British First Army, called No. 1 Reception Camp. Here we were under canvas and quite miserable as the camp was pitched on a windy slope. The officers' mess was in a marquee which took a terrible beating from the wind, and for lights we had lanterns and candles only. We soon found out what the war was all about in Tunisia. Our first shock was to find that First Army wasn't an army at all, but only a two-division corps with a few extras. The 5th Corps consisted of 6th Armoured and 78th Infantry divisions, a Guards Brigade, a Commando, a parachute battalion and "Bladeforce". This latter was a battlegroup made up of the 17th/21st Lancers, the "Death or Glory" boys of Balaclava and Omdurman fame, a U.S. tank battalion, a motorized company of the Rifle Brigade, a battery of the Royal Horse Artillery, a few armoured cars of the Derbyshire Yeomanry, plus the usual minimum of Services troops. No wonder they had bogged down into trench warfare after their initial lengthy advance the previous November. As one English officer said, "Same old story, sending a boy to do a man's job."

Soon after we arrived the senior officer on our draft, Alec Ballachey, went to Rear corps and was told what our individual postings were to be. Corkett and I were to go to the Guards Brigade, he to the 3rd Grenadiers and me to the 2nd Coldstream. The others were slated for the various Line regiments of the 6th Armoured and 78th Divisions. Ballachey said he saw a list of the draft with all the regimental postings opposite our names. It suited me just fine. Not because I was a military snob, but because the Coldstream motto, Nulli Secundus — "Second to None" — seemed good enough for me. When I was told a couple of days later that Corkett was going to the Coldstream and not me, because his name started with "C" and mine with a "G", and that I was going to the 2nd Battalion, London Irish Rifles, a Territorial Army unit, I was far from pleased. But the Guards needed fewer replacements than the Irish, who had been badly cut up in a show with the *Afrikakorps* the week before. Hence the alphabetical cut-off and my name moving down onto their list.

The other battalions in the 38th Irish Brigade, to which the London Irish belonged, were the 1st Royal Irish Fusiliers, nicknamed the "Faughs" and the 6th Royal Inniskilling Fusiliers, known as the "Skins". The Faughs were Regulars, the Skins were a new battalion raised for wartime service and the London Irish were a unit of the Territorial Army, or Militia as we call weekend amateur soldiers in Canada. Thus, in this one brigade there were representatives of the three different classes of British soldier. Most of the men were volunteers. The high proportion of Irishmen, or Londoners of Irish descent, originally LIR, had been much reduced. Some Scottish Rifles and Lancashire Fusiliers had been drafted in as reinforcements because the Irish had been badly cut up in a successful, but costly counterattack at Bou Arada less than a month before my arrival. Their casualties had totalled 248 all ranks, including more than half their officer strength. Therefore, the variety of British accent to be heard within the battalion by that time was considerable.

The Brigade Commander was a veteran of the Great War. He was a Regular and came from the Faughs. His name was Nelson Russell, but he was known to all as "Laddie" Russell. He had white hair, a red squire's face and he wore a Military Cross from his earlier engagements.

Loaded into 8-cwt trucks we left the transit camp by

moonlight. Between the *djebels*, over the bridged *wadis*, past cactus patches and olive groves we rolled toward the front. It was a chilly night and we huddled in the truck boxes in greatcoats.

Finally we arrived at our destination, the reverse slope of a rock-strewn ridge near Bou Arada.

Brigade Headquarters was in a French colonist's farm. We dossed down for the night on an earthen floor beside bags of grain. Next morning the BM, the Hon. Frank Douglas-Pennant, now the 5th Lord Penrhyn, briefed us on the tactical situation on the brigade front. "I call this 'putting you in the picture'," he drawled. Then he pointed out the German positions on a ridge in the distance. "The Boche can see us now", he said, "but we seem to be just out of range of his guns, so don't worry. Of course, we do get *Stuka* dive-bombed occasionally. They know this farm is a headquarters."

That night we went forward after Last Light, as the route was both in view of the enemy and in range of his guns. I was welcomed by Major Conroy, who after the war became a colonial judge and Sir Dairmaid Conroy. He was OC Headquarters Company and told me that first thing in the morning I would be guided up to "F" Company, where I would be the company 2IC. It had been a stage by stage journey, but at last I had arrived at the Front.

The London Irish proved to be rather a scruffy lot. To begin with they wore black buttons. Such items I had always scorned, having been educated in the really impor-tant military matters — such as the beauty of well-shone brass — by the RCR back at Wolseley Barracks in London, Ontario. Most of the chaps were Southern Irishmen who had been working in London, (England) when war broke out, but their homes and their hearts were in Dublin. Some of the officers had Irish names, but they were really Englishmen — stockbrokers, journalists, solicitors, actors and things like that. The colonel and a few of the senior NCOs had been regulars with the Royal Ulster Rifles. They wished they were back with the Royal Ulsters and made no bones about it. Some officers resented the colonel because he had been an Other Rank. The colonel in turn resented some of the officers because they had been stockbrokers, journalists, solicitors and actors when he had been sloping arms on the barrack square. But he loved his men. So much so, that he was reluctant to see them get killed and was said by some of his superiors to lack aggressiveness. So he was shortly removed.

Nevertheless, the battalion had fought well less than a month before I joined. One company had gone in with the bayonet singing, *"You are my sunshine."* It had really been a fine battalion, the men keen as mustard and the officers and NCOs capable fellows. When I left them after 10 weeks of fighting, I was proud to have been one of them.

But on February 14, when, in the cold North African moonlight, I was shown where I was to doss down until "stand to," I was not thrilled at the prospect of soldiering with chaps whose greatcoats had black buttons and who wore funny green hackles in strange Irish bonnets.

The enemy Hermann Goering Jaeger Regiment, was two or three miles across the plain. It was a quiet period. The worst features were the food, which was bully beef and hardtack every meal, and the fact that *Stuka* dive-bombers screamed in punctually every day at 4 p.m.

One such afternoon the air alarm went and the CQMS and I dove under a heavy table in the Arab farmhouse we occupied, not having time to make for the narrow slit trenches along the courtyard wall.

It was then that I shed my first blood for King and Empire. As a bomb shook the plaster down on us, CQMS Jones twitched madly and one hobnailed heel caught me right in the kisser and a copper-rimmed toe in the eye.

As the *Stukas* streaked off home, so their crews could freshen up in time for the evening's *bratwurst und sauerkraut*, Jones helped wipe the blood from my pallid features. Through my watering eyes I could see the crowned Irish harp that was his cap badge. When I re-entered the dust-filled room where my blanket roll was, I saw huge chunks of the roof scattered all over, one heavy piece of stone lying exactly where my head had been resting when the alarm went.

It must be the "luck o' the Irish", I thought to myself. Later I heard that Corkett had been seriously wounded on his way up to join the Coldstream. It seems the vehicle he was in was straffed by a *Messerschmitt*. I was glad to be a London Irishman from that hour on, even though they didn't shine their buttons. I was also glad that my name started with a "G".

Artillery duels and infantry attempts to 'dominate' no-man's-land by patrol activity gave the Tunisian battle-front its special flavour in early February, 1943.

The term "artillery duels" is misleading. All the opposing gunners did was shell each other's infantry. "Duelling", that is actually shelling one another, was impossible. Each side's gun lines were too far out of range of the other fellows for that — which was just great for the gunners.

No-man's-land was the Goubellat Plain, a great valley bottom criss-crossed with *wadis* and *nullahs*, flecked with cactus patches and dotted with red and blue roofed farm buildings. On the other side of the valley the Jaegers held the high ground which blocked our route to Tunis. The British line, following January's unsuccessful infantry and tank clashes out on the plain, was now drawn along the top of a series of hills and ridges running south from Medjez el Bab to Bou Arada.

By day, the 2nd London Irish Rifles occupied sandbagged farms and dugouts on the reverse slopes of their positions. Concealed observation posts and prepared, but unoccupied, machine-gun pits were located on the forward slopes. These were pivots upon which we could frame our defense during the hours of darkness to ward off possible night attacks, or raids at dusk or dawn. Daylight assaults were unlikely. Approach over the open ground would mean suicide for attacking enemy infantry. Tanks could not get at us, because the gradients of the forward slopes were much too steep. But infantry, attacking under cover of darkness, could have played havoc with our lightly held positions.

As always, our companies were 'below war establishment'. In simple English this meant the London Irish were short of men, and officers too. At one time the Irish had five Canadian officers, Major Chisholm, Capts. Curry, Gale and Galloway, Lieut. LaPrairie and a WO2, CSM Keyes.

The nights were chilling. Greatcoats and balaclavas were worn as, standing breast-deep in two-man slit trenches, we peered into the silent dark, straining our ears for possible enemy movement. To keep our blood warm, and thus to keep alert, we created a soothing mash inside our bellies by nibbling hardtack and lacing it with periodic sips of the King's red rum. Occasionally, some rationed whisky, personally purchased from NAAFI, provided a welcome variation on this alcoholic theme.

About every ten minutes one member of the slit trench team would crouch down below the lip of the trench, cup his hands to hide the glow of the flame, and light a cigarette. When the butt began to burn his lips he would again stand watch. Then the other chap would slide a bulkily clad form down between the narrow earthen walls for his tryst with Lady Nicotine.

Because of our manpower shortage, company officers performed this nightly task in exactly the same manner as any rifleman.

But this static vigil was the cushy job. Night after night some poor sods went mucking about in no-man's-land on patrol. Sometimes these were only standing, or ambush patrols. Such patrols were put out several hundred yards ahead of our main positions to wait hopefully for an unsuspecting German patrol to cross their line of fire. If no enemy came they had little or no excitement. But, not being dug in, they had to stretch out on the naked earth. They could communicate only in whispers. They could neither smoke nor warm their veins with a gulp of rum. Their seven or eight hours of exile in no-man's-land was no fun.

Then there were the reconnaissance patrols. These were quite unpleasant affairs. Usually an officer and a junior

NCO went out on these fact-finding expeditions. Answers to specific questions were always required of these patrols. "Is Stop Farm occupied by the enemy?" "Is the road-junction at map reference 13572468 mined?" "Is the blurry white square on this aerial photo a machine-gun emplacement, or only a disused corn bin?"

Trying to get answers to these questions was difficult and dangerous business. One false move and an enemy grenade or a stream of tracer could end the patrol's quest for information. It sometimes ended the lives of the seekers after truth as well!

Fighting patrols were the worst type. Death was their portion, painful wounds the least fearful of their products. Their object was to close with the enemy and destroy him. Often it was the would-be destroyers who died in the night. There would be a sharp explosion, a flurry of small arms fire, or both. Mission accomplished or another failure? We would know before the sun came up.

In my diary for February 15, I wrote:

"There was considerable activity out on the plain last night. For the first time I heard the sounds of the battlefield . . . a patrol clash on Grandstand Hill between the Royal Irish Fusiliers and the Hermann Goering Jaegers. The Boche put up numerous illuminating flares (I am told this is a habit of theirs) and bursts of automatic fire and the explosion of hand grenades could be heard. Gibbs (Major Colin Gibbs, OC "F" company) said he could distinguish Tommygun fire, but could not hear any *Schmeisser*. There were also several long bursts of MMG, which, according to Gibbs, were from a German weapon. Since the firing started at 8.55 p.m., just after a flare went up, Gibbs concluded that a British patrol was revealed thereby and opened up on by the Jerry machine-guns. Why they replied with Tommyguns and grenades seemed a mystery, since he believed they would be out of range to use these weapons effectively. Anyway, in such a manner is the story of the battlefield read . . . by sounds, by suppositions."

At about 9.15 p.m. the two MMGs belonging to the

London Irish, which had been moved into the *nullah* between "G" Company HQ and Battalion HQ, opened up and plastered the Hun positions heavily for nearly an hour. During the night the gunners threw over a number of shells in the enemy's direction. Gibbs said, "The one thing we've got is artillery superiority."

About this time Division warned the forward troops that there was a possibility of a German attack in about three days' time. This information was supposedly gleaned from wandering Arabs. These "Wogs", as the British called them, strolled back and forth across the battle area, sometimes with farm carts, and were a menace to both sides. They gave every scrap of information they could think up to gain the friendship of whomever they happened to be talking to. Much of the information given to us proved false. It was believed they favoured the enemy, as the Arabs definitely hated French colonial rule and the Germans had promised them many benefits when the French yoke in Tunisia was thrown off as the result of a Nazi victory in Africa.

One day some Arabs told us that the Boche had instructed them to drive their cattle well behind the German lines and to evacuate their farms as severe fighting was imminent in that area. At the time our Intelligence people pooh-poohed Jerry's ability to attack, saying he was merely tricking the Arabs into coralling their cattle and carting seed grain behind his lines, so that it could be used to augment German rations!

A week later our Intelligence people were proved wrong! Some of the "Wogs" were German soldiers and the farm carts were not retrieving seed grain for planting behind the German lines, but were carting mortar ammunition forward and stacking it in cellars and garrets to be used to support their up-coming attack!

On February 22 I wrote in my diary,

"The patrol last night was quite an affair. It consisted of one rifleman and myself. We wore caps, comforters and leather jerkins and carried a Tommygun and two grenades each. Our faces were blackened with soot. We left the FDLs at 6:40 p.m. and arrived back fifteen minutes after midnight. Our route was a semi-circle of about five miles. During the circuit we visited eight features to see if they were enemy-occupied. Six of these were farms, one a hillock and the other a *wadi*.

"The night was moonlit and very eerie. As we neared each farm Arab dogs, the terror of every night patrol, began yapping. We lay still for ten minutes or so on each of these occurrences. Then, figuring the dogs had vanished, we would start inching forward again on our bellies. But the slightest move on our part always started the dogs barking again. Finally, we decided that if the dogs barked as much as they did and no enemy MG fire followed, the farms must not be occupied! Then we acted more boldly.

"We alternated as 'cover-man' and 'searcher'. The cover-man placed himself so that he could send a stream of bullets into the door of a house, if necessary, while the searcher approached with great stealth. The searcher then kicked the door open quickly and ducked, sticking close to the outer wall. If nothing happened he rushed indoors and got into the shadows. Then he searched the two to four rooms of the dwelling for traces of enemy visits, while the cover-man guarded the entrance in case some enemy appeared on the scene in the meantime. It was a rather unpleasant way to spend an evening.

"Once we had a fairly bad scare. Crossing a small *wadi* we came into an olive grove and on the skyline just beyond we thought we saw a large Boche patrol moving directly toward us! For several minutes we held grenades with the pins drawn, ready to toss them into the centre of what appeared to be a group of about twenty men. But it proved to be nothing more than a patch of cactus swaying slightly in the breeze.

"We returned without incident, got a good slug of rum into us, removed most of the burnt cork from our faces and lay down to sleep. We felt incredibly safe from all danger, even though the enemy began shelling the area of our little stone house as we dozed off."

Forty-eight hours later my diary recorded,

"Two men from the Carrier Platoon have been captured! This morning they set off for a waterhole to fill their bottles and cans. They were not seen again. Finally, late this afternoon, it was decided to send out a patrol along the route they had followed to see if they could be located. The patrol found some pages from a German illustrated magazine, which had been used as toilet paper, a German chocolate package and a pair of homemade sponge rubber sandals for tying onto the soles of ammunition boots to render them noiseless. The water cans, still unfilled, were also at the well. The assumption is that the Boche observed our chaps' habit of going to that waterhole and decided to obtain a prisoner. As a result, a small patrol lay up close by, awaiting their expected arrival. From the human excreta and stained German papers lying about, it appeared that four or five men made up the ambush, and that they had lain in wait some time."

And so we slept or lazed by day, and moved about at night amid the sand and gravel, cactus patches and fears of North Africa. We did not know it, at our level, but battle was soon to be joined.

The *bête noire* of the British at this time was the great Field Marshal Erwin Rommel of *Afrikakorps* fame. One day we received a message from Battalion HQ stating that Rommel had been evacuated from Tunisia in a very ill condition. It was directed that this information be made known to all troops, as it was believed such knowledge would boost their morale. This attitude irritated us, but the fact was, the men did feel that the Desert Fox could outsmart our generals anytime.

Gibbs said, "I suppose the High Command is breathing more freely now."

Rommel had indeed left Africa for health reasons. General Sixt von Arnim succeeded him and soon launched a furious attack against the British front. His attack failed. Several weeks later, with Monty's Eighth Army pressing in from the south, the First Army began its drive on Tunis. The stalemate of artillery duels and infantry capers in no-man's-land was over.

My own part in holding back von Arnim's abortive attack was very minor, of course. But it was like a boyhood dream come true.

Stuka Farm. Ground over which bayonet charge took place near Bou Arada, Tunisia, February 26, 1943.

CHAPTER VI

NAKED BAYONETS AT STUKA FARM

Playing at war as schoolboys, my friends and I often charged imaginary Germans with imaginary bayonets. On February 26, 1943, when I actually shouted "Fix Bayonets! Charge!" on the Tunisian battlefield, our bayonets were steel, the Germans were real and the bayonets' intended use was a wartime rarity. Very few men charged with the bayonet during the Second World War. It wasn't that kind of war.

But that chilly morning when I gave the order that launched men of the 2nd London Irish Rifles against the fire of the Hermann Goering Division our bayonets were fixed. As I have already recounted to some extent, things had been quiet for days. The 2nd London Irish, dug in on a forward slope overlooking the Goubellat Plain, busied themselves by night staring into the dark to detect enemy movement, or sending out fighting patrols to 'hot things up'. By day they slept in reverse slope positions, the dangerous daylight face of the ridge in the care of a few concealed observers, who could call down mortar or artillery fire on any aggressively-minded Germans.

"F" Company, of which I was second-in-command, occupied a farm which was regularly the target for a pair of *Stuka* dive-bombers. It became known as Stuka Farm. Today it is among official battle honours of the London Irish Rifles and this is why.

During darkness, every hour on the hour, either Colin Gibbs, the company commander, or I, would visit the platoon positions to make sure everybody was alert.

Staggering down narrow, winding paths among cactus and underbrush, across rocky or sandy stretches, we faced the added hazards of our own wire and our own sentries with nervous fingers.

This particular morning, Gibbs left our dugout to make the "Stand To" rounds. I snuggled into my damp, grimy blanket until the field phone jingled and I had to put it to my ear. A voice from "G" company crackled that the enemy seemed to be in the *nullah* below.

Scrambling to my feet, I pushed aside the frosty groundsheet that served our dugout for a door. Reaching the foggy outside I saw Gibbs panting up the slope toward me.

"Boche"! he shrieked, "Boche! there are about thirty of the bastards in the *Nullah*!"

Pausing, he gasped that one post had been overrun. He was on his way to organize a counterattack. I was to take No. 12 Platoon and occupy Stuka Farm before the enemy did.

What he said was true. Bursts of fire could be heard from below. The familiar chatter of a Bren gun answered from "G" Company to the left. I made off on my errand, panting up a rough slope in greatcoat and webb equipment.

Soon I reached No. 12 Platoon. Sgt. Jimmy North and his twenty-five or so men were moving back to the farm at the end of "Stand To", rifles slung according to our routine. He had heard the firing, but thought it was only windy replacements shooting at nodding cactus in the mist.

"North", I barked, "the Jerries are through our wire. We've got to get to the farm before they do. Follow me!"

Shouting to his platoon to double, the two of us dashed along some low ground to where we could approach the farm under cover. Within scant seconds the platoon was with us, soon, at my command, to shake out into extended order.

My plan was to move toward the farm so that it could

be entered at all points at the same time, and every door and window, gate or gap in the wall manned without delay. Then all of a sudden hell was upon us!

The low ground in which we crouched was laced with mortar fire. Jagged chunks of metal tore into human flesh. I hugged the earth between two obviously fatal victims. Screams from the wounded added to our terror. Then machine-gun tracer began fanning out across the slope ahead as if a thousand neon signs had exploded in our faces.

To retreat was impossible. The enemy's mortar *stonk* was moving behind the shuddering, shapeless khaki bundles that were No. 12 Platoon. Only from within the farm could we fight successfully. And it seemed to be in enemy hands already!

Shouting to Cpl. Johnson to move in a wide left hook to behind a haystack, I indicated we would assault the farm from two directions. His section would provide me with covering fire and then he would follow on, into the farm behind my assault line.

I got to my feet. "Fix Bayonets!" I yelled. I heard Sgt. North's bayonet click on, followed by *click, click, click* on either side.

"Charge!" I roared. Breathless and terrified we raced across the open field. The tracer was all around us, but only one man was hit before we reached the farm. Soon we were within the thick walls, the stables, the living quarters. No Germans were there. Our bayonets remained unbloodied.

Three minutes later we heard guttural shouts. Soon stick grenades came hurtling through the windows. MG 42's chipped the stone walls, or bored through the plaster. For several hours we held out, Germans occupying one room, London Irish the next. But we stayed and they didn't, though they nabbed three of my men and frog-marched them into temporary captivity.

We had assaulted a tactical vacuum, but we had stopped the enemy. We had won the race for Stuka Farm, with fixed bayonets we were prepared to use.

Dusk fell and the battle continued as the enemy, firm on a small knoll which overlooked our farm, kept us within the farm walls with mortar and machine-gun fire.

Sgt. North and I spent most of our time going from post to post joking with the men and keeping them on the alert. To attack the knoll was out of the question, so I decided that the only sound plan was to make a fortress out of our farm and withstand any further enemy attacks. Since the enemy were on higher ground, and since, so far as we knew, the other two platoons were liquidated, it would have been suicide to attempt to dislodge them. I decided that counterattack was the problem of the battalion commander, who could call on the Brigade for its counterattack force, always held in reserve and centrally located.

Despite the enemy fire, three stretcher bearers, who had been in the farm all along, went out to the crest of the ridge and managed to bring in one lad who was badly wounded in the shoulder by a mortar fragment. They bandaged him up and I located a bottle of whisky in my quarters and gave him a drink to quiet his nerves. I then replaced the bottle in my kit and went to the wireless truck where Lance-Corporal Stratton was attempting to get through to BHQ.

Just before noon, after continuous duelling with LMQ's and rifles, the Germans worked around in some low ground and assaulted the farm. The main attack was beaten off, but several of them entered one wing of the courtyard and carried off the three SB's as prisoners, tossing stick grenades into our part of the courtyard. During this assault the Jerries shouted to one another, but since most of my defenses were riflemen in slit trenches within the yard, and not right at the gates, we could not see them. Had any of them attempted to rush through the gates we would have easily shot them down. Only in one place did I have men positioned right at an open window. I had just crawled into the room and snuggled up to the wall beside the gun when several rounds came through the window, one of them hitting Rfn. E. Janes, the Bren gunner, square in the front of his helmet. He toppled back, the gun clattering to the floor, however the bullet failed to pierce the helmet. He got to his feet, removed his helmet, upon which there was a great dent, put it on again, back to front, picked up the Bren, shoved the muzzle out the window and fired back at his opponent. All this despite the fact that enemy bullets were continually smashing the window sash and whizzing past his head!

During the morning the CSM and Lance-Corporal Stratton made their way from man to man distributing chocolate bars, hardtack and oranges which they had found in the cookhouse. This cheered the hungry troops considerably, as the morning's business had cut out all hopes of a proper breakfast. At 11 : 30 a.m., having got in touch with BHQ by wireless and informing them that we were holding on, and giving our scanty information on the remainder of the company, I detailed a small patrol under Sergeant Udall to leave the farm and work its way around through a gully to the knoll to see what was happening, as the enemy fire had completely stopped. At this time the CSM, disregarding my orders and my private property, was getting slightly drunk on my whisky. He then saw a couple of Jerries sneaking up from what had been our night positions, which they had overrun. Instead of waiting until they got up to the gap in the wall which he was covering, he jumped out through the gap and rushed up to them, apparently intent upon making a capture. As a result he was shot and killed. His body lay in a grotesque attitude throughout the day. One of the men told me he was quite drunk. Going to my bottle I found its contents half gone. I smashed it against the wall. The CSM had come to me earlier during the morning, after I had given the drink to the badly wounded man, and had asked that each of the garrison be given a drink. I had refused his request, but didn't have enough sense to hide my bottle. He apparently felt the need for "Dutch courage".

In the afternoon a platoon of Royal Irish Fusiliers and six Churchill tanks of the Lothian and Border Horse counterattacked towards the knoll. They withdrew again, for what reason I do not know. It appears that it was the sight of this counterattack coming in that had caused the Germans to leave the knoll, thus lessening the pressure against us in Stuka Farm. Later our counterattack force became confused, due to lack of information. The commander, thinking Stuka Farm was in enemy hands, asked Brigade for further orders. He was told to attack the farm and pass through and down onto the forward positions. By this time the enemy was active again. Sergeant Udall, whose small patrol was still in slit trenches outside our "fortress", risked himself by bringing word across open ground that the counterattack was being launched despite our tenancy of the farm, and that the officer in charge had said it was too late to call off the artillery fire plan. Everything seemed to be complete confusion, except in Stuka farm. As a result, I got through on the wireless to Brigade and said I was leaving the farm for the cactus patch behind it. Not because of the enemy forcing me out, but because our own artillery was going to shell me to cover their counterattack. We then broke cover and dashed across the plateau and down the slight reverse slope into the cactus patch just as the Fusiliers appeared on the scene. This attack swept forward unopposed, moved through the previously overrun forward positions and "restored the situation". The enemy fled into the *wadis* on the plain. Our 3-inch mortars got in some fine shooting.

Earlier in the morning, Corporal Hogan, in an effort to dislodge enemy who were in and around his concealed position, called down fire on his observation post and on himself. In doing so, he had to whisper over the field phone lest the Germans hear his orders. As a result, a prong of the enemy attack was broken off just as it was about to launch an assault on Stuka Farm coincident with the one which we ourselves beat off on the other side. Had this pincer movement succeeded we would probably have lost the farm.

Toward evening our wounded were brought in, along with several German prisoners, one of whom was a sergeant in paratroopers' uniform and equipment. *"Soldat? Unteroffizier?"*, I queried him. *"Nein, Feldwebel!"* he replied arrogantly, pulling down the shoulder of his paratrooper smock to show me his silver-edged epaulette.

Several of the Jerries spoke English, and they told us that they had been brought from Germany through Italy by train, then flown to Tunisia. The paratroopers were used to "thicken up" the attack. The *Feldwebel* surrendered by running towards the counterattack, holding his *Schmeisser* above his head. He stated that he had seen enough fighting during the war to date and had decided this was a good time to give up!

As darkness fell Major McCann, Second-in-Command of the Inniskillings came to the farm to get a report of the action and to see what the exact situation was. He brought two more Royal Irish Fusilier platoons, which took up position in front of the farm, but not so far down the slope as the London Irish positions were. By 7:30 p.m. Gibbs came hobbling in, wounded in the leg, and Willcocks was carried in with a bad knee wound. A number of "F" Company who had been captured during Gibbs' counterattack at 7 a.m., but released by the Fusilier counterattack, also showed up. So did Lieutenant Wade and ten men of the Carrier Platoon. They had all been scuppered before dawn as the enemy stole up onto the knoll. Wade and his men joined us in the cactus patch shortly after the second counterattack had cleared the knoll. By 11:30 p.m. two motor ambulances arrived up behind Stuka Farm and the wounded were evacuated. My batman Murely was killed in the initial dawn attack, after I had left him in the dugout to join North's platoon.

Rifleman Burton, who was Lieutenent Howell's batman, was getting 11 platoon's breakfast ready as the attack developed. He joined me in Stuka Farm about 10 o'clock in the morning, and worked like mad all day. Late in the afternoon he got hold of some Compo rations, carried them across the open to a Wog hut, and cooked a dixie full of stew, which he then carried to all the positions in the cactus patch. He managed this despite the fact that enemy small arms fire was still humming around, and numerous mortar bombs were bursting here and there. He also proved himself a wonder at reviving some of the "shell shocked" cases. He merely pummelled them until they came out of their "trance". Five or six of these lads, who had bolted when we launched our bayonet charge were rooted out of slit trenches toward evening, and sent to the farm. All were scared to death and in a lamentable mental state. Burton's treatment did a great deal to bring them around.

My own close escapes during the day were many, death and capture both eluded by the narrowest margins. Besides the time when the two lads on either side of me were knocked out just before the bayonet charge, and the actual charge itself across open, machine-gun swept ground, my two most noteworthy escapes took place very close together. After giving the wounded chap a swig of whisky in the cookhouse, where he was being attended by the stretcher bearers, I had barely left the room when three Germans entered with machine pistols and Lugers, and kidnapped the three stretcher bearers. Had I been administering the whisky, or otherwise off guard when they entered, I would have been shot in my tracks, or taken prisoner. According to Rifleman Marchant my foot was hardly clear of the gap in the wall by which I left when the order "*Hande Hoch!*" was given by three paratroopers. While our men were being marched out of the courtyard and down the slope into temporary captivity, I was crossing the adjoining courtyard.

I had just entered the stable where the wireless truck was parked, and where I had my headquarters, when a stick grenade came hurtling over the wall and blasted one of my men out of his slit trench. Hearing shouts in German outside the farm I ran across the next courtyard and entered a corner room. Here Thompson, the company clerk, was keeping watch. What was probably a German egg grenade came hurtling through the window and exploded on the far wall. The room was filled with flying plaster and clouds of dust and smoke. But no harm was done to either Thompson or myself. I then rushed back to the wireless truck and tried to silence its dreadful humming sound, as I was afraid that if the enemy managed to force an entry into the centre courtyard they would hurl a grenade into the stable to knock out the wireless set, which was giving itself away with its noise. I frantically pulled wires and turned knobs but nothing happened, so I jumped out of the back of the truck and scrambled underneath it. From this position I aimed my pistol at the entrance through which the enemy might come — but fortunately none did! I had more wind up at this stage than at any other time during the day. I was sure the wireless set's humming would attract the Germans, who would toss their grenades in to damage it, then follow up with a burst of automatic fire which would completely finish me off, too!

The night was quiet. "Under orders" from Burton, who had attached himself to me as my new batman, I got some sleep in the stable beside the wireless truck. By the time "F" Company got organized with the released prisoners and other missing men, we mustered about forty or fifty, and with the addition of Wade's ten Carrier personnel, we made a fairly strong group. I placed all these men within the farm walls for the night. With the Royal Irish Fusiliers out in front, a large number of my men got a fair rest. At First Light I moved all the "F" Company back into the cactus patch. It was a far better place from which to support the flanks of the Fusiliers, should the enemy launch another attack. Thompson managed to get a strength statement made up. It showed "F" Company's casualties as two officers wounded, eight Other Ranks killed and nine Other Ranks wounded. Nine more men, listed as missing, showed up during the day, reporting in from God-knows-where. All loudly proclaimed that they had become separated from the Company through no fault of their own!

The enemy had withdrawn across the plain and things became quiet. I spent the evening in Stuka Farm with the Irish Fusilier company commander, Captain Desmond Gethin, and his 2IC, Capt. Brian Power. They had set up in one of the rooms with the company cooker and so we were quite cosy. The fact that they had a bottle of whisky also proved comforting. Nick Kingsmill arrived at about 10:30 p.m. and informed me that "F" Company was to come under command of the 6th Inniskillings.

Shortly afterwards Nick and I led the company across the cactus-strewn countryside, through several *wadis*, under a brilliant moon. We arrived at our destination, a mile and a half away and there we were allotted some disused slits and told to sleep. Prior to turning in I went over to Lt.-Col. "Heaver" Allan's HQ in a camouflaged tent, and gave him a report on the Company. Wade and I wedged ourselves into a slit trench with only one blanket between us and we nearly froze to death, to say nothing of the terrible cramps we got in our legs and the pains in our backs from being crowded together in the one-man trench.

I had been very annoyed, on looking for my kit in my old room at Stuka Farm, to find that the Royal Irish Fusiliers had gone through all my belongings and taken my old RCR cap badge, my commando knife, five pairs of socks, a balaclava, my handkerchiefs and other belongings. The unwanted remainder of the kit was just thrown in a heap on the floor of the old company office.

Just before Nick's arrival a wireless message arrived from BHQ to the effect that Course No. 5 and an Anti-Malaria Course had been cancelled. I don't recall what Course No. 5 was, but Thompson, the company clerk, told me that our candidates for both courses had been killed in the bayonet charge.

Rifleman Burton (left) distributing rations in cactus patch at Stuka Farm, Feb. 26, 1943.

CHAPTER VII

THE IRISH BRIGADE FOUGHT ON

The winter months which the First Army spent in the trenches of Tunisia were far from pleasant. If either side held the initiative then it was the Germans. Down south the Americans had come reeling back from the Kasserine Pass. Up north the abortive attempts to wrest Sejenane from Von Arnim's hands had proved bloody and fruitless. In the centre, holding the front between El Aroussa and Bou Arada, lay the 38th (Irish) Brigade. For the men with the shamrocks sewn on their battledress sleeves the winter was one of vigilance, constant patrolling, incessant Stuka bombing and the memory of that February day when the Hermann Goering Division hit them so hard that they were dislodged from their dug-in defensive positions for twenty-four hours.

One night we were sitting in the back of a stationary 15-cwt truck. Rain beat a tattoo on the canvas cover, but we were quite snug although our damp battledress was steamy and the air was blue with cigarette smoke that made our eyes smart.

Outside, in the North African winter, some muffled thuds indicated that somebody's artillery was carrying out a 'shoot' in the distance. Now and then a burst of small arms fire could be heard. Perhaps a nervous sentry had fired at a shadow, a stray dog, a lost goat or a swaying cactus plant. Or maybe two hostile patrols had bumped, poor sods.

But for us their fury and their fear were remote. We were in a safe reserve position. At the moment ours was the boring rather than the exciting side of war. As the night wore on, the King's red rum warmed our bellies and we began discussing our friends and our foes.

"The Yanks were a shower at Kasserine Pass", Major Jimmy Dunhill ventured.

"But they did pretty good at Bizerta," said a subaltern.

"They get better as time goes on", added a third chap.

"I still rate them the world's worst troops", insisted the major. "Not counting the Italians, of course, who are too bloody awful to even rate."

The conversation continued, somewhat inanely. Not everyone agreed with the major who had the anti-American and anti-Italian bias. However, he was adamant. After hours thinking about the subject, he had concluded that the best fighting troops in the North African theatre were the Algerian *Goumiers* — those swarthy killers whose normal existence was one of tribal warfare. He had general agreement on that point.

Then he ranked the other troops in the theatre, saying that the next best were the British Guards Brigade, then the French Foreign Legion, followed by the German and British paratroopers in that order, then the ordinary German infantry and finally the ordinary British infantry. The American infantry, he maintained, was miles behind all the others. As the only Canadian present I was spared possible embarrassment, since no Canadians had yet fought as units in North Africa, nor did they ever.

"What about the armoured fellows?" I asked.

"I'm talking about fighting", he answered, "whites-of-their-eyes stuff, not blokes with a foot of steel between them and the Boche."

The conversation became even more nonsensical. My opinionated companion refused to even list the Italians: "I'd rather have the Orange Lodge," he said.

After the war, a German colonel who had fought in Poland, the Low Countries, North Africa, Sicily, Italy and

118

finally in Russia told me that the best fighters he ever saw were the Italians who counterattacked Patton's 7th Army on the Gela beachhead!

The troops who fight the best do so, not because of their nationality, but because at that specific time they are the best trained, the best disciplined and the best led on the field.

At Kasserine the Americans fought without adequate training. They lacked discipline and their leadership was poor. So they were taken to the cleaners. Six months later the British CIGS wrote that the American "setback at Kasserine, and the temporary deflation that followed, had been gloriously avenged by Patton's exploits in Sicily." And Patton said that the U.S. 7th Army was "the best group of fighting men in the world." Yet many of them had fled at Kasserine. Since then they had been trained, disciplined and provided with good leadership.

Cato, a Roman who lived about 50 BC, wrote that "an agricultural population produces the bravest men, the most valiant soldiers." This is not particularly true today in the era of advanced military technology and mechanization. But for infantry fighting on the open battlefield, the farmer or the outdoorsman is more at home and more likely to fight better than the city-bred who loses direction without street signs and is jumpy in the dark. That is why the Algerian tribesman performed better in North Africa than the American boy from the Bronx or the gondolier from Venice.

Since the basic fighting unit is the infantry battalion there seems to be much truth in the statement that "there are no bad battalions, only bad battalion commanders." It is they who train, discipline and lead. It doesn't matter whether the battalions or their commanders are British, German, Italian, American, French or Canadian.

With the coming of Spring reinforcements began to arrive from England. To take their part in the African Adventure alongside the 6th Armoured and 78th Infantry Divisions and the Guards Brigade, came the British 1st, 4th and 46th Divisions. Furthermore, on the southern frontier Monty's irresistible Eighth Army was crashing through the

Mareth Line and Erwin Rommel was on his way to Berlin to report to *Der Fuehrer* and dose himself with headache pills.

Left to battle the advancing Eighth Army on one side and to parry the First Army, plus Patton's U.S. Second Corps on the other, Von Arnim placed his back toward Cape Bon and prepared to fight it out. Then came the 7th of April. At German Headquarters they could hear the noise of the First Army moving into gear. The Allied traffic was pointed toward Tunis itself, and Von Arnim knew that no matter how much he wished it weren't, the stoplight of the German defense was out.

On April 4 I left the battalion and was posted to Brigade HQ as a Liaison Officer for the impending offensive toward Tunis.

At 4 a.m. on April 7 a murderous barrage was brought down on the German positions in the vicinity of Oued Zarga . . . 4,000 rounds of 25-pdr; 1,000 rounds of medium and 200 rounds of heavy. Such was the 'softening up' process on the Brigade's objective. Then the infantry attacked; 6th Inniskilling Fusiliers and 2nd Hampshires, the latter temporarily under command of the Irish Brigade, until the London Irish were battleworthy again. Resistance was almost nil. Shortly after dawn the two forward battalions were on their objectives and the 1st Royal Irish Fusiliers were exploiting through their newly dug positions.

At the time I was attached to Brigade Headquarters as a supernumerary liaison officer.

In looking over my diaries I came across the following entry for April 6: "This morning I went on a message to 78 Div. HQ. having to speak directly to the GOC, Major-General Eveleigh. I went by jeep at 70 m.p.h. — what a ride it was! As we drove into our area tonight we passed the Royal Irish Fusiliers moving up to their assembly area, loaded for bear and carrying picks and shovels. Each company was ominously followed by four stretcher bearers. Their heavy equipment, ammunition, wireless, etc., was loaded on mules. The scale for this attack is 72 mules per battalion. Out of the dark the marching men 'blinded' at my driver and me, as we bowled along in a captured German vehicle. The top was down and the windshield flat, making it look like a sports model. 'Look at the bloody touring car', I heard one man say, and his marching comrades mumbled their disapproval of the wheel-borne officers in good round army language!"

During the morning of April 7 the Army Commander, General K.A.N. Anderson visited us. An hour or so later we were subjected to *Stuka* and ME 109 attacks all along our front. So far as I recall, little or no damage was done by these *Luftwaffe* raids. The absence of the RAF was noticeable. According to one cynic they were refighting the "Battle of Britain" in the cafés of Constantine!

Before sunset the attack was pressed again and many prisoners fell to the men with the shamrocks sewn on their battledress sleeves. Mainly they were from the 3/755 Grenadier Regiment and had little or no stomach for fighting. In fact, one Jerry surrendered to a platoon of ours and after a lengthy explanation guided them to a *wadi* wherein sat over twenty Boche — armless and harmless — waiting to surrender. He had been their emissary of defeat! That day the Irish Brigade made five thousand yards with less than seventy-five casualties.

The weather at this time was cold and the wind was razor-sharp. We wore greatcoats and leather jerkins, mufflers and mitts. Yet, in one of the press-clippings which arrived from a Canadian paper we read: "CANUCKS SOAK UP SUN IN AFRICA" . . . it was the Canadian Press at its best. The reporter was probably lolling around on the sandy beaches of Algiers, five hundred miles from the Tunisian front!

The attack continued and the prisoners marched to the rear. It was during this phase of the operation that I was singled out by an ME 109 pilot and personally *straffed*! Going up the winding trail to the top of the Djebel Bir El Mahdi I saw the German plane coming toward me, its cannon blazing. I dumped my motor bike and took to the ditch while the bike dug itself into the earth, its wheels still spinning. The enemy plane passed by and one of the shell cases fell within two feet of my face. Without thinking, I reached out to pick it up and burned my fingers. It was, of course, red-hot!

During the night the Royal Irish Fusiliers had captured the Djebel Bir El Mahdi and before First Light our eager Brigadier ordered Brigade HQ to upstakes and make for the Mahdi where he intended establishing his HQ with the Fusiliers. When we arrived small arms fire was still spasmodically occurring. For the first hour after dawn a heavy fog cloaked the Mahdi. Then it lifted. What a sight met our eyes!

There on the forward slope, slightly ahead of the Irish Fusiliers' dug-in positions, and in full view of the enemy, lay the 6th Black Watch! They had been dispatched to take over the Mahdi from the Irish Fusiliers immediately the latter had seized it. By some error the Irishmen had not been notified of this and the stealthy Black Watch had crept through our lines unnoticed. Then, when the fog lifted, they were revealed lying on the ground and standing around in little clumps wondering *"Whateffer the scor-r-r-re wass?"* I'll never forget our BM's vocabulary when he began blasting the unfortunate Black Watch CO. Before the latter had an opportunity to realize that he was being told off by a mere BM the Brigadier hove into view and instructed the unhappy and very embarrassed Scot to gather up his hackle-hung battalion and get "behind the Irish". The Watch had a pleasant day in the valley below. Next day they took over from the Fusiliers and everything turned out *"a' richt"*.

After the Scots had departed, the battle proceeded and the North Irish Horse began a sweep out to the right and forward toward the Medjez-el-Bab sector. As buckshee LO I was given the job of keeping contact with the North Irish Horse and found that the LO from these mounted Micks was none other than Captain Randolph Churchill, the much-publicized son of the PM. He proved an amusing companion during the day. We sat together in his scout car, getting the dope over his wireless and then I took the information to my Brigadier. Several times we dove into his slit trench, as the *Stukas* were fairly active during the day and the ME 109's were straffing every half hour or so. Once, while we cowered in our slit he asked me why the Canadian Army wasn't taking part in the African campaign. I replied, "Why don't you ask your father? He knows a hell of a lot more about these things than I do".

London Irish with captured German trophies. Author seated on right wearing German helmet. Tunisia, March, 1943.

Churchill was interesting to talk to, having recently, for some obscure reason, been with his father at the Casablanca conference where he had met such people as Roosevelt, Eisenhower, Sir Alan Brooke and so on. He described Eisenhower as a very *nice* fellow and said he had a wonderful gift for getting people to work together without petty squabbles and arguments. It was an odd switch of scene for him, I thought, from being with his great father, President Roosevelt, and all the other warlords divining world policy, to sitting with me in our forlorn little slit trench on a godforsaken battlefield in Tunisia.

During the afternoon our Ack-Ack shot down a *Stuka* dive-bomber, a very difficult thing to do, and also an ME

109. In my diary I wrote: "a glorious sight to see the bright orange dot burst into a great sheet of flame, consuming the devilish apparatus as it plunges earthward, its pilot a dark twirling starfish swirling down, down, down". The Tommies cheered wildly when the human pin-wheel finally buried himself in the Tunisian soil. There was no pity in their Irish hearts.

On April 11 the Irish Brigade, which by this time was only the Royal Irish Fusiliers and the Inniskillings, the Hampshires having returned to their own brigade, lay up for a couple of days near the Mahdi. The enemy was pulling out fast, and other formations swept up the tag-ends to the flanks.

My attachment to the First Army was at its end. The night before I left the Front I sat in my tent and by the light of a candle wrote the last entry from the Tunisian battleground in my diary; it was as follows: "Awakened by aerial machine-gunning — the prelude to a harrowing day! Did nothing but lie in the sun (the first this Spring) and jump into slit trenches. Jerry was over about every forty-five minutes bombing vehicles on the plain. On one such occasion Bobby Lowry, the IO, jumped into the officers' latrine trench for protection and emerged covered with s——t! About 2100 hours, as we were eating dinner, the Boche swooped over the farm and dropped a bomb in the gully below. All of us, except the BM, hit the floor. What a shambles . . . benches turned over and dishes went flying. The mess servants also went flat, one chap carrying a bucket of water which doused several of us as we dived for shelter."

For the next few weeks the Irish Brigade fought on. With their fighting comrades of the veteran 6th Armoured and 78th Divisions and the thousands of new arrivals from Britain, they used their new-found strength to kick Rommel's successor, Von Arnim, out of Africa, and all this by May 12. By then I was back with my own people in the United Kingdom. When the news broke that the Germans had been turfed out of Tunisia and later that the pipers of the 2nd London Irish had led the victory parade in the city of Tunis itself, I was proud that I had taken part in at least the first week of that mammoth drive which culminated in so great a victory for Britain and her Allies. More than 200,000 prisoners, Von Arnim himself among them, as well as 1,000 guns, 250 tanks and thousands of wheeled vehicles, had been captured. It was the first British victory, it might be recalled, since November 1918!

It was not the last I was to see of my former Irish comrades. Little did I think, though such was to be the case, that I would be fighting beside them in Sicily three months later, again in Italy seven months after that, at Cassino in May, 1944 and in the Po Valley in the late autumn of that year.

CHAPTER VIII

"DOWN DOORS!"

I left the Front on April 14, going by truck to Souk el Arba. Here, with the other members of our returning Canadian draft, I was accommodated for the rail journey to Algiers in a boxcar marked *40 Hommes — 8 Chevaux*. Despite the "forty men — eight horses" capacity notice, the officers were assigned four to a boxcar, so we were able to erect our camp beds, one in each corner of the car. The only trouble was that during the nights as we slept, our beds kept sliding toward the open doors which could not be closed. However, the train moved so slowly that if any of us had slid out the doors not much damage would have been done either to the beds or to us.

At Souk el Arba we caught up on all the news of the past two months since we had separated. Of the officers, one had been badly wounded, one had been wounded and captured, another had been captured on a patrol and one had been taken with acute appendicitis and had spent all his time at the Base. In his own words he had "missed all the fun". Of the NCOs several had been wounded. These included CSM Bill Waudby, of the RCR, whose soldiering days were ended by serious head wounds received during an attack near Sejenane. Fortunately, no one had been killed.

We arrived at Algiers five days after our rail journey started. Once, while our train was halted at a station with a sign which said Kroubs, we saw three American 2nd Lieutenants wearing steel helmets and sitting in a jeep. We asked them how far it was to Algiers. A particularly stupid looking one sitting at the steering wheel answered, "Jesus, we ain't seen Algiers for months. We're all goin' up Front."

He jerked his thumb in the direction of Tunisia for emphasis.

Padre "Rusty" Wilkes and Lt.-Col. Spry at Scordia, Sicily in August 1943.

As it happened, we were about 300 miles from Algiers and 150 miles from the Front Line. We reached our destination on the 19th after four nights in our boxcar boudoir. After five days of buying and drinking wine in Algiers we embarked again on the *Duchess of York*. The naval personnel on board were short-handed and because most of the British troops returning on the ship were battle neurotics, disciplinary cases, non-combatants or for various other reasons unemployable in this role, the Canadian officers and NCOs on board were asked if they would volunteer for Ack-Ack duty. Most of us did. I was detailed as captain of a four-man Oerlikon gun crew. We were quite the team. The other three were an Ordnance Corps captain, an HLI of Canada CSM and a *Van-Doo* sergeant. Three days later we were attacked by German aircraft in the Bay of Biscay and had a taste of war on the High Seas.

The alarm sounded just after dinner. As gun crew captain, I had only to inspect the crew members on duty twice a day and take post if Action Stations sounded. I made off and, dashing to P-4 Oerlikon found that Capt. McBride, the RCOC chap, was on the gun, it being his tour of duty. Sgt. McMahon, who, despite his Irish name was a *Van Doo*, was 'next for duty'. He arrived at the same time I did, taking over as ammunition passer.

The alert lasted two hours. The enemy, two Focke-Wulf *Condors*, attacked three times. They seemed to single out the *Duchess* as their target, gliding in from out of the sinking sun across the golden water to drop their bombs. McBride got off a sixty-round magazine without result while dozens of gunners on all the ships also blazed away. Tracer filled the sky with hundreds of shimmering red "jewels". Smoke from the heavier guns burst into little black clouds and the chattering and booming of the mixed weaponry provided a very noisy sunset ceremony.

When their first sortie ended, the *Condors* circled into position for their next attack. I ordered McMahon to hand the gun over to McBride. The latter was obviously anxious to get a few shots off, which he did. Then I took over, anticipating a third attack. The second and third attacks were closer in. Huge geysers of water shot up into the air all around our ship as the bombs hit the sea. I found that firing back at the enemy aircraft was exhilarating. This 'hitting back' made all the difference. The first two attacks, when I was just standing by, were terrifying. But when I took over the gun, got my sights on the aircraft and blasted away, I almost wished there were more targets! I think the Germans knew the 'ceiling' of our guns, for they swooped over us quite slowly, too low for the heavier anti-aircraft guns and just beyond the effective range of our Oerlikons. It was a strange experience, quite different from the battlefield. I felt that our little gun turret was the enemy's sole target. No doubt everyone else felt the same way about theirs. The HLI chap arrived all right, but the two planes streaked off to France after their third attack, so he didn't get a turn on the gun. It was an amazing exchange of death-dealing missiles, but as far as I know nobody got hurt.

On May 2, having gone around the west coast of Ireland, then through the narrows between Ireland and Scotland, we entered the Irish Sea and berthed safely in Liverpool harbour. A few hours later we were on the train for Aldershot, sleeping that night in Albuhera Lodge.

Rumour had it that 1st Canadian Division was in Scotland preparing to leave for an unknown overseas destination. In a few days this was confirmed when I was sent northward to rejoin my Regiment at an undisclosed location. I was met at a suburban Glasgow railway station by the adjutant and taken by jeep to the unit area twenty-five miles south in Ayrshire. Things were much different than when I had left the battalion for North Africa three and a half months before. For one thing we had a new CO and a new Second-in-Command. Other officers had gone elsewhere and been replaced by new arrivals from Canada. Some of these were old friends who had been kept at home in training establishments as instructors and administrators.

My Company HQ personnel near Regalbuto. L. to R., Pte. D. Smith, Pte. R.W. Miller, Pte. J.D. Sheehy, Pte. S.C. Harland, Pte. D.H. Blackman, MM, Pte. E. Amond, CSM J.L. Goodridge, Pte. A.V. Drake, Pte. J.A. Bancroft, MM. Seated, Pte. M.M. Millard, MM.

There was a great hustle and bustle about our hutted camps. New equipment was much in evidence, new weapons caught the eye. It was easy to see that an expedition was in the offing. Vehicles were being waterproofed; that meant an assault landing. Speculation in the Mess was hushed, but active. Would it be Norway, or Burma, or Italy? No one knew but the CO, Lt.-Col. Ralph Crowe and his 2IC, Major Billy Pope. And their lips were sealed.

I was given command of "B" Company, much to my disgust, as I had been commanding "D" Company when I left in January. As it happened, my "D" Company CSM, Jim Goodridge, had been posted to "B" Company during my absence. My Second-in-Command was an old friend, Capt. Charles Lithgow. I knew none of my three subalterns, two recent RMC products direct from Canada and a very unmilitary but comical chap who had been some sort of man-about-town before the war, and was also a new arrival. I got my batman, Pte. Harry Armitage, transferred from "D" Company and, looking over the rank and file, decided that my 'team' would be as battleworthy as any. At the time the establishment permitted three majors per infantry battalion. There were only two on strength, Billy Pope and the OC "D" Company, Tommy Powers. Both Slim Liddell and I wondered who would get the vacancy. Two captains were senior to us, but they had not served with the battalion for two years, having been back in Canada serving at training establishments. Both were Permanent Force officers as, of course, was the CO, who apparently did not favour either one. One day the Colonel summoned both Slim and me and astounded us by saying he had considered that either Slim or I should have the vacancy, but had decided he would wait to see which of us performed better when we first met the enemy! He said that although I was senior to Slim as a captain, and had three months battle experience with the British in North Africa, Slim was older, married and a Permanent Force soldier. If I were promoted major and Slim were killed as a captain it would be a hardship, pensionwise, on his widow. In my case there was no widow to consider. He then said that this would be an unfair solution in my case, because of my seniority and battle experience. Faced with

130

this dilemma he decided to promote neither of us. His reasoning made no sense to either Slim or myself and we left his presence dumbfounded.

I immediately purchased two sets of brass crowns and when I landed in Sicily had them in my small pack ready to receive my promotion! The possibility that I could be killed I ignored. As it was, I was promoted some three months later, six weeks after Crowe had been killed, and I in turn, as acting CO, promoted Slim three months later. In the meantime both the captains who were senior to us were given rifle companies after Crowe's death in Sicily and also awarded their majorities. The deaths of Crowe and Pope expedited my promotion, but Slim had to wait, as shortly after we landed in Italy two of our majors who had been on Staff jobs were returned for regimental duty, filling the existing vacancies!

My promotion saga in 1943 was almost unbelievable. I was made an acting major on 8 September. In November I was dropped to captain as one of the majors from the Staff who joined us filled the vacancy. A couple of days later we were notified that as from 5 August the War Establishment had been amended to provide for five majors per infantry battalion instead of three. I was promoted to the confirmed rank of major and back-dated to 5 August, to avoid the confusion of being a captain, an acting major and a captain again in the same period. Three weeks later I was commanding the battalion and the three weeks during which I held this appointment was recognized several months later by my being shown in Orders as having been an acting lieutenant-colonel. In theory, I held successively the ranks of acting major, captain, confirmed major, acting lieutenant-colonel and confirmed major in just under six weeks.

A funny thing happened the day the CO summoned me to tell me that Major Jerry Nelson was being posted to the battalion from Divisional HQ and would fill my vacancy, necessitating my stepping down to captain. As I entered the Battalion HQ gate the sentry gave me the "Present Arms", which my major's crown demanded. I left the HQ building by a different door and returned to my billet where I told my batman to remove the brass crowns from my shoulder straps and replace them with captain's stars. He had just completed this job when the field phone rang and I was again summoned to Battalion HQ. As I approached the gate the same sentry spied me and began the three-movement "Present Arms", the salute to which I had been entitled the last time he had seen me. Halfway through the movement he noticed I was a captain. "Jes — us — Christ!" he blurted out as he stopped the movement and replaced the rifle on his shoulder, giving me the proper "Butt Salute", in perfect timing with his three syllable expression. He must have wondered how and when my miraculous transition took place!

The officers were none too happy. Crowe and Pope were both intense people and perfectionists. For several years they had been on Staff jobs and they were out to whip their newfound battalion into the peak of fighting efficiency, no matter what. They treated the junior officers as though they were pupils in a boys' school and they instituted numerous madcap schemes to keep everyone on tiptoe. Actually, they were good for the battalion. They got our fighting spirit up to the point where we longed for the day of battle so we could get away from all the criticism we incurred for not meeting their standards. Crowe was an Anglican and Pope a Roman Catholic. Their insistence on church parades and their constant references to the blessings of their respective Faiths seemed neverending. They pushed religion more than the padre did. The only officer who didn't seem to mind was Sam Lerner, the 2IC of "C" Company. Fortunately for him, he was Jewish and thus in these religious matters only an onlooker. Strangely enough, Pope and Crowe were our first two officers killed, and the only ones killed during the thirty-eight day Sicilian campaign which was to occupy us that summer, although we didn't know it at the time.

Landings on the Ayrshire coast and fast marches inland gave us a good idea of what was going to be expected of us. A month after I rejoined — on June 13 — we removed all our cap badges, regimental flashes and divisional shoulder patches for reasons of security and entrained incognito for Clydeside. We were soon filing up the gangplank onto the *SS Marnix Van Sint Aldegonde*, a Dutch vessel now serving as one of His Majesty's Troopships. For three weeks we lay in the Firth of Clyde taking part in landing exercises, from which we were quickly and secretly reembarked.

Finally, on June 28 just before dark, we noticed that a large convoy was forming around our ship. During the night we put to sea and the next day at noon a message was posted on all notice boards. It read:

> The following message has been received from the Rear Admiral of Force V:
> "We are on our way to the Mediterranean to take part in the greatest combined operation ever attempted.
> "We shall be able to give you further information later."

Soon after, we were issued tropical bush clothing and ordered to pack away our long-familiar battledress. Those of us who were still serving with the battalion when winter came to the Appenines four months later would don it again. But some took off the only clothing they had worn for several years and saw it for the last time. After the heavy, tailored battledress, the sight of the troops in the loose fitting, shapeless bush clothing was a bit of a shock. But like everything else in the army we got used to it and when, in a few weeks' time we were burned brown with the Mediterranean sun, our bronzed faces, forearms and knees contrasted nicely with the sandy coloured material, also highlighted by our bright red divisional patches and blue, black and amber regimental flashes. Good soldiers are always proud of their dress and it wasn't long before we got the 'hang' of how to look smart and soldierly in the new garb.

On Dominion Day the CO briefed the officers of the Regiment on what the future held. Then we in turn, with maps and large scale drawings told our troops what our job was going to be. The first thing that struck us all, officers and men, was that the practice landings we had recently done on the Ayrshire coast had been on a section of beach and hinterland that was remarkably similar to where the

Sicilian landing was to take place. The road exits from the beach were almost identical. The distances to the exercise objectives the same as to the actual objectives — an airfield and a coastal battery in Sicily. In fact, in our Scottish exercises those exact objectives had been simulated. The beaches were sandy as well. The only real differences, it seemed, were that tall vineyards had to be crossed in Sicily once we cleared the beach, and that our enemies would be real, waiting for us behind minefields, barbed wire and blazing weapons.

We were told that although Italian troops had not fought well in the Western Desert, they could be expected to put up a stiff fight on their native soil. Fortunately, this was not to be the case. We were also told that there were 75,000 Germans in Sicily as well, held in reserve for counterattack purposes.

There followed a period of boat drill, lectures on the Italian Army and the people of Italy, specialist information on the environment we would encounter in Sicily and the readying of weapons and other assault equipment. Our convoy increased after we entered the Mediterranean and it was a terrific thrill to see the big battleships and ocean liners emerge from the foggy distance, some coming direct from the United States, others from various North African ports. We had been told that we were now part of Montgomery's famous 8th Army and we marvelled at our good fortune and wondered if we would measure up to the fighting standards of the Desert Rats. The American convoy carried troops to join other Americans sailing from North Africa, the two groups to become Patton's 7th U.S. Army.

These convoys, labelled Forces "H", "W" and "F" rendezvoused with our Force "V" between Malta and Sicily. The magnitude of the enterprise became apparent when, off Cap Bon, convoy after convoy covered the sea as far as the eye could discern.

All ranks were light-hearted, but there were solemn moments. The two mornings before the assault Holy Communion was held for Prostestants and Catholics and, at the former service, the Communion wine had to be replenished several times as the battle-destined troops filed past until almost one hundred per cent 'took the cup' and ate 'the broken bread' of Christian salvation.

Gourock, Scotland. Embarking for Sicily, June, 1943. Full marching order.

The afternoon of the 9th a *sirocco*, the dread gale of the Mediterranean, sprang up and monstrous white-capped waves created uneasiness as to the success of our landings. But the winds abated as quickly as they had begun and we prepared ourselves for battle.

I think nothing conveys my thoughts at the time any better than the three letters that I wrote to my family during the voyage.

At Sea,
June 1943

Dear Dad:

Here I am on the Atlantic again, and once more Mediterranean-bound! I hope I will be as well cared for by Providence in this Campaign as I was during my first.

When you receive this letter you will have long since known about the world-resounding operation which is as yet unborn. I shall have played my part, and God grant I will have come through unscathed.

We are told that this combined operation is the greatest ever attempted — presumably it is the long called for "Second Front". Let us hope — and you will know by the time you read these lines — that it will be successful.

When I look around at the faces of my men and those of my brother officers — my closest of friends — I am sobered by the realization that many of us will be among those who will not survive the terrific impact of the attack. They are all such wonderful chaps, even those with the most glaring faults.

As for myself I have implicit faith in the Wisdom of God, and if it be His design to carry me through I am sure that He will — and I pray for His protection and His strength.

Let me say that no son has ever been blessed with such loving and good parents, and fine young brother as have I, and I want to come home to you and enjoy the warmth of your affection once more. Thank God, however, that I am fit in mind, body and Spirit so that I can match myself against the enemy in these tremendous days for the greater glory of Our Empire and the destruction of Evil.

My bank statement was received, and thanks for your trouble in preparing it. My will, made in 1940 is now out of date inasmuch as dear Charles is left in cash a fairly small amount, such being my holdings then. Since I am richer now by several thousands of dollars I ask you to see that, should anything happen to me, there is practically equality in the division of my Estate — three ways — Mother, Charles and yourself — a thing not possible under my Old Will. If you or Mother see fit that for Charles' benefit the money should be devoted to his education in some form or other, then I leave it to your good judgement to lend him or allot him more than his ⅓ if you and Mother so desire. I know that however you and Mother decide to use my Estate, should I not be spared to enjoy it myself, will be of satisfaction to me. My wish is that what little Estate I have be kept among my parents and brother, and that Charles not be left with the mere $500 (I think it was) I willed him at the time my Estate was so small.

God Bless you,
Your Son, Strome

4/5 July 1943
Dear Family:
As I write this letter our convoy is sliding through the Straights (*sic*) of Gibraltar — my third such passage in six months — 30 Jan. 25 Apr. and tonight. It seems another age since my last adventure; and yet, in another way it just seems a day or two ago!

I am very proud and happy in the knowledge that I am going to lead a Company of so fine a Regiment in an Assault Landing such as we are going to do in the early morning of next Saturday. I talk to them in their mess deck, telling them of the specific jobs, etc. and I am a lucky man indeed to have such a good lot of lads under my command. The average age is about 24, although there are a number who, claiming 20, look about 18. In their shorts and open-necked, rolled-up sleeved shirts they look like a bunch of Boy Scouts. It is hard to believe that these Western Ontario school boys of 1939, and in some cases later, are the "tough assault troops" which will be the newspapers' probable description of them.

They all have fighting spirit, but are schoolboyish in their enthusiasm; it seems a shame that so many of these splendid fellows will be dead or wounded before this week is out.

Today (Sunday) we had services on board, asking God's blessing on our venture and committing ourselves to his care. The CO read Psalm 91, the Soldiers' Psalm. I am sure that many of the men are very sure that God is close to them in this great and dangerous undertaking. I know I do. I have great pleasure in going as a "veteran", telling my men of various sensations under fire, etc., to, I hope, their benefit.

My Company has been given the toughest job of the battalion and I imagine it is because the CO has faith in my wartime experience. "B" Company — my lads — will attack and destroy a 4-gun coastal artillery battery about 1½ miles inland — then an airdrome 3 miles further inland is to be attacked and captured and again the boys of "B" Company have a "front seat", and take a bow.

This great operation is history in the making and I am going to be among the first ashore.

I am amazed at the fact that I am not excited, I imagined I would be quite excited with the great uncertainties of taking part in such a show.

I assure you I feel it a great and high honour to be so positioned. I am proud that my Regiment is to take part in such a terrific, hazardous and glorious undertaking and I am happy that I have been entrusted to the command in the initial stages of a "force" of two companies (practically a ½ battalion). Last night I poured (sic) over air photos and maps and made my plan of attack on the battery position. The CO was quite satisfied when I gave it out at the Conference today.

It seems strange so much is afoot and you know

nothing of it, and yet when this letter arrives the invasion of Sicily will be history!

If through God's good grace I survive the ordeal it will be a great experience, and, with my Tunisian fighting, will make me an experienced soldier indeed, and I am fortunate to have had these opportunities.

Rest assured that my first thoughts are of you all at my home, which I hope will be happy and peaceful forever. I thank God I can play my part in this great struggle for the Honour of our Race and the survival and greater glory of the British Empire. Your loving son and brother.

Strome.

At Sea
8 July 1943

Dear Folks:
Well, here's my last letter for some little while, I guess, as tomorrow night is our last normal night aboard and will in all probability be rather busy. The next night we go into the assault.

Both officers and men are in good spirits as the day of battle approaches and it is marvellous how cool and self-confident one and all are. Men who in 48-hrs will be gliding in little craft to the beaches of Sicily, the unknown ahead. No doubt this is due to the old saying that "All men think all men mortal save themselves". It is, however, fortunate that such is the human thought. Personally I have no evil foreboding and am very proud of my men in their calmness. I do hope we get a decent show. Latest Intelligence adds a snag as a sandbar with 9 feet of water between it and the beach necessitates a slight change in point of landing and the navy tells us the shore will be quite rocky where we land. However, that is the fortune of war.

Tomorrow we expect heavy air opposition; a nasty thing. I know, having had air attack on my trip back from Africa. Attack at sea is rather nerve-wracking.

Tomorrow morning there is a Protestant communion

service in the officers' lounge at 0830 hrs, which I shall attend. Our spiritual welfare is well looked after. I intend asking God's blessing on my company as we prepare to leave the mother ship, and have the Company repeat the Lord's Prayer in unison. I do not wish to be picturesque or dramatic, but I believe in committing one's endeavour into the Hand of God even as did Oliver Cromwell, Robert the Bruce, "Chinese" Gordon and other God-fearing commanders in our Empire's glorious past. Besides, prayer is a great strengthener and I know that it will renew with Faith and Courage at least some of my gallant fellows and thus they shall have this last piece of armour to uphold them in this the most critical moment of their lives so far.

May God bless our enterprise with success and a minimum of bloodshed, even of Italian blood.

I know your prayers are ever with me and I thank God for it, as it is an unseen shield before me.

It seems so cruel my knowing the news that will break on Saturday, and yet in no way can I prepare you for the worry you will undoubtedly undergo.

Be of good cheer whatever befalls, and through God's good Grace I shall write you soon again.

Your ever loving and appreciative Son, and Brother,

Strome.

Now, almost forty years after the event and reading these letters, I marvel at the attitudes we had, and beliefs we held and the spirit with which we carried out the duties we were assigned. They were, of course, the attitudes, the beliefs and the spirit by which the war was won.

Crowded into the tiny LCA's (Landing Craft Assault) we tossed for a while on the swelling waves, then in broad daylight made a run for the beach. The prow of one flat-bottomed craft ground to a halt on the sandbar. A few spouts of water indicated that shells were falling around us. Spasmodic, ineffectual enemy machine-gun fire could be heard.

"Down doors!" I shouted. The naval rating let the hawser go and as the prow door fell into the water like a ramp, we splashed waist deep or deeper through icy waters onto the enemy shore.

Regalbuto, Sicily, August 2, 1943.
Dressed for fighting in hot weather.

CHAPTER IX

THEY DIED IN SICILY'S SUNSHINE

"Have you seen much of death in the sun — in the morning?" That was the question Major Billy Pope, the battalion's second-in-command, continually put to the young and apprehensive subalterns during the feverish weeks of preparation for the assault on Sicily. "Well, you will," he would reply to his own question, flashing a grin and twitching the scar on his cheek which was the result of a motorcycle accident, but which Billy tried to pass off as a sabre cut received in a student duel.

The road from Pachino to Mount Etna was to see much of death in the sun — and in the shade, too.

Alas, it was Billy of the close-cropped head, round as a cannon ball, with china-white teeth under a Zorro moustache, who was the first of our lot to find out what death in the sun was like. He was cut down at Valguarnera while attacking a German tank single-handed, using an infantry anti-tank weapon and a bomb which he had failed to arm!

That evening, when our battalion rested, the CO, Ralph Crowe, another would-be Cavalier, with tears in his eyes reminded his senior subordinates that Billy's death should never have been; that it was an object lesson for all of us. We were not to expose ourselves needlessly. The Second-in-Command had no business stalking enemy armour and we, the company commanders, had even less business putting ourselves in positions of great danger when our men were supposed to be properly led by the sound application of our tactical training and by accepted techniques of command and control. He was so very right. But one week later to the day, Ralph Crowe fell at the main point of his battalion's attack, rifle in hand, ten yards in front of a *sangar*, a stone breastwork, over which poked the snout of a German MG42.

Crowe was the second to die. He too, died in the sun. There was plenty of sun in Sicily in July 1943. There was plenty of white dust, plenty of putrid flesh, animal and human; plenty of burning hot days and stinking hot nights. The mud and the snow came later, in Italy. By then, many more Royal Canadians had learned how to die; but fortunately many others, including myself, had learned how to live — or at least how to reduce the odds on dying.

Sicily wasn't all death in the sun, but it was an adventure for all. For me, it was my second campaign. Except for the CO, whose untimely death removed him from the scene 14 days after the landing, I was the only member of the battalion who had been in a battle.

Crowe had served in the Waziristan campaign on the Northwest Frontier in 1936 while on exchange with the Indian Army. What he had seen or heard, other than the crack of an occasional Waziri rifle, I don't know. Certainly machine-guns, mortars, tanks and all the other lethal paraphernalia of modern war had been, up until that memorable July 10, experienced by only one Royal Canadian — and that one was me.

The landing at Pachino had been almost bloodless, but most disconcerting. First of all, we were supposed to go ashore under cover of darkness. But that didn't happen. We went ashore in broad daylight! Secondly, we were to land almost dryshod. But, when I stepped from my assault craft into the chilly Mediterranean up to my armpits, I realized that we had been misled again. Thirdly, we were told that once we had crossed the narrow strip of sandy beach we would find cover in vineyards where the vines were almost six feet high. Our sense of tactical nakedness was extremely unpleasant when we found that the vines weren't as high as our soon-to-be-sunburned bare knees!

The night before the landing I had dined off snowy linen at a round table in the ship's luxury dining room. Billy Pope, Slim Liddell, Ian Hodson, Sam Lerner and Johnny Praysner were at the same table. Billy jokingly referred to our meal as the Last Supper. It was, but only for him. The rest of us all survived the war, although three of us were wounded.

The lowering of the assault craft with us packed in spoon fashion, to be tossed about, vomiting over one another from seasickness, while spasmodic enemy shelling sent up geysers of water, is a vague, fading memory now. I remember distinctly only two things that happened as we stood in the ship's passageways, a long queue of khaki clad, equipment-laden infantrymen. Each man grasped the bayonet scabbard of the man ahead to keep the line intact. My batman, Pte. Harry Armitage, pointed to the water closet door, barely visible in the eerie blue light. We were on a Dutch ship and the slot which indicated whether the WC was occupied or not, showed the first three letters of the Dutch word *vrij* meaning "free".

"Look sir," Armitage whispered, "V.R.I. — that must be a good omen." These three letters, the Royal and Imperial cipher of Queen Victoria, that is, Victoria Regina et Imperatrix, was our Regimental badge! A week later Armitage left me, shot through the throat.

The second thing I remember about the shuffling line of assault infantrymen in the narrow companionways that night was a remark made by the War Graves Commission representative, a chap named Gray. He was standing at the exit to the boat deck, directly under one of the blue lamps, which gave his face a gruesome, hideous hue. "I'll be seeing you soon," he remarked, with every good meaning. "Not me, I bloody well hope," was my acid retort.

The fighting in Sicily lasted exactly 26 days, so far as The Royal Canadian Regiment was concerned. The first day was fought under a scorching sun to capture an airfield. This brought in about 400 Italian prisoners. It cost us one officer wounded, six men killed and perhaps twice that number wounded. One of our men was killed on a two-man scout patrol and before the stretcher bearers got to him some Sicilian peasants had braved the dangers of the battlefield to steal his boots!

During the first day the company commanders were summoned by wireless to Battalion Headquarters for orders. Billy Pope, who had landed in the support echelon, had made his way up to where my company was digging in. We decided to go to headquarters together. We crossed one corner of the airfield but were sniped at all the way. As always, Billy had a plan. He decided that we were too valuable for both of us to be shot together. "I'll run 200 yards and go to ground", he said, "then you close up on me, drop, and I'll go for another 200 yards and so on." Oddly enough, while making this skin-saving plan we were standing bolt upright in the middle of a field with bullets singing all around! However, we soon began to carry out our movement scheme. At the second lap Billy stood up. "You know," he confided to me in a high-pitched voice, "I'm not scared at all. I thought I would be."

"Let's get to hell out of here," I answered him, "I am."

A couple of nights after our landing in Sicily, the CO told us that the battalion was to mount on a squadron of tanks and, by combining a sort of shuttle service with marching periods in between, make speedily for a spot about seven kilometers from a place called Modica, and sixteen miles from another place called Ragusa. By now we had rounded up all the Italians on coastal defense. We had broken the crust, so to speak, and were supposed to thrust inland to find and fight the Germans, who were said to be organized into hard-hitting mobile groups in the hinterland.

Our mechanized column got off at about 2 a.m., although the tankmen figured they had hardly enough petrol to make the trip. When the tank commander said that he was short of fuel, Billy Pope thought he had the answer. From the recesses of a German staff car he had found abandoned earlier in the day, he produced four jerricans of gas. The laugh was on him. The tankmen wanted 2,000 gallons!

We waited until the tanks got their needed fuel and

then the CO led off into the void in his carrier. We company commanders followed in the open staff car, with the troop-laden tanks grinding up the dusty road behind us. The whole move was a nightmare. It turned quite cold. We wrapped ourselves up in our gas capes, which always produced a clammy, sweaty condition. Billy was at the wheel wearing a Navy duffelcoat with a parka hood. He looked quite snug, and undoubtedly was. Every once in awhile he would fall asleep and have to be nudged to keep the car from swerving off the dusty ribbon of road which stretched ahead. Since we had absolutely no knowledge of the enemy's whereabouts, we all expected to be shot up at any moment. As dawn broke the column was slowed down by the CO who, by the excellence of his map reading, had got the head of his column to the exact spot ordered.

Jumping out of the staff car we four rifle company commanders got our attack orders from the CO. We then got our dusty troops into concealed forming-up places. The men looked as though they had been dipped in flour, the tanks having churned up so much chalky roadway that they had been in thick clouds of dust the whole journey.

I gave my orders in double quick time. The CO had pointed out a large, walled famhouse as my objective. It was on top of a low hill. My plan was to attack with two platoons — about 60 men. The third platoon would be used later, if needed. After approaching under the cover afforded by cactus fences and folds in the ground, the two platoons assaulted by rushing straight for the several iron gates leading into the stone-flagged courtyard of the farm.

To our surprise we found the place occupied only by a farmer and his wife! Unperturbed by the deadly, two-pronged assault of about five dozen Canadian soldiers, this pair welcomed us with bread, cheese and eggs. They were as unconcerned as if it were an everyday occurrence to be awakened from their early morning slumbers by infantry assaults. They said, through my interpreter, Pte. Tonellato, that they had seen neither German nor Italian troops anywhere in the district for days.

Not until the day Billy Pope was killed did we bump

into the Germans. But on our right flank the 51st Highland Division and on our left flank the Americans, had a succession of sharp, bloody encounters. Strangely enough, our initial advance had been up an empty corridor.

On July 14 General Montgomery paid us a visit. Col. Crowe introduced us as we stood at attention in front of our companies, and mentioned that I had been in the North African campaign.

"I was with the 78th Division," I said.

"Oh, Eveleigh's crowd, great fellow Eveleigh. I have him in my army now." This was the first hint we had that Monty's Eighth Army, of which we had, for just four days, been so proudly a part, was being enlarged by divisions from the First Army which was still resting in North Africa after its capture of Tunis.

Following the bloody clash at Valguarnera, where Pope was killed and my batman Armitage wounded, we pushed on to Nissoria where Col. Crowe died. Our losses then began to mount.

Harry Armitage had been my batman for more than a year before we landed together in Sicily. We waded ashore side-by-side, the cold Mediterranean lapping our armpits. He dug my first slit trench and several more for me in the days that followed. I landed with a tommy-gun and four loaded magazines. I soon realized that I couldn't do my job and also be a walking arsenal, so I told Armitage to chuck his rifle and handed him my tommy-gun and the ammo. I taught him how to walk in my wake, eyes peeled for my protection as I studied the map, peered through my binoculars or searched the ground with the naked eye. He could brew a good cup of tea and prepare my food while I checked the platoons, told them off to their tasks, or returned, dead beat, to my resting troops from a reconnaissance or an O Group. I also taught him map reading and how to carry orders and come back with information. He was to be one of my battle-winning factors. Unfortunately, he only lasted a week after we landed.

Our orders were to attack down a forward slope and

push the Germans out of the village of Valguarnera. I had crawled up to the crest of a ridge and was peering through a scrubby hedge in an attempt to locate the enemy defenses, when Armitage crept up beside me. He had just guided the company to its forming-up place down the slope behind us and was joining me to report that the company was now in position. As I wanted him to see the route I intended to follow during the attack and point out where he was to join me if we got separated, I told him to crawl closer until we were almost cheek to cheek. Just as our heads came together he jerked. There was a loud gurgle and he began gasping for breath. Blood poured from his throat. He had been shot right through the windpipe.

That morning, as he had done every morning for many months, Armitage had shone my cap badge until it glittered like the Star of the East. In fact, it must have shone so brightly in the glaring sun that a German sniper took his bead on it, only missing my forehead by several inches. A few yards down the slope was our medical officer, Jake Heller. He ran forward in a crouching manner when I shouted for a stretcher bearer, dropped beside the wounded Armitage and applied his skilled fingers to the gushing throat. He bound it with a first field dressing, but it was only his skill and speedy response, despite the bullets now whizzing about, that saved Armitage's life. My poor batman, unable to speak, looked at me with the eyes of a dying stag.

Ten minutes later we launched our attack. In the first few yards four of my section leaders fell to the ground behind me — Cpl. W.N. Roberts, shot in the foot, Cpl. F.R. Biggs, drilled through the shoulder, Cpl. A.H. Hall and L/Cpl. H. Johnston also received bullets somewhere in their anatomies. Pte. W.J. Huff got a bullet in the eye. Then the enemy ran off and we reached our intermediate objective without further casualties.

None of these wounds proved mortal, but I was sure Armitage would not survive. Happily, I was wrong. Less than a month later his first letter arrived. "Dear Sir", it read, "I hope this letter finds you OK and carrying on in the usual manner. I'm terribly sorry I let you down so early in the game. . . . I can't talk yet, but there is hope, I guess. . . ."

148

While all this was going on, the other companies were suffering light casualties as well. Major Pope was dying, ripped open by machine gun bullets and, on our right flank the Hastings and Prince Edward Regiment, our good friends the 'Hasty P's', were soon to ambush and destroy a column of troop-laden vehicles. These were either our opponents fleeing to their next position on the Assoro Heights, or reinforcements coming up to hold Valguarnera. In any event, these vehicles came along below a ridge on which the Hasty P's had just arrived, providing the Bay of Quinte boys with a shooting gallery.

Pope's death was tragic in that it should never have been. He was eager to be in the thick of the fray, where, as Battalion Second-in-Command, he had no place. From somewhere he acquired a Piat gun and with it he attacked a Tiger tank. Unfortunately, he forgot to arm the bombs and fired two of them, both of which hit the tank but failed to explode. The tank swivelled its turret and filled him full of lead. His wireless operator, Plankenhorn, who had accompanied him on foot with his radio set, had his first field dressing and emergency ration cut right out of his battledress trouser pocket without one scratch to his skin!

A day or so before the Nissoria bloodletting I had led my company in an advance to contact Slim Liddell's company. We were to clear the enemy off some low hills to our immediate front. We got on our objective without any real opposition. Some sporadic mortaring had somehow set the long dry grass on fire and we avoided being burned by hopping over the wall of flame as it rolled toward us and landing on the blackened and smouldering stubble over which it had swept a moment before. To add to the confusion, several of our accompanying tanks blew up on a minefield and, finally, the two companies received orders over the wireless to pull back to a tight defensive position for the night.

While our men were digging in, Slim and I were summoned to battalion headquarters for further orders. As we arrived, Crowe and the officers of his headquarters group were eating a greasy supper of stew off an improvised table in the barnyard of a dilapidated farm. Seated around the table on broken chairs, a wooden box and a long bench they looked grubby and unkempt. Piles of manure lay all around and the body of Lt.-Col. Bruce Sutcliffe, the CO of the Hastings and Prince Edward Regiment, lay under a blanket, stiff and still, about fifty yards away. He had been killed by a lone shell while scanning the cliffs of Assoro, his battalion's objective for a night attack.

Slim, sweat streaming in rivulets down his flame-fanned body, arrived at the barnyard meeting place naked to the waist, carrying his sooty, damp bush shirt over his arm. He looked exhausted from the long walk back from the hill. He saluted and then almost collapsed on an old box near one end of the table, content that he had done a good day's work. I felt the same way, but being a few years younger than Slim, I was not quite so near to a state of collapse. Besides, I still had my shirt on.

Slim had hardly found time to open his lips and exhale the journey's fug from his lungs when Crowe barked out:

"Capt. Liddell, what do you mean, coming into an officers' mess improperly dressed?"

There were times when the enemy was the least of our worries.

The next day we bumped the enemy — Germans, although there were still Italians in the vicinity. The CO detailed me to produce a fighting patrol of platoon strength. The idea was to probe the high ground between two hilltop towns, Leonforte and Assoro, to see if the enemy were holding it in any strength. We were also to knock out a bothersome gun if we could pinpoint it. I chose Lieut. Harry Keene as the patrol leader and detailed Lance-Sergeant Sandy Leith and two corporals as section commanders. I then told them to pick their own men. There was no difficulty in this; we had too many volunteers.

The patrol was a disaster. I went with it to lend moral support, though such was probably unnecessary. At that stage of the game I didn't like the idea of detailing a brother officer to take on such a dicey task on his own. We drew enemy fire at noon and Cameron, our lead scout, was hit. Then Leith and Keene's batman were both wounded.

Soon one of the Bren gunners got a slug in the upper arm and another had his water bottle shot off his hip. The impact of the bullet spun him around and knocked him down. He thought he was bleeding to death when he felt so much wetness streaming down his body! In a few more minutes a grass fire had started. The flame and smoke were choking. I decided that, although our first casualty, Pte. Alvin Cameron, had fallen in a very exposed position, we could not leave him to the mercy of the grass fire.

It was not certain that he was dead so I called for volunteers to bring him in. Harry Keene and one of the stretcher bearers, Pte. J.A. Bancroft, said they would come with me. We went out very cautiously at first, but finally began walking around in full view. We located Cameron but he was quite dead. Strangely enough, a breeze had diverted the grass fire so the three of us turned to go back.

It was then that the German sniper who probably got Cameron opened up on us. A couple of bullets sang overhead in quick succession and we took to our heels. Cpl. J.E. Norton saw what was happening and rushed up to a small mound from where he intended to give us covering fire as we dashed to safety. As fate would have it, not one of us was hit, but Norton got it right through the stomach. Bancroft had just reached the mound when Norton fell forward, dropping his rifle. He bent down, placed the wounded corporal's arm over his shoulder, then seized him around the waist and jogged down the hill where he tried to bandage him behind a large protective boulder.

He did a good job, but Norton was dying and he knew it. I tried to cheer him by saying we'd soon have him back to a doctor, but he merely said, "I'm finished, sir." He was unconscious by the time a jeep ambulance arrived.

After clinging to our positions in the crags, pushing forward here and there, always drawing fire from high above us on the cliff tops five to six hundred yards away, we were withdrawn. I was able to report on several enemy positions, none of which could be reached frontally in daylight. It was a costly little effort, but the results were better than we had expected.

Shortly before Norton had been hit, he and a private named Lloyd Maxted had come upon a 3-inch mortar which had been abandoned by another Canadian unit the previous night. With it were about fifty bombs. They lobbed these over in the direction from which the enemy fire had first come. Two days later, having pushed on, I took the opportunity to visit the suspected enemy position with Goodridge, my company-sergeant-major. We found two badly wounded Germans, and two dead ones, chewed up by mortar fire. We counted more than sixty German helmets and numerous rifles and sets of equipment scattered about. From these now deserted *sangars* Goodridge and I could look right down the ravine where I had been operating with my patrol. It was from here that Cameron and Norton had been killed. It pleased us to find the two German bodies, because it made us feel that the score was more or less even.

We experienced the most severe fighting of the campaign when we attacked a small village called Nissoria. It lay astride our main axis of advance toward Mount Etna. Here, Colonel Crowe was killed and every company suffered losses in dead and wounded. We failed to take the village, but some days later an item appeared in the papers back home which took some of the sting out of our failure. The article was headed "Huns Amazed at Red Patch Devils". Datelined at Nissoria, Sicily, July 27 (CP), the story read:

> The Germans now are calling the Canadian 1st Division troops fighting in Sicily "The Red Patch Devils". The battle patch worn by the Canadian troops here is a bright red rectangle carried near the shoulder.

> One prisoner told a Canadian officer today: "We see the Red Devils coming and we fire our mortars hard. But the Red Patches just keep running through the fire.

> "I can't understand it. Other troops we fought lay down and took shelter when the mortars fired right on

top of them. The Red Patches are devils. They keep coming."

Certainly, at Nissoria we continued to advance under the intense mortar and MG fire without turning back or seeking shelter. However, I think the truth of the matter was that we had no other choice. We had to keep going, though I remember cowering momentarily in successive gullies which ran across our line of advance. Eventually, we were pulled back to reform and two other battalions attempted to carry the village. Both failed. Later the enemy pulled out on its own and hightailed it in half-tracks for Regalbuto.

Some of our cynics said that the whole Red Patch Devil story was concocted by a war correspondent. This may have been so, but the fact remains that so far as The Royal Canadian Regiment was concerned, the whole four rifle companies did move forward with the road to Nissoria as their axis, and they did not falter until the Colonel was killed and control was lost. Three companies outflanked the position, and had the advance not been rigidly planned beforehand, they might have reached the final objective, Agira. They had indeed kept "running through the fire", and had done so successfully. "D" Company had not been able to avoid getting pinned down and its casualties were the heaviest.

Crowe's death was heroic like Billy Pope's, but like Pope's was uncalled for. Having committed all four of his companies to the attack, he was moving up on foot on a centre line much too far forward for a battalion commander, when, because of the smoke of battle, the apple orchards and the gullies, he lost visual contact with his companies. According to one of the few of his command group who survived, he was calling out, "RCR, RCR," in the hope of getting a response. Suddenly he came face to face with a German machine-gun post in a *sangar*. He seized his runner's rifle and, as he levelled it at the enemy, was cut down by a burst from the machine-gun.

Regalbuto proved to be another bloody encounter. The town was divided by a precipitous ravine which did not show on the maps. The enemy were pushed out of

Regalbuto, but not before the 48th Highlanders had moved in on the extreme left and threatened to cut the enemy off from their line of withdrawal. Before the 48th were sent into action we had plunged into a totally unexpected deep ravine.

Both sides of this great scar on the terrain were almost sheer cliffs, cut into terraces. Although we began the descent long before midnight, daylight was upon us while we were still crawling up the other side. To our extreme discomfort we found that snipers were in some of the houses on our left rear. One of these knocked a branch off a scrubby tree that was between CSM Goodridge and me as we sat about four feet apart trying to communicate over our wireless with battalion headquarters. Fortunately, one of our snipers, an American named Eddie Amond, saw the German and fired back. Whether he hit him as he claimed, or merely convinced him that his lair was discovered remains unanswered. At least, he never fired on us again. Tank fire wounded a number of men, however, and one of our sections was captured in a gully.

We perched on our precipitous hillside in the blistering heat for fourteen hours, unable to get over the crest. It was swept by machine-gun fire from two tanks. Finally, Goodridge asked me if I would give permission for the troops to open their emergency ration. This was a tin box the size and shape of a sardine tin. Inside was some compound which was a "last resource" meal. On the tin in embossed lettering were the words ONLY TO BE OPENED AND CONSUMED ON THE ORDER OF AN OFFICER.

I told Goodridge that ten or so hours without food was not, according to my standards, an emergency. Some three months later, when I was lying wounded in a base hospital at Catania I was asked by an inspecting medical officer if I had any complaints. "Yes", I replied, "I have. The food is so bad and so inadequate in quantity that I had to use my authority as an officer and order myself to open my emergency ration and consume a portion of it to keep from starving to death." He thought my complaint rather facetious.

A day after the Regalbuto fiasco we were bombed by American Flying Fortresses. This was unpleasant as I had just been assuring my men that they were friendly planes. Their bombs made rubble out of Regalbuto and certainly scared us. Fortunately, only two or three Canadians were injured and those only slightly.

A couple of days later we received our first fresh rations. Up until then we had lived on Compo rations, mostly canned stew, canned fruit, bully beef and hardtack. Now we got meat, bread and, in keeping with typical army logic, we also got an issue of lemons. My company had a ration strength of 99 at the time and thus we received 99 lemons. They were rather useless as a food, but I suppose were meant to be good for purposes of nutrition. The most ridiculous part of the matter was that we had by now arrived almost at the foot of Mount Etna and before us were acres and acres of lemon trees, all loaded with the yellow fruit. The lemons issued to us had come all the way from North Africa! I forget now what most of us did with the lemons, but I seem to remember a few curves being pitched with small oval objects which were the wrong colour to be mistaken for No. 36 grenades.

The Sicilian campaign was far from bloodless. But by later standards it was not too costly. In the RCR we only had two officers killed, the Colonel and the Second-in-Command. Perhaps thirty Other Ranks lost their lives, not many more. Over seventy all ranks were wounded and twenty (mostly prisoners of war) were listed as missing. Illness and injury took their toll. It was, however, a hard campaign from the standpoint of discomfort, long gruelling marches, the stench of burning grass, and unburied dead, including soldiers, civilians and mules, and the incredible heat, with thirst, hunger and painful sunburn our constant scourges. Lack of sleep, caused by the continuous movement, and bowel trouble caused by contaminated fruit and water helped wear down some troops. Fortunately, the training in Britain had turned us into the right material from which to make hardy campaigners. Besides, we were young.

The Sicilian fighting ended on August 6. We moved into a sunbaked, lonely rest area near Scordia and went back to scrubbing our webbing, shining our brass, mounting quarter guards and holding study groups on "lessons learned during the campaign". We also had many a drinking party with strange Sicilian wines under the olive trees in the cool quiet of the nights. We welcomed newcomers to take the place of those who had died, been hospitalized or had quitted our ranks for other reasons. Then we readied ourselves for our next assault — on the Mainland of Italy.

"B" Company Orders Group, Messina, Sicily, on eve of invasion of Italy, September 2, 1943.

CHAPTER X

THE POINT OF THE ARROW

We had a new CO for the mainland fighting. After Crowe's death Major Powers commanded until the campaign ended. Then Lt.-Col. Dan Spry arrived from North Africa where he had been waiting it out with General Andy McNaughton, GOC-in-C. First Canadian Army, who had come out to visit the 1st Division once the campaign had ended.

On September 2, Spry took his four company commanders, Major Nelson who had joined us from the Staff, Lithgow, now a company commander, Liddell and me, to a hilltop on the Straits of Messina. There we had the weird experience of making a binocular reconnaissance of our objectives on the Italian mainland about two to three miles across the blue water.

At 4:30 a.m. on September 3 our assault went in, the landing taking place on the Reggio de Calabria beaches. Covered by air and naval bombardment and 630 guns of both the British 8th and U.S. 7th Armies, firing from positions in Sicily, our Division and the 5th Yorkshire Division crossed the straits. We found that the Germans had fled northward several days earlier and the Italians surrendered in droves. The landing was costly in ammunition spent, but loss of blood was negligible. Except for a stray shot or two and some bombs dropped on the beach by a couple of German planes it was a regatta.

* * * *

"The Mayor of Motta, I presume?"

With these colourful words Dan Spry greeted me

shortly after dawn on October 2, 1943.

Followed by a queue of wireless operators and orderlies, he plodded up the steeply inclined main street of Motta Montecorvino to where I stood, my walking stick under my left armpit, my right hand raised in salute to the peak of my cap.

Two companies under my command had just captured the little hilltop village amid a downpour of rain and a crashing of artillery shells. The last *Spandau* fire had died away. The enemy was screeching down the winding road to the west in half-tracks. Motta belonged to us, and had only cost us one officer killed, one man killed; one officer and a dozen men wounded. The darkness, the rain and our gunfire had shielded us from shooting accuracy on the part of the enemy. The blood-smeared tile floor in the house I had selected as my headquarters showed that our opponents had not gone unhurt. It had been their first aid post, and a busy one! In the middle of the street, one of our supporting tanks burned less fiercely than earlier. The villagers began to emerge from their cellars, blinking in the sunlight, overjoyed that *Tedesci* had gone.

"Sir," I replied to the Colonel's greeting, bringing my right hand down smartly to my side, "the town is yours!"

Spry, as I stated earlier, had arrived to take command of the RCR just before we landed on the Italian mainland. We had been ashore since September 3, yet this had been our first fight.

After landing, we bivouacked for the night and the next morning marched into the towering mountains behind Reggio. We reached our objective after twelve hours of uphill climbing, with a four hour halt at midday. For two and a half days we remained on our heavily-wooded mountain perch. At night it either poured rain or cloaked us with dense and chilling fog. Here "C" Company hoisted a large Union Jack, probably the first British flag to fly in the mountains of Calabria since the British landed at Reggio in 1806 to beat the French at nearby Maida. On September 7 we marched a few miles farther to Gambaria. Here the battalion paraded next day to be told by Spry that Italy had surrendered. At first, in our folly, we thought the war in Italy was over!

For days we moved northward, sometimes in vehicles, mostly on foot. Occasionally, light mobile troops ahead of us exchanged shots with German demolition parties. But we merely trudged down demolished railway tracks, often still burning with strange blue flames, or crossed countless ravines at the bottom of which shattered concrete bridges testified to the work of the enemy's engineers.

The Calabrians took us for Americans or English. "German man no *buono*," screamed out one hoary-headed native, "*Americanos buono, Inglese buono*! Kicka da ass for German man!" Such were the salutations they accorded their liberators, as we marched past peach orchards, fields of watermelons, and vineyards heavy with grapes.

As we pressed north, hordes of Italian deserters in their cheap, grey uniforms streamed past us in the opposite direction, hungry, unshaven and humiliated. Once they had considered themselves the legions of a modern Rome, but their Caesar had been filled with hot air. Now it stank in their nostrils.

On September 11 the RCR stumbled on a complete Italian division. It was intact, but hidden away in a leafy valley complete with all its transport, 15,000 men and a major-general. The latter, Guido Bologna by name, parleyed through subordinates until a meeting was arranged with Colonel Spry. Then Bologna arrived in a shiny limousine, complete with flag, motorcycle outriders and an entourage of aides-de-camp.

Dan Spry was ready for him. An RCR Guard of Honour was drawn up. A bugler sounded a brassy salute. Spry stepped forward, saluted the Italian general and asked if he wished to inspect the guard. Bologna accepted the honour. It was all very chivalrous. Then the Italian made his big request, not without tact. He wanted to surrender, but not please to a mere *tenente-colonello*. It must be to an officer of his own rank! In due course, Major-General Guy

Simonds, General Officer Commanding the 1st Canadian Division received him and accepted his sword and his 15,000 men.

Some Italian officers were emotional. One fat, aging and highly-scented staff officer had tears in his eyes. In his mortification he tore off his wealth of medal ribbons and flung them on the ground. It was a gesture of despair. Later, as these emissaries left the open-air conclave, one of his subordinates stooped and retrieved the ribbons, handing them surreptitiously to their owner. They were sewed on a cloth panel, for affixing to the tunic with dome fasteners. No doubt there would be repeat performances.

Such was the comedy which preceded the tragedy of the months to follow.

The capture of Motta was a classic example of a vanguard action. The division had advanced across the Foggia Plains into the Daunia Mountains with a main guard which was "to seize and hold Campobasso until relieved". Campobasso was said to be the headquarters of Field-Marshal Kesselring, commander of the German 10th Army. Ahead of the divisional main guard moved a vanguard consisting of the 4th Princess Louise Dragoon Guards (PLDG), which was an armoured reconnaissance regiment. Then followed "C" Squadron of the Calgary Regiment of Tanks, "B" Company of the RCR in troop-carrying vehicles, and other supporting arms detachments.

When Spry gave me my orders to join the vanguard as its infantry company, he introduced my task in his usual picturesque way. "We have all seen the war maps in *The Times*" he said, "and noticed how the progress of our troops or that of our opponents has been marked with broad black arrows. Well, Strome, tomorrow you are to be the point of the arrow."

When the PLDG drew fire from the outskirts of Motta, the tanks tried to blast the opposition out of the town. It didn't work. The vanguard commander, who was also CO of the PLDG, then ordered me to attack. I debussed my company under cover of a wood, got Major Bob Kingstone, my artillery colleague, to plan a covering shoot, and then raced up the road in a carrier that the PLDG had loaned me. A troop of the Calgarys reported to me and, under cover of their fire, two of my platoons, one under Lt. Doug Bagg, the other under Lt. George Hyman, launched their attack. Hyman was hit three times, his batman killed and a corporal wounded, before they had gone ten yards. Bagg's platoon was pinned down and drew fire from both flanks every time they raised their heads. It only took a moment to realize that two platoons were not going to be enough to carry Motta. My third platoon, under Ian Wilson, was on another axis, supporting a detached squadron of the PLDG.

The enemy began to shell the road. It was now six o'clock. I decided the best plan was to attack again after dark. I whistled back in the carrier to report to the vanguard commander, only to find that the rest of the RCR had closed up, and that a battalion attack had been ordered.

Spry decided to put "A" Company under my command and let me carry on when darkness fell. By 11 p.m., having explored every possible approach, "A" Company managed to enter the single, S-shaped street of the town and capture two prisoners. Then it came under machine-gun fire and suffered numerous casualties. Shortly afterwards a veil lowered by a torrential downpour solved our problem. I moved Bagg's platoon up with "A" Company, then through it. Bagg stole down the street, gained the centre of town without casualties, then managed to send a fusilade of shots after ten vehicles full of Germans which were disappearing around a long curve into the valley below.

Later in the morning "C" and "D" Companies tried to move forward, mounted on tanks, through the low ground to the flanks. It was no go. Three of the Calgary Regiment's tanks supporting "C" Company were knocked out and both approaches were taped with mortar fire. German shells fell in the village periodically during the day. Italian civilians and our troops were sent scurrying each time!

At 4:20 p.m. Spry came back from a visit to Brigade headquarters with orders for us to attack in an hour's time.

The attack was to begin without tank support, and without a tell-tale barrage. We were to "tiptoe through the tulips" — or to employ the advantage of surprise, as the military erudite put it.

The attack began before dusk, but by the time we reached the edge of our battalion objective it was dark. We moved over muddy fields, our feet swollen to the size of footballs with great lumps of red clay. As we approached the objective, a scrub-covered ridge, the two leading companies, "A" commanded by Capt. Tommy Cantley and "D" commanded by Major Ted Price, were given covering fire by both tanks and field artillery. They began the ascent.

"C" Company had been left in the position it had reached when its tanks had been knocked out earlier in the day. I had "B" Company close behind the two forward ones. Spry and his retinue walked with me.

A road curved along the base of the ridge. As we came on this Spry and his group remained with my three platoons and I took my Company HQ and set up in a small clump of brush about twenty yards beyond the road line. Suddenly, a half-track came whizzing down the road between us! It was full of men. They were Germans! Right behind them came a small civilian car and it sped by at top speed, too. Dead beat from our cross-country move none of us was quick enough to realize that they had to be enemy! So nobody fired! Certainly we missed a chance that would not present itself again. A few seconds later a loud boom testified to a demolition some yards along the road.

Minutes later "A" and "D" Companies reached the top of the ridge only to come under murderous machine-gun fire. Cantley was badly wounded, losing an arm later on as the result. One of his platoon commanders, George Slack, was killed. His platoon sergeant, Sgt. Albert Chipchase, was also killed and about fifteen men were wounded.

Several Germans were captured. The next morning a few German dead were found as we moved forward. They were all parachutists. In a haversack belonging to a huge, blond six-footer we found two pink see-through nighties, a

162

pair of lace panties and a flask of cologne.

The pattern of enemy tactics was plain. They were falling back from defensible feature to defensible feature; fighting sharp, bloody delaying actions — then withdrawing in haste while we bound up our wounds.

Our pattern of tactics was also plain. We were to continue to attack each enemy delaying position in turn. Next on our list, we learned at 10:30 the following morning, was San Marco, another hilltop village like Motta.

This time "B" and "C" Companies were detailed to lead the attack. We went in single file through close country toward our Forming-Up-Place. I crossed the Start Line and went forward to a little hillock from where I thought I could best control the two leading platoons in their assault. Here I got caught in machine-gun fire, enemy shelling and our own barrage, and was hit.

I managed to crawl into a dried river bed and snuggle up against the sandy bank. Enemy tracer kept biting the bank a foot above my head. My company did not show up, and I feared capture. By now I was almost paralyzed, but fortunately I had my pipe. Lighting up, I smoked away and by nightfall things quietened down. Around 8 o'clock I heard someone call my name in a low voice. It was my batman, Pte. Roy Lang. With him was Cpl. Driscoll, a stretcher bearer. The latter put a field dressing on my wound, gave me morphine and wrapped me in a gas cape. He promised to return at first light and take me to the regimental aid post. He also answered my most pressing question: Where was everybody?

The attack had been delayed, then the line of advance switched. My sergeant-major had received the message on the wireless, but could not get to me because of all the shelling! San Marco fell at the break of day.

A month later, after hospital stays in Italy and Sicily, I was back with the battalion. But it was not until December 8 that I led "B" Company in another attack. By this time we were out of the mountains and pushing up the Adriatic coast.

I have never been a German-hater. I think very few fighting men were. But there were times when the Jerries did get under your skin. Loving your enemies may be the right thing to do, but the gulf between love and hate is a fairly wide one. My attitude toward our wartime opponents was like a compass needle and most apt to swing somewhere in between the two emotions. Some of them were pretty good fellows.

After being wounded I had a short sea voyage in the saloon of an ex-English Channel steamer, the *St. Andrew*, with other wounded being ferried from Bari on Italy's Adriatic coast through the Ionian Sea to Catania in Sicily, where No. 5 Canadian General Hospital was located. Another Canadian was beside me and across the aisle sat a thin-lipped German captain with an Iron Cross ribbon in his button hole. His straight black hair was brushed closely back on his skull. His eyes were icy and his nose was sharp. His demeanor was aloof, as if he were sitting among inferior beings. He had been wounded too and his bandages showed through a slit in his trouser leg as he sat there with his arms crossed over his chest. He was not happy to be a prisoner of war.

Two other Jerry prisoners, also slightly wounded, were aboard. One was a huge, blond, hulking paratrooper. Like the captain, he also wore the ribbon of the Iron Cross.

"Look at those three Jerry bastards," my companion blurted out. "Why don't we throw them overboard?" Whether his idea was improper or not really didn't matter. With a piece of shrapnel in my back I was almost unable to stand up, whereas my friend was being evacuated with asthmatic trouble and could hardly breathe. We just couldn't have carried out his suggestion.

"That black-haired s.o.b. is the worst looking of the three," wheezed my pal. "I bet he'd shoot his own mother if Hitler told him to." Then he got a little more vehement. Looking directly across at the Jerry he almost shouted, "God damned Nazi, to hell with you." This verbal effort brought on breathing problems and he quietened down. The Jerry was looking directly at us, his eyes coldly quizzical as if he were thinking, "I wonder what they're talking about."

A little later, in a somewhat calmer tone, my opinionated chum began pointing out how cold the German's eyes were, how his thin lips indicated that he was cruel and sadistic, how his face betrayed the typical Nazi killer and so on. I agreed, and for a few minutes we discussed this particular German and his kind in more uncomplimentary detail. Just then a British medical orderly came around passing out cigarettes. He offered a package to the German captain.

"No thank you, Orderly," the German replied in Oxford English, "I don't smoke. Please give my issue to those two chaps over there," indicating us with a nod of his sleek head.

When we recovered from the shock, I meekly said, "Well, I guess you know what we think of you," and tried to smile rather apologetically.

"Don't let it worry you," he replied. "Are you Canadians?"

Mindful of his security lectures, my comrade replied, "Perhaps." Then, forgetting himself he asked the Jerry, "Are you a Panzer Grenadier or a parachutist?" With a smile the fellow answered, "Perhaps," adding, "but the important thing is I'm a regular soldier." Then he went on to say he wished that the war could be fought by professionals only, as modern armies were too big. My friend said that that wouldn't be fair, as the Germans would undoubtedly have the biggest army.

"True," replied the Jerry, "but my point is, we would be fighting against gentlemen. These big volunteer armies get so full of poor types, don't you think?"

By now my wound was beginning to throb, so I decided to leave the conversation. As I turned my head away I heard the Jerry say, "My home is Cologne. It is a beautiful city. My mother lives there."

"Have you been to Cologne recently?" taunted my

friend, "they say it's nothing but a heap of rubble." I thought it a rather unkind remark.

In November 1943, our battalion was enjoying a brief respite from battle in the cold and wet of Italy's Abruzzi mountain range. Our commanding officer was still Dan Spry, eventually to be nicknamed "Durable Dan", and destined to become the youngest major-general in the Allied forces.

One day there arrived the unwelcome news that we were about to be favoured with a visit by the Minister of National Defense! This was iron-jawed James L. Ralston who had won his DSO commanding the 85th Nova Scotia Highlanders in the First War. He was doubtless a fighting soldier (or rather he had been) but he knew beans about military protocol — so we found out.

The battalion formed up in a hollow square on a sloping, wind-swept hillside. A table was set up in the centre of the three-sided formation so that the Minister could use it as a platform. Last minute instructions were given out, the final word coming from Dan Spry.

"After the Minister has finished speaking," he said, "I will call for 'three cheers'. There will be 'three cheers'. There will be no 'tiger'."

He then explained that the calling for a tiger was unmilitary, poor form — and just not done. And no one would try it — or else!

Soon the Canadian warlords arrived, in a convoy of motorcycle-escorted cars. The Minister approached, surrounded and followed by countless red-tabbed gentlemen of considerable rank.

The introductions were run through as stiffly and stupidly as expected. The Minister then jumped up on the table, his trouser legs shoved into a pair of flight boots, his hands jammed into the pockets of his tightly-buttoned suit coat. On his head was a trim fedora hat. His jaw jutted out. What he said, I cannot remember.

He ended his talk, stepped down from the table and

the great moment arrived. The Colonel gave the order, "Remove headdress. Three cheers for the Minister of National Defense." We did as we were bidden — and did it splendidly. The Colonel saluted the godlike figure in the flight boots, proud of our response. There was a slight pause. Then the Minister vaulted up on the table again, whipped his fedora from above his well-pleased eyes and waving it above his head, called for "Three cheers for your colonel, boys!"

This was the first shock.

Only a few days before, the Colonel had made it known in no uncertain terms, that the men under his command were men and not boys. The word "boys" was all right in some circumstances, but not officially, semi-officially or even demi-officially. And certainly not on parade!

We obeyed the Minister's wish. We gave three cheers for the Colonel. And it came from our hearts, for he was much respected. Then the Minister exceeded the bounds of regimental propriety. "And a tiger," he bawled out. There was some hesitancy on the part of some, and there were funny looks on some faces. But we again obeyed our visitor from Canada. Beaming at the response, the Minister went one further. "And a tiger's pup," he shrieked in glee. And the skies of Italy echoed to a tiger's pup.

The Colonel's face got more deeply red each time his views on the proprieties were transgressed. But although only 30 years old, he had grown relatively wise in the ways of the world. He knew that a mere soldier can never cope with the words and deeds of a politician. His face broke into a sheepish smile. Inwardly I think that most of us smiled back at him. Even though he would never use the term himself, we became his "boys" on that grey and windy day. And we remained his boys until he went on to bigger things.

Late in November, after a semi-operational role in the Daunia Mountains north of Campobasso, we found out that our battle-cry was now, "Rome by Christmas!" The Fifth U.S. Army, which was more than half British in make-up, but commanded by U.S. General Mark Clark and designated U.S. for propaganda purposes, was bogged down at the foot of Monte Cassino. Eighth Army was to attack the enemy's winter defense line on the Sangro River, capture an Adriatic port called Pescara and then swing left through the Appenines and drive straight across the peninsula to Rome. This movement would bring Eighth Army in behind the Cassino defenses and thus, it was hoped, make the Germans pull out to avoid being attacked in their rear. When they pulled out they would have to flee north of Rome, thus Fifth and Eighth Armies would join hands in the Eternal City.

On December 1, a grey and misty morning, we left the mountain top village of Duronia, where we had stopped when the Germans melted into the "deep purple", as Colonel Spry called the mountainous Appenines — that colour signifying the highest ground on our operational maps. In TCVs we moved back along our October-November axis, to the Foggia Plain. Then we swung north toward Termoli and a concentration area on the banks of the Sangro River, which the British 78th Division had just fought their way across, with heavy losses.

Our journey was painfully slow, even hesitant, as if some unseen hand sought to stay our progress to that place where so many of The Regiment were to fight their last battle. Traffic jams ahead of our convoy were so thick that by nightfall we were only half-way to our destination and in a steady drizzle had to spend the night sleeping packed into the cramped space of our vehicles. One cause of the traffic tie-up was that the ground installations of the Desert Air Force had been put on a route which crossed ours. The DAF were moving north to set up shop on the Foggia landing fields, now ready for Allied use, so they could be in range to bomb the Ploesti oilfields in Roumania, as well as pound the enemy's rear areas from the Sangro to the Po.

Our concentration area was near enough the front to receive a bit of shelling by extremely heavy, long-range guns. Evidence of stiff fighting was on every hand, the towns of Fossacesia and Rocca both being smashed up beyond description.

The worst feature of the 'conc area' was that the ground was widely sown with S-mines, our abbreviation for

Schuminen, deadly little wooden boxes filled with explosive which, when stepped on, sent a shower of metal pellets up between the legs, often reducing the testicles to a bloody pulp and blowing off a foot on the way up. We lost a few chaps that way, whereas any who survived the experience would never become fathers.

We were just south of San Vito, through which we marched the following day, winding our way through the British gun lines as darkness fell. The din was terrific and the gun flashes lit up our weary pathway with great sheets of light, fading into pitch blackness for a second or two, then breaking out into more man-made lightning as they roared again.

Buried where they fell. Some RCR graves beside the Ortona Road, December, 1943.

CHAPTER XI

THE GATES OF HELL

It was dark and drizzling as we marched down the winding road from San Vito into the muddy valley below. Shells screamed above us from our batteries behind the town. A mile away machine-guns stuttered in the vineyards across the Moro River. Up the road came a British battalion. Footfalls and heavy breathing passed in the night.

"Blimey, it's the ruddy Canadians," came a voice out of the blackness. There was a pause. Then another Briton added his bit. "Ow did y'leave our wives back 'ome?" he croaked. Again, a pause. Then in distinctly Canadian tones came the reply.

"Satisfied," it said.

On November 30 the Army Commander's message had arrived with instructions that it was to be read out to all troops. It contained the words: "WE WILL NOW HIT THE GERMANS A COLOSSAL CRACK."

I read this out at the head of my company.

"Holy Christ!" I heard a faint voice gasp.

"Cut out the talking!" roared my sergeant-major.

And so we had arrived at the Sangro battlefront, to relieve an almost fought-out British 78th Division still thinking about its wives back home.

On December 7, Lt.-Col. Dan Spry received orders for The RCR to "burst through" the bridgehead over the Moro, which the Hastings and Prince Edward Regiment had seized during a bloody struggle the day before. The Staff always used colourful words like that. Especially when the "bursting" was to be done by someone else.

There was one aerial photo of our attack area. Each of the four company commanders had about two minutes to memorize the features on the photo. It was an exercise in futility.

"A" and "B" Companies were to lead off. When Slim Liddell reached a road running parallel to our Start Line, about 500 yards away, he was to turn sharply to the left and advance another 1,000 yards to seize a low ridge. I was to conform on his left. Then "C" and "D" Companies would follow up, pass through us and capture the village of San Leonardo. It was an L-shaped attack — easier said than done.

At 4:30 p.m. Slim and I lined up our companies in a sunken road. "A" Company was to go over the top, then head straight through an apple orchard which masked the road where he was to turn left. My company was to jump off five minutes later. This would allow us to form on "A" Company's left when it turned. We would then sweep down to San Leonardo on a two-company front, clearing the enemy out between the road and the river.

The enemy, of course, had different ideas. They always did.

Slim and his men had hardly gone 50 yards when a mortar concentration came down on top of them. Among the jets of black smoke and clouds of dust we could see his men falling. Cpl. L.F. Meister, MM, and his entire section were wiped out to a man. I watched Slim stroll on. He seemed unmindful of the smoke, dust and hot steel that surrounded him.

I looked at my watch. "Let's go," I shouted. I scrambled over the lip of the sunken road with CSM Vic Lewington beside me. Using my walking stick, I waved the men over to the right to avoid the continuing inferno in Slim's wake. Soon a machine-gun opened up on us. Some of the leading men fell, including two section commanders, Cpl. W.R. White and L/Cpl. J.N. Duffey, both hit in the legs.

171

The winter skies were growing dark and this shielded us from the enemy's eyes. The machine-gun stuttered again and we veered farther right as the red tracer sped by. The leading platoon under Lt. Kitch Wildfang finally reached what appeared to be the road and turned left. But we could not locate "A" Company on our right!

Obviously, we were lost. I halted the two platoons behind me just as Wildfang came hurrying down the road. "Sir, there's a signpost ahead that says Ortona," he rasped out in throaty tones. We were on the wrong road, heading northeast instead of southwest. Our two swings right to avoid the enemy machine-gun fire had not been sufficiently corrected because of the dark.

An hour later, having retraced our steps silently, with German voices shouting from post to post on the high ground to our right, we reached the correct objective. We weren't all that long behind "A" Company, its right flank having been constantly harassed by fire after it made the L-turn. The follow-up companies had run into trouble right on the rim of the bridgehead. By stealth they had worked their way forward. Now, as we dug in on the firm base position, "C" Company patrolled forward toward San Leonardo.

Before dawn broke Lt. David Bindman captured eight panzer grenadiers single-handedly. Then the enemy came to life, counterattacking with tanks and pushing "C" Company back into the firm base position. "D" Company, slow to get started, was still wedged in between "A" and "B" Companies.

A few chaps were wounded. When the enemy armour got too close for comfort Col. Spry called down artillery fire which drove them off. Then Bindman was sent out to patrol along the battalion front with a small detachment. He returned with two more prisoners. An hour later he was mortally wounded by a tank shell.

The morning was one of confusion. Our "firm base" had been occupied by the enemy. As we dug in during the night, most of them had crept away. At daybreak three

Germans jumped out of a machine-gun post six yards from the root-house where I had joined Wildfang's platoon and established my headquarters! They surrendered. During darkness Lt. Freddie Sims had taken them for one of his own section posts. We were so intermingled neither side could tell friend from foe. Even so, we found that two of Freddie's men had been captured. Their rifles and equipment were found in a lean-to. In the corner was Pte. Brown's paybook. He had tossed it there without his captor seeing it. Despite his name, the book revealed that he was Jewish and a native of Warsaw, Poland. He did not want to become a prisoner of the Nazis with that background showing!

That afternoon Spry ordered me to push on to San Leonardo. The Seaforths were entering from the south. Together we cleared the village, Wildfang's Platoon capturing several Germans.

Meantime, the other three companies were withstanding a ferocious infantry counterattack. They had been taken in flank as they prepared to follow us. The bloodshed that resulted gave the name "Slaughterhouse Hill" to the ridge. Sgt. A.J. Hocking and L/Cpl. C.J. Davino were both awarded Military Medals for their efforts in breaking up the enemy attack. Sgt. R.W. Menzies and L/Cpl. R.M. Stuart also killed numbers of the enemy. Menzies survived, but when Stuart's body was found later it was crouched over his rifle, the finger on the trigger and his remaining clips of ammunition laid out on his slit trench lip, ready for instant use. There was a bullet hole between his eyes.

Having smashed the enemy counterattack we spent a day or so burying the dead under desultory shellfire. Then we went into reserve for three days.

During this time Spry left us to command 1st Brigade. Major W.W. Mathers, a Permanent Force officer who had arrived from Canada two weeks previously, took over. On December 17 Mathers received orders to attack through the Van Doos, who were holding a hamlet named Casa Berardi, and enter Ortona.

Mathers' plan was for "A" and "B" Companies to lead, but the I.O., Lt. Walter Roy, persuaded him that since this was almost always the pattern, perhaps the other two companies should lead this time. Mathers agreed. "C" and "D" were ordered to seize an important crossroads on the outskirts of town. Then the lead platoon of my company was to patrol silently by dark into the centre of the built-up area, create havoc and thus cover the arrival of the entire battalion, which would seize the place, presumably intact.

The Army Commander did not want the town destroyed. It was to serve as Eighth Army's winter headquarters, and since it was a seaport, as a main supply point.

The RCR attack began at 11:45 a.m. on December 18. It was a walk into catastrophe. Enemy mortar fire struck heavily as the troops crossed the Start Line. Somebody thought it was our own barrage falling short. The barrage was called off. This allowed the enemy machine-gunners to pop up and bring their weapons into play. "C" and "D" Companies were cut to pieces. Both company commanders and all six platoon commanders were killed or badly wounded. "D" Company, advancing along Ortona Road, was reduced to a dozen men cowering in a roadside ditch. "C" Company pushed on until flank fire from both sides of a gully caused their ranks to disintegrate. It was then that A/Cpl. C.G. ("Red") Forrest gathered up 21 survivors, organized a defensive position and fought back with rifle and grenade, winning himself a nice DCM.

Mathers, following "A" Company along a railway track, paused to take stock of the situation. He raised his arm to wave the attack forward, only to get a sniper's bullet clean through his biceps.

The attack collapsed. Up forward Major Jerry Nelson lay bleeding to death. Capt. Chuck Lithgow was carried past me on a bloody stretcher. Our attack had been along a deadly axis. For Mathers and Nelson it had been their first attack; for me, my fifteenth. But it was not to be my last. Fate had spared me for a great many more.

The Royal Canadian Regiment dug in among its dead, dying and wounded. Its effective fighting strength was now 18 officers and 159 men. We had just entered the gates of Hell, of hell on earth at least. Weak from loss of blood,

Major Mathers had been evacuated. Major Ian Hodson, yellow with jaundice and wracked with malaria, was hurried up from the rear to take command. It was the evening of December 18, 1943.

At 3 o'clock next afternoon a squadron of tanks arrived and Hodson was ordered to renew the attack. He detailed me to command the two assault companies. He kept the remnants of "C" and "D" Companies under his own thumb as a reserve, beefing them up with B-Echelon personnel.

Capt. Tommy Burdett took over "B" Company. At "A" Company's head was Capt. Dick Dillon, MC, as Slim Liddell had become *hors-de-combat* with a twisted knee. I directed the attack by wireless from the squadron commander's tank. The barrage worked perfectly. "B" Company faltered briefly under some heavy fire, but Burdett showed great dash and got them onto the crossroads in jig time, receiving the Military Cross for his leadership.

When I arrived about ten minutes later, the objective looked like a smoking dungheap. It was pitted with acrid craters and littered with "D" Company's dead from the day before. A shell-pierced stone house stood in the midst of this inferno. I went inside with my artillery officer, Bob Kingstone, to make my defensive fire plan. Soon CSM Lewington arrived with the signallers and company runners. One of these went into the cellar where he captured a six-foot-two paratrooper wearing an Iron Cross ribbon. Lewington, shot through the buttocks during the attack, sat on a rolled up feather tick and kept our uncooperative prisoner quiet under the muzzle of a Luger pistol.

Hodson led his reserve forward on my success signal. Half way to the objective he came under small arms fire. Our attack had passed by some enemy weapon pits without spotting them. There was a sharp exchange of shots and the enemy faded into the dusk.

Next day Hodson's illness became acute. The Brigade Commander ordered him out and I assumed command of the battalion. It was a bloody command. We were on our preliminary objective, but Ortona was still a mile away. Five officers were dead, four were wounded, two were battle exhaustion cases. Slim was injured. Spry was gone from our midst. Now Hodson had to go. Among the other ranks, 51 had been killed and 127 wounded. Sickness and battle fatigue had removed others. We began to wonder *who* had been hit by the "colossal crack" the Army Commander had referred to three weeks before.

December 21 was the regimental birthday. The RCR had been formed on that day in 1883; it was our Diamond Jubilee! "Men die, wars end, but the Regiment lives on", we had always been told. So, by field telephone I invited Spry to return to the fold and "drink a Health to the Regiment." Within the hour his jeep approached. It came under shellfire and he had to crawl along a ditch to reach us. Capt. Sandy Mitchell, my battle adjutant, prepared some grog and we raised the china cups the RSM had found in an adjoining house. Dan Spry said: "Gentlemen, The Regiment!" Just then Padre Rusty Wilkes, MC, arrived with a dozen wooden crosses under his arm. He joined in the toast, before beginning his ghastly task of shoving about thirty stiffened corpses into the narrow graves the Pioneers had dug outside.

As we drained our cups, Lt. Buck Bowman, MC, reported back from a fighting patrol he had led to clear snipers out of a house about 500 yards to our flank. At the same time Wildfang had led a patrol to flush out a sniper's post which was irritating his platoon. As he brought in his wounded he met our old paymaster, Capt. Cec Hollingsworth. Having caught the birthday spirit in the relative safety of the Field Cashier's office, Hollingsworth had decided to make his way up to the front line to wish his former regiment "another Sixty Years".

Three days later we renewed the attack. This time we tried to outflank Ortona and cut its garrison off.

We moved through the Hastings and Prince Edward Regiment into a tangle of shell-torn vineyards. Concrete posts and wire made the muddy waste almost impassable. My command post was established in a hole about eight feet square and four feet deep. We covered it with a tarpaulin. Into this space were jammed the battle adjutant, the I.O., two signallers, the RSM and me. RSM Archie McDonell and I lay in a T-shaped relationship. Rain trickled in under the tarp. Screaming rockets called "Moaning Minnies" fell around us all night. Every time one hit close by, McDonell's involuntary reflexes caused him to kick me in the stomach. I would have kicked him back each time but my own feet were wedged in behind the wireless set.

At first light I went forward to "A" Company. There I found a stone house with a loft from which we could see the landscape ahead. Summoning the company commanders I issued my orders for the attack. "A" Company was to capture the first objective. When I pointed out this feature and the ground to be covered in reaching it, Dillon, who commanded "A" Company, said: "Are you serious?" I replied that I was and there was no argument.

The attack was a failure. Dillon was wounded, as was Buck Bowman. Thirteen Other Ranks were either killed or wounded. The task proved impossible, the vineyards were thick with Germans.

I returned to my command post where a new draft of eight officers and 144 men stood in the rain, bewildered. I welcomed them, "putting them in the picture" as best I could. Dividing them up into four equal groups, I pointed out the "B", "C" and "D" Company areas, detailed an officer in charge of each group and sent them off to reinforce the bleeding platoons. I held "A" Company's detail until I heard the result of its attack. This did not take long. Two stretchers, Dillon on one, Bowman on the other, passed by the goggling eyes of the newcomers. Then came some walking wounded, followed by another stretcher with Lt. Jimmy Joice of "C" Company on it.

Confused fighting broke out in the Hastings area and up ahead. I ordered "B" Company to move up and protect "A" Company's left. In the process Burdett was slightly wounded, but he captured a large house into which I was able to move my command post. Night fell, and with it came relative quiet.

At dawn on Christmas morning I renewed the attack. "A" Company, now under Capt. Ernie Jackson, who had come up with the draft, suffered twenty casualties. "B" Company got off lightly, but among its dead was Cpl. J.E. Norton, brother of the Cpl. Norton killed at Assoro in Sicily. Having the same rank and the same initials, the brothers were known to all as "Norton 28" and "Norton 95", the last two digits of their regimental numbers. Both were good fighters. As "B" Company trudged forward I saw Norton with his Bren gun on his shoulder. I wished him luck. With a grim smile he walked on to his death in the vineyard ahead.

During the day the battalion advanced 800 yards through the tangled, rain-swept vineyards and suffered heavily. At our Command Post the Christmas cheer was limited to Yuletide colours — we had a crock of red and green peppers soaked in olive oil! The peppers went down well with the bully beef, some farmhouse bread we came upon and some homemade wine. The olive oil helped restore our weapons to working order, after the mud and grit had been scraped out of the moving parts.

Outside our building men were dying. In the muddy vineyards they found their peace on earth — the Christmas message throughout the ages. But they didn't hear any angels sing, only the stutter of machine-guns, the crack of rifles and the screaming, whining and thudding of shells and mortar bombs. They were as far from Bethlehem as Man could ever get.

Command post was constantly raked by machine-gun fire, keeping us inside the thick stone walls. We were in good wireless communication with all companies. As dusk fell Sandy Mitchell found a mandolin. I put in a multiple call to all company commanders on the wireless. With Sandy strumming, we sang *Silent Night* and other carols. Then we added our Christmas greetings, which were rather impolite, but heartfelt.

The next day enemy resistance weakened. One platoon silenced an 88-mm gun and took a few prisoners. The remaining Germans evaporated when a tank squadron lumbered up through the mud to help us, knocking out two sniper-infested houses on the way.

On December 29 we were relieved by the *Van Doos*, commanded by Major Jean-Victor Allard. He reached my command post wearing a U.S. helmet, carrying a U.S. carbine and talking French to a guide wearing an Italian uniform!

A belated Christmas dinner was served to us in a cemetery, during a rainfall. The canned turkey tasted wonderful. Our sergeant cook, Val Alcock, and his company cooks had slaved to prepare the meal and get it to us hot. But it was far from a happy Christmas. Of the 41 officers who had landed at Pachino less than six months before only nine remained with the battalion, and six of us had been wounded. We landed 756 strong. Now, more than 550 of these originals were among the killed, wounded, missing or prisoners of war. Or, they had gone out with jaundice, malaria or other ailments. Some had been wounded, returned and wounded again. New faces had appeared as reinforcements and had been evacuated or buried before we even learned their names.

New Year's Eve brought added tragedy. A ruined monastery collapsed under shellfire, killing nine "B" Company men. These included my former batman, Pte. Roy Lang, who had come looking for me when I lay wounded between the lines at San Marco the previous October.

Mathers returned from hospital on January 7. He was promoted to the rank of lieutenant-colonel and I became Second-in-Command. Several weeks later I was shown in Divisional Orders as having been an acting lieutenant-colonel for my 18-day period of command. I never wore the rank badges, but my pay account was credited with $61.75 extra, as the rank merited.

The war had lost its glamour. Too many had died on the road to Ortona. There were to be fifteen more months fighting before I hung out my washing on the Siegfried Line, that fanciful thing we had sung about in Canada four and a half years before. In the meantime, Duty would continue to call all of us; and Death some of us. And we would continue to follow their calls.

There was another factor which made us feel less enthusiastic about the war. On January 1st it was announced that General Montgomery was leaving the Eighth Army and returning to England for another high appointment. His successor was Sir Oliver Leese, a smooth-faced baronet with about as much personal appeal to Canadian troops as a suet pudding in a Sam Browne belt.

In July when we had come into Eighth Army, we immediately identified ourselves with Monty and his men as if the glory of El Alamein and the Mareth Line was already our own. At the end of the Sicilian campaign Monty had arrived one day in an open car to where our whole brigade was formed up awaiting him. He had us break ranks and gather round his vehicle. He then gave us permission to smoke and extolled the fighting virtues of Canadian troops and flattered us by telling us how much we had helped in the conquest of Sicily. He had said, "I regard you now as one of the veteran divisions of my army, just as good as any, if not better. I knew the Canadians on the Western Front in the last war and there were no finer soldiers anywhere. I wonder what they would say to you now if they could speak to you? I think they would say something like this: 'Well done. We have handed you the sword and you have wielded it well and truly'."

We lapped it up. Then we marched back to our bivouacs fairly satisfied with ourselves. Later that week we received a printed personal message from Monty with the instructions, 'To be Read out to All Troops'. It gave a brief review of the campaign and ended with the words: 'Well done, indeed. Together you and I, we will see this thing through to the end. Good luck to you all.' It was signed, 'B.L. Montgomery, General, Eighth Army.'

The most remarkable thing about General B.L. Montgomery, as we Canadians knew him in our early days together, was his lack of remoteness. Six distinct levels of command existed between the man with the rifle and "Monty". These levels were platoon, company, battalion, brigade, division and corps. Yet, to the private soldier the

Army Commander seemed to be his own personal commander, with no one else really in between. In Sicily and up to the Sangro the Canadian infantryman saw his platoon, company and battalion commander, like he saw himself, as just another member of Monty's Eighth Army. The generals in between, Canadian or British, just didn't seem to exist.

It was this remarkable ability of Montgomery to project his personality over the heads of all his subordinate formation commanders, right down into the forward slit trench, that made him the soldier's general. Above him, of course, were such remote military personages as the Army Group Commander and the Theatre Commander. But they were shadowy figures, as far removed from our war as Mackenzie King or Gracie Fields.

When talking to our troops none of us would have referred to our battalion commander as "Ralph" or "Dan", or spoken of the brigadier, the divisional commander or the corps commander by their christian names. Yet, in bivouac or on the line of march, or going into the attack, I have heard company officers discussing the Army Commander with their men as "Monty". "Monty" has ordered this, "Monty" has planned this, "Monty" has promised us this. I did it myself. We never employed the vague "they", which became the term for our unknown masters after Monty left the theatre and the Eighth Army lost its Desert Rat character.

I was present at the now famous lecture given by Gen. Montgomery in England early in 1942. That was the first contact for most of us with the new boss soldier of the part of England where we were stationed.

Montgomery walked onto the stage. What his first words were, I don't remember. What the body of his lecture was about, I don't recall. But I do remember him saying, very early on in his stage appearance: "There will be no smoking. You may cough for two minutes. Then there will be no coughing."

Here was somebody different! We listened to his lecture. Nobody smoked. And nobody coughed, once he had begun. When we left the lecture a new era in our wartime lives had commenced.

Shortly afterwards we took part in Exercise "Tiger". This was the most severe test of endurance the Canadians had been put to. My own unit marched 170 miles, fighting mock battles, during the eleven-day exercise. We slogged off 32 miles the last day on the homeward stretch. Montgomery was the author of the exercise. In our minds he was an overbearing martinet — a proper bastard. He demanded that we undergo hardships. To toughen us, he broke many in the process. We thought his methods were madness. But his system of training prevailed, and when we eventually went into action we knew he was right.

If he was hard on the troops, he was harder on the officers. During "Tiger" he drove past a dead-beat Canadian battalion. The men were hungry and footsore. They failed to stand up and salute Montgomery. The General stopped his car, lectured the troops on their unsoldierly conduct, and then drove off to find who their commander was. He fired him on the spot. His reason? The CO was totally unfit to command men in battle, because his men's conduct reflected that he was a slack disciplinarian.

He left us for the Western Desert in August, 1942, and most of the troops said, "Good riddance".

But experience is a great teacher. Montgomery's success in the Western Desert was so amazing that even back in England we decided his training methods, under which we had suffered, had been the best. When we found out we were to fight under his command we were happy. When we ended our five weeks of warfare in Sicily successfully, we realized it was because we had been moulded into a hard, disciplined fighting force by the hand of Montgomery, the *bête noire* of our days in southern England. We had joined him abroad and now he was leaving us.

Only a month before he had sent us one of his printed messages, the one which told us we were going to hit the Germans a colossal crack. It had ended, "Good luck to you all. And good hunting as we go forward."

We did our best, but it was on New Year's Eve 1944, while hitting the Germans this colossal crack that the weather, the terrain, our exhaustion and the enemy combined to stop the Eighth Army cold for the first time since El Alamein, fourteen months before.

Those of us who survived those next fifteen months of the Italian campaign under Leese and then his successor McCreery, a tall, boney figure in riding breeches, ended up in the Rhineland in the First Canadian Army, which was part of Monty's 21st Army Group. By then things were on too large, too international and too impersonal a scale to inspire us. Monty was at the peak of his fame, but the remnant of his old Eighth Army, that had served under him in 1943 was only a small part of his great victory machine, 21st Army Group. He had become remote. But some of us remembered the farewell message he had sent us in Italy. It had ended with the words:

"What can I say to you as I go away?

"When the heart is full it is not easy to speak. But I would say this to you. You have made this Army what it is. You have made its name a household word all over the world.

"Therefore, YOU must uphold its good name and its traditions.

"And I would ask you to give to my successor the same loyal and devoted service that you have never failed to give to me.

"And so I say GOOD-BYE to you all. May we meet again soon; and may we serve together again as comrades-in-arms in the final stages of this war."

We had upheld Eighth Army's good name. We had been loyal to his shadowy successors. Life had become less glamourous when a dull, spiritless and unblooded Canadian Corps headquarters had been brought out to Italy to exercise intermediate command over us. We were still in the Eighth Army, but in name only. Those who were able to say that they had marched with the Eighth Army when Monty was at its head became a race apart — at least in their own minds.

CHAPTER XII

VINEYARDS OF DEATH

General Harry Crerar stood in the frozen mud. Behind him was the battered husk of the stone farmhouse we used as our Battalion HQ. He leaned on his walking stick. Slowly his gaze shifted in an arc from left to right.

"It's just like Passchendaele," he murmured. "Just like Passchendaele."

"Yes, sir," I answered him. "Yes, sir," echoed the other officers, as though confirming the General's knowledge of such things.

He may have been right. None of us knew. We had no memories of Passchendaele. We had been unborn, or babes in arms; or at best school boys when that ghastly drama had been acted out twenty-six years before.

The General had reached the Italian front just a few days earlier. He was the commander of the newly-organized 1st Canadian Corps. With him he had brought the yet-to-be blooded 5th Canadian Armoured Division to help make up the Corps. He had also brought along his likewise un-blooded Corps HQ, fresh from the training camps and staff college theories of England.

We of the 1st Canadian Infantry Division had served in three different corps already. We had landed in Sicily as a division of 30th Corps and in Italy as a division of 13th Corps. Recently, for the shattering experience of the Ortona fighting, we had been under 5th Corps. Just as the fierce contests for the Moro River and Ortona ended, news reached us that we would be joined by the "Mighty Maroon

Machine", as 5th Armoured Division was nicknamed. Together we would constitute the 1st Canadian Corps. The prospect hadn't thrilled us a bit. We were jealous of our six months as Eighth Army campaigners. We knew that, compared with the outlook on life which we had grown accustomed to, Canadian attitudes would be restrictive and often petty.

Our fears were soon realized.

Pte. Fred Peltier was one of the first to become aware of the new regime. He drove the battalion water truck. Across the front of the cab of his truck, painted in bold white letters were the words GUNGA DIN, the name of Kipling's heroic Hindu water boy. The truck (and Peltier) became known by this moniker throughout the battalion — and affectionately so. When throats were parched and lips were dry or cracking, Gunga Din never failed to arrive with cold, clear water; just like the water boy of Kipling's famous poem.

Now, some of the romance of war was to be erased. Peltier's truck was to be nameless. And so was every other truck whose driver had neatly painted a fond name, perhaps that of a wife or sweetheart, on its cab.

There was no place for sentiment, or even humour, in the minds of our new Corps staff.

We cursed them for their academic approach to war; for their immaturity toward the wants and ways of fighting troops. Gradually, our Eighth Army glamour wore off. Where it didn't wear off fast enough, our new Corps HQ rubbed it off. By now, Montgomery was back in England planning the Second Front. Like our repainted vehicles, our new leaders were nameless.

The war bogged down and became a replica of the early months of World War I. It was trench warfare, but not of the sophisticated kind that developed in 1915. Two ramshackle barricades of unconnected slit trenches and fortified farmhouses, the gaps between them sometimes filled with primitive barbed wire entanglements, stretched across the torn vineyards and sodden meadows north of

Ortona. One barrier was German, the other Canadian. A broad gully lay in between. This gully was no-man's land.

With Lt.-Col. J.W. Ritchie, near Rimini airfield, September, 1944.

Between January 4 and April 20, only three attacks were mounted along this Adriatic Front. All three were failures. It was largely a winter of endless patrolling, a costly and futile pastime.

The first of the three attacks was staged by the newly arrived 11th Infantry Brigade of 5th Armoured Division. On January 17 they marched past the RCR positions in single file toward their Start Line.

"We'll show you Red Patch bastards how it's done," shouted a cocky member of one of the attacking platoons.

Some of the "Red Patch bastards" laughed when the battle-humbled tyros passed by a second time, in the opposite direction. They straggled back, leaving their dead behind them, and in some cases their weapons — in all cases their pride.

They were good fellows, really. They just hadn't had time to learn. But they did learn. And that first experience, which cost them more than 200 men, was where their learning began.

Even the battle-wise still caught hell on occasion. On January 30 the experienced Hastings and Prince Edward Regiment got nowhere in a daylight attack against a village named Tollo. This attack was to give the Germans the impression that the Canadians were offensively minded. This was to keep the Germans from thinning out their Ortona front to provide troops to counterattack the precarious Allied beachhead at Anzio.

After meeting with near disaster, the Hasty P's were ordered to renew the attack next day. More than a third of the battalion's assault strength was lost in these two efforts. I saw Major Stan Ketcheson coming back in a jeep with a grey face, wrapped in a grey blanket, with the grey winter sky behind him. He had been lucky. He was one of those who came back.

For the remainder of the winter, life for the infantry was one long round of reconnaissance or fighting patrols. The RCR provided 64 of these patrols.

The Germans were good watchers. They rarely patrolled forward of their own lines, other than to establish ambush patrols on our likely routes into their territory. Night after night Canadian patrols walked into a line of fire, or got caught in a mortar concentration. They never seemed to accomplish anything, although one patrol from the Seaforths of Canada got close enough to an enemy post to destroy it, killing and wounding its occupants.

Fortunately, the static front allowed for a rotation of troops into forward, support and reserve positions. Even when in the forward slit trenches, it was possible to thin out during daylight. The enemy had no covered approaches. They could have easily been detected preparing any daytime attacks. Surprise by day was highly unlikely. Little groups of our chaps could march out from reverse slope positions and manage six or seven hours of eating, bathing and sleeping in Ortona. Sometimes even a few hours fun were possible.

Casualties sometimes occurred in Ortona, since the enemy shelled the town almost daily. This usually happened at 4 o'clock each afternoon. This was thoughtful of Jerry, and most troops avoided the streets around that hour.

Ortona was a fortress. It was wired, sandbagged and barricaded. But officers' and sergeants' messes, wet canteens and recreation rooms all flourished. Further back was San Vito to where the troops could get 48-hour passes. It was out of shell range, and two days in that paradise was much sought after.

Life behind the lines had its lighter moments. An article headed "WATSON COMES IN" which appeared in the 1st Canadian Division's newspaper, *The Red Patch*, of February 19, 1944 reveals this. Beginning, "With the Canadian Corps in Italy", the article continued:

"Ace sprinter, when the stakes are down, of the Canadian Corps in Italy, is Capt. Russ Watson, member of the headquarters staff of a division.

"Challenged to a 100-yard race by Capt. C.N. Smith, former Royal Canadian Regiment paymaster, Watson showed he is in a class all by himself when, despite the last-minute entry of two outsiders, he crossed the finishing line a winner by a good 100 yards.

"'It's the life I lead', said Capt. Watson as he munched an orange after the race. Though he covered the cobblestones of San Vito's main square in 10:3 seconds, equalling the Canadian Army record, he was not even breathing (hard).

"The outsiders were two senior padres, Rev. Rusty Wilkes and Father Cherrier, both majors. Their entry, it is understood, was part of their training program for a baseball team they are organizing.

"The race, sponsored and announced by popular Major A.S. Galloway, of the Aylmer Galloways, second-in-command and acting commanding officer of the RCR's during recent actions, was held in brilliant moonlight before a large crowd of distinguished Canadian and Italian sports followers.

"At race time official starter, Capt. Edward McIntyre, who held the 20 pound stakes, was quoting odds of one to three against Major Wilkes, slim, greyhound type of racer. Capt. Watson, whose solid appearance belies his nimbleness, was quoted at 200 to 1.

"There was disaster right at the beginning when Major Wilkes slipped at the foot of the town hall steps and fell on the stone track. A great groan went up from the crowd, standing tensely along the sidelines, waiting to cheer their favourite home.

"Major Wilkes gamely picked himself up and sprinted in chase of the other runners, but he had lost too much ground. Also, he had not counted on Capt. Watson's amazing natural ability and condition.

"With his arms swinging high over his head, his knees hammering his chest, Capt. Watson drove out like a full-blooded stallion and from the 50-yard mark it was evident that only an accident or a miracle could stop him from winning.

"There was neither, and Capt. Watson was able to

pull up and look back over his shoulder as he crossed the finishing line. The crowd's acclaim drowned out the thunder of the guns in the valley below, as the winner modestly shook hands with the men he had beaten.

"First to congratulate Capt. Watson was Major Galloway who cracked his light stick lustily and doffed his soft hat as he said:

" 'Well done, Sah.'

"Later, in an exclusive interview with The Canadian Press (TCP), Major Galloway made this statement:

" 'Watson is alert, he never passes a fault. You may quote me as saying he is a Royal Canadian.'."

The article, written by Douglas Amaron of the Canadian Press, had repercussions. The brigade commander, Brigadier Dan Spry had, as CO of the RCR, caused signs to be erected throughout his battalion's rest area bearing the words "Be Alert", "Never Pass a Fault" and "Are *you* a Royal Canadian". He took some umbrage at the prostitution of his authorship. Somehow or other the *London Free Press*, Russ Watson's home town paper, reprinted the story, causing some enthusiastic local Nazi-haters to believe that we were not quite earnest enough in our crusade to free the World from Hitler's awful scourge and recorded this publicly. The newly-appointed CO, Lt.-Col. Willie Mathers, considered the whole episode to be very much beneath the dignity of his Second-in-Command. The best sum-up of the whole matter came from the lips of Benny Potts, an officer noted for the common sense contained in all his observations. "You can smell the *vino* between every line", he chuckled.

Colonel Mathers was finding life rather difficult at this time. He was an enthusiastic CO, who had many good qualities, including plenty of personal courage. He had displayed the latter less than two months before when he took a sniper's bullet through his upper arm while reforming the assault wave of his battalion, which had been hard hit as it attacked astride the railway track from Orsogna to Ortona.

He had recently been back to the Canadian Reinforcement area at Avellino and on his return brought a case of *Lachryma Christi*, that is, "Tears of Christ" wine, which he considered with some justification to be a good wine. He kept this near the Orderly Room in a niche where some of his personal gear was stored. This space was also used by various officers resting in the battalion headquarters area before taking out a night patrol, or after returning from a patrol, and still rather unsettled after having so recently exchanged shots with the enemy. Here they were able to wash up and steady themselves. The room was in a one-storey stone cottage, typical of those which dotted the landscape. It was reinforced with sandbags and was comparatively safe. In this relative comfort a front-line soldier could relax, for the enemy was perhaps a mile or more away. To assist in the relaxation some of Willie's *Lachryma Christi* began to disappear. However, warfare always generates cunning and the bottles were always refilled — with local *vino bianco*, a vinegary concoction fit only for rubber palates. The poor colonel, not realizing the evil that lurks in the hearts of men, including one's brother officers, could not understand how his precious wine was deteriorating. Eventually, I think he caught on. He accused no one, though he stopped offering it to those occasional visitors from other units or higher formation who had always looked rather aghast at his supposed knowledge of wine, after swallowing a mouthful of it while he lauded its outstanding virtues.

And so life went on. And war, said to be long periods of boredom, punctuated with short periods of fright, proved to be just that. The weather was foul. Freezing rain, high chill winds and occasional snow flurries made life miserable in the extreme. The patrol program went on, too. The size of regimental cemeteries grew, slowly but steadily, aided by spasmodic fits of shelling or mortaring, to which our enemies treated us from time to time. In this way both sides waited for spring.

Mule trains took rations and rum up through the shattered vineyards to our forward positions. The nightly trip up and back by the ration parties was employment of the vilest kind. These parties were often caught in a random shoot by German artillery or Moaning Minnies, as the enemy wisely tried to snap our supply line and leave the forward troops hungry, thirsty and without the necessary warlike stores.

One night CQMS Johnny Dadds received wounds from which he died the next day, and CQMS Cec Whyte was so badly hurt he never returned to the field. This was the night when most of the rum jars were smashed. The tawny liquid ran down the mules' flanks, causing more tears in the slit trenches than did the death of a comrade.

By January, 1944, the Canadian Volunteer Service Medal came out for every serviceman with eighteen months voluntary service to his credit. Six months overseas service added a silver maple leaf clasp to the award. In Italy, we had both officers and men who qualified for the clasp, but did not have enough total service to receive the ribbon to pin the clasp on. We laughed at this as a typical piece of military foresight. One young lad, killed at Ortona in December '43, even lacked enough service for the clasp! How he got into a forward slit trench some four months after enlistment astounded us. He was his own little Hong Kong disaster. Virtually untrained, he went to his death in a soggy Italian vineyard.

The day the rolls of CVSM ribbon arrived, I had mine sewn on beside my Africa Star ribbon. I had just stepped outside our shell-shattered headquarters in all my new-found glory when I bumped into a visiting British corps commander, Sir Charles Allfrey.

"What's that medal ribbon you're wearing?" he barked, quite bug-eyed at a colour scheme with which he was not familiar. I explained, rather modestly, that it was really nothing, as it was on issue to everybody in our army.

"Well, I think it's a damned good idea," he replied. "The Americans are simply plawstered with ribbons, even before they get to the front. Jolly good show, this Canadian ribbon, I would say."

The Americans gave a medal called the Purple Heart

to all those unlucky enough to get themselves wounded, or injured during operations. It was handed out almost immediately on the casualty being hospitalized. In early '44 a story circulated that a U.S. staff officer, sent to a base hospital to confer these awards, did so only to be told on leaving one huge marquee that he had just decorated all the chaps in the VD ward!

When it came to gongs for bravery, the Americans had such a lavish system of awards that it was utterly impossible to compare the "fruit salad" on their chests with the occasional daub of colour seen on British or Canadian breasts. It is probably true to say that for every MM and DCM given to a British and Canadian soldier, our American allies got ten Bronze Stars and five Silver Stars.

There are those who feel that the generous American distribution was perhaps much better than our stingy quota system. I must agree, since far too many of our good soldiers went unrecognized.

And still the patrols went out. The lucky ones came back to an enamel cup with an inch of rum in the bottom. The unlucky ones stayed out and their skeletons were recovered in the spring.

On April 19, Major Ted Littleford led "C" Company in a well-planned raid. The battalion was to be relieved by the 2nd/4th Gurkhas. The idea behind the raid was to 'hot things up' so that the Germans wouldn't sense that a handover was taking place.

Relief in the line is a very dangerous operation of war. If it is noisy the enemy realizes what is going on. He then shells or mortars the outgoing and incoming troops, catches them in the open and causes undue casualties to our side. If he waits briefly and then puts in a quick raid, he hits the new troops while they are still off balance and before they are familiar with the ground.

If the line is too quiet during a relief the enemy gets suspicious. Then he can do the same things to upset the procedure or bash the newcomers.

Either the enemy must be led to believe everything is

normal on our side, or we must hide our goings and comings with activity to keep him busy. The usual thinning out process would begin at 'last light'. Section by section, platoon by platoon, company by company the Canadians would hand over their slit trenches and observation posts to the men from Nepal.

Having decided that the relief would be masked by a hit-and-run raid, our planners got busy with their maps and aerial photos. The plan looked pretty good. The best approach had been selected. The best FUP had been spotted. The most energetic company commander had been warned and he had decided to use his two best platoons. Nothing would be left to chance.

"It's going to be a sharp little party, one that will leave Jerry stunned — and with a very bloody nose," said the CO. And he told the selected company commander that he was a lucky man to get the opportunity to hit the Hun. It looked like there was an MC in the offing. Maybe an MM or two, or perhaps some prisoners for souvenirs.

Map enlargements were made and orders memorized. In the afternoon Littleford was flown over the area in a light aircraft to study the trails, contours and landmarks and to pinpoint enemy positions. A sand table model was studied. But it was an exercise in futility.

By dusk, as the battalion began to thin out to the rear, the raiders filed into the tangled vineyards of no-man's-land and made for the FUP. The little group, about 40 men, had been selected to kiss the enemy goodbye — and they were going to do it with a real smack!

However, they didn't get close enough!

No one really knows why things went wrong. The raiders shook out into their attack formation and began to climb a low escarpment. When they reached the crest they came under the red-hot spew of machine-guns. Littleford went down. One platoon commander was killed, the other wounded. Eight men fell as the bullets struck. Some were wounded, some killed. The *Spandau* fire never slackened. Then the *nebelwerfers* started up. Their bombs pounded the earth.

For a few moments the raiders returned the fire, but the show was over. The mortally wounded company commander ordered them back and then died. Back they went. Some of them didn't make it.

Meanwhile, the battalion rapidly completed the handover to the Gurkhas without enemy interference and soon the convoy's wheels were rolling the lucky platoons to a training area 50 miles to the rear. Each man now had a new lease on life — at least until the training period was over.

But back in the muddy vineyard, below the escarpment, their dead comrades lay stiff in the April dawn. No one would ever know why it happened that way.

By then the little brown men from Nepal occupied our trenches and our sandbagged houses. And did their business in our latrines.

"Bad luck about Littleford," I said to one of his closer friends. We were having a whisky together which probably dulled our true emotions.

"Yes," he replied. Then parodying an old English music hall number, he raised his voice in semi-song, emitting the words: "They made him what he is today. I hope they're satisfied."

Some time later, when the Germans withdrew from their winter line to conform to the battlefield pattern, which had been changed by the Cassino operations on their right, the Gurkhas moved forward unopposed. With them went the Canadian Graves Registration people to recover the remains of the raiding party, now fleshless skeletons. We were notified that the skeletons of Major Littleford and several of his men had been found. It was good to hear that Littleford's skeleton was found where he fell, well ahead of his troops. A good regiment takes pride in that sort of thing.

I once heard an old fellow tell his friend, "Everybody in this world is crazy but you and me. And sometimes I think you're a bit odd."

Well, there are a lot of funny people in this great

gathering we call the human race. I don't know whether the navy and the air force had many oddballs, but certainly the army had its share.

I remember once, during the winter on the Ortona front, seeing a battalion commander studying an aerial photo of the enemy territory the other side of no-man's-land. Suddenly he called to the artillery rep. Ross Zavitz, who was dozing in the corner of the sandbagged room which served as Battalion HQ.

"Come here quick," he shouted.

The gunnery officer opened his lids with a start and bounded across the room to where the colonel had his eyes glued to the stereos.

"Yes, sir!" he answered excitedly "What is it?"

"Get onto your gun position right away. I want a shoot on these three vehicles on the road here."

The gunner stopped in his tracks. His mouth fell open. He couldn't believe his ears.

"But sir!" he said, "that aerial photo is dated December 5th. This is February!"

"I know, I know," replied the infantry colonel, "But they may well be back there. Now's our chance to clobber them. Don't argue. Shoot."

So a concentration of 25-pdr shells went whirring overhead, expertly plotted to hit the non-existent vehicles as they reached a point a thousand yards or so farther on — and, as the gunner later remarked, "six weeks after they had left the road, if not the country."

"Good," said the colonel, as he leaned back from the big photo mosaic, so carefully laid out on the farmhouse table, "that will show those Jerries we're not asleep!"

But it wasn't always the top boys who made such mighty military decisions.

In an attack in the Appenines a young platoon commander led his troops up the slope of an emeny-held hill. A machine-gun opened up on his flank. Quickly, he

196

decided to lay down a smoke screen, thus blinding the enemy.

"Mortarman!" he cried out. "Mortarman, three rounds smoke, line of my arm." And he pointed in the direction where a curtain of smoke would obscure his men from aimed enemy fire.

There was no response to his command. The fellow with the 2-inch mortar continued to plod up the hill, his weapon held tightly in both hands. The officer repeated the command. Again, no response from the mortarman with the platoon weapon. By now the platoon had apparently protected itself by descending into a hillside depression. A few yards farther on a couple of German paratroopers manning a rearguard sniper's post stood up and surrendered. The platoon battle was over.

The mortarman trudged up to the lieutenant. "Sorry about that, sir," he said, in all seriousness. "But I couldn't fire the mortar, sir. The barrel is full of platoon headquarters' breakfast. Six eggs, sir, with grass stuffed in between so they won't get broken."

Well, we won the war anyway.

Which reminds me of the time one of our successive colonels got a bullet through his upper arm. Loss of blood weakened him and as he sat propped up against a farmhouse wall, a corporal tried to apply a first field dressing.

"I can't get this damned dressing on, sir," he said. "The wound is in too awkward a position. But I don't want to cut the arm off."

The colonel bit his lip, now blue with the chilling tremors of shock. But he was a brave fellow.

"Cut it off," he replied grimly, "cut it off. I won't be the first man to lose a limb in battle."

"Holy cow, sir! I don't mean *your* arm," replied the first aider. "I mean the arm of the shirt. It's a *Viyella*. A shirt like that costs a lot of money."

CHAPTER XIII

THE ROAD TO ROME

We left the Ortona front because General Alexander, now in overall command of the Allied Armies in Italy, had decided that the great bastion of Monte Cassino which had stopped the U.S. Fifth Army in its tracks since early December must be taken, that the Hitler Line of which Cassino was the main pivot must be breached and that Rome must be captured that way. The Ortona front was a dead end. The idea that Eighth Army could outflank Rome from the Adriatic had come to naught in the muddy vineyards along the Arielli River.

Most of the Eighth Army was moved across Italy to join up with the Fifth Army and the French Expeditionary Corps. The move was secret. Everything was made to look as though we were training in the Naples area for a seaborne landing somewhere up the coast of Italy, presumably behind Rome. This deceived the enemy and while he looked anxiously along the coast above Rome, we trained for tank/infantry warfare in a remote valley.

In three weeks summer came. Ortona was soon forgotten. The Adriatic mud was replaced by Liri Valley dust. Filthy battledress was stowed away and crisp bush clothing made its appearance. The sun burned our cheeks, throats, and arms mahogany. It was good to be alive.

On May 11 the CO assembled his officers on the verandah of a villa to observe the flashes of 2,000 Allied guns on the night horizon almost 60 miles away. It was the opening chorus for the drama of Rome's capture by the combined efforts of the British Eighth Army and the U.S.

Fifth Army. Three days later we were in the thick of it ourselves.

With Lt. Jack Davis on Senio Front, February 1945.

An Indian Division had broken the Gustav Line, which screened the more formidable Hitler Line and hinged on the huge mass of Monte Cassino, topped by its famous monastery.

In the hot summer sun the Canadians passed through the wreckage of the Gustav Line. First to bump resistance in the hinterland was our No. 7 Platoon under Lt. Geoff Wright and No. 8 Platoon under Lt. Jack Morgan. There was a sharp fight; 12 men were killed and 20 wounded. Morgan was among the dead. Wright's performance won him a Military Cross. A self-propelled gun was attacked by Cpl. R.D. Deadman, who silenced it by firing a two-inch mortar from the shoulder. He got the Military Medal for this.

The Hitler Line was breached. Its pivot, the town of Pontecorvo fell to the RCR, but it took ten days to do it. On May 24 our Scout Platoon penetrated this bastion, taking 70 prisoners. Lt. Bill Rich climbed the church tower and rang the bell. It was the signal that the town was in our hands. In the open warfare, fought through the poppy-flecked wheat fields and farmlands of the Liri Valley, Rich and his scouts had always been in the van. This fact was testified to by his own Military Cross and an MM for Pte. J.J. Griggs, one of his most aggressive scouts.

Clever tactics paid off. Although the Princess Patricias and Loyal Edmontons ran into very stiff opposition and got badly clobbered around the Acquino airfield, the Hitler Line battle was not too tough. Not for the 1st Brigade anyway. The RCR buried two dozen of their number and only 60 were wounded. You couldn't do much better than that.

The most thrilling sight during the battle, which I spent at Battalion HQ, was that of the Polish troops moving up the precipitous slopes of Monte Cassino, like thousands of ants. It was the Polish troops who took Monte Cassino, but if the British, Indians and Canadians had not swept all before them in the valley below, the fall of the Monte and its massive monastery would have been long delayed.

Enemy aircraft was active every night, and the skies

were often red with our burning ammunition dumps, or vehicles that had been straffed. One low-level attack sent the adjutant Birnie Smith, my batman Pte. Gelinas and myself scurrying for a slit trench. We all found the same one, at almost the same time! I was slower than my batman, faster than the adjutant. We looked like an orgy of fishworms, as we ate dirt and wriggled in fear of our lives.

Six days of rest, while the 5th Armoured Division swarmed through the breach the Red Patch division had made, was followed by another mobile operation. The ground now became unsuitable for the use of tanks and 1st Division was ordered into the forefront again. It was a pursuit battle, with few casualties and large numbers of prisoners taken.

Lt.-Col. Jim Ritchie had succeeded Lt.-Col. Bill Mathers during the brief rest period. His first triumph came when the village of Ferentino fell to our leading company. A rearguard of ten Germans surrendered. Ritchie entered the hilltop hamlet to the cheers of the local inhabitants. He was greeted with shouts of *Salute il Commandante*! Flowers were strewn in his path. More tangible evidence of these foreign hosannas appeared when both a rose and an egg were thrust into his hands by weeping villagers.

Like an emperor with his orb and sceptre, the Colonel strode through the village street. Five miles further on was Agnani. By now the Germans were in headlong flight to Rome and northward. Partisans had roped in the last few enemy stragglers.

Except for heavy shelling of the approaches to the town, which denied immediate entry, the "capture" of Agnani was almost a repeat of the Ferentino episode. It was, however, more dramatic. Some 600 Partisans lined the streets, fanfares were sounded by their trumpeters and cheer after cheer burst from the crowds as the RCR marched into the town square.

Two days later Rome fell to the Fifth Army. The Canadians went into rest and it was eight weeks before bullets sang around their ears again.

With my bride on our wedding day in Toronto, May 29, 1948.

A chat with Field Marshal Montgomery at Staff College, 1952.

The twenty-six days of the Liri Valley operation had not been without interesting sidelights and experiences. The arrival of the French Expeditionary Corps had added something new. In its wake followed what one of our chaps cleverly styled *hors de combat*. These were "ladies of joy" who were provided by the realistic French culture to keep their warriors content during lulls in the fighting. They arrived in vehicles, had tents pitched for them behind the French Front Line and set up shop. Another feature of the French contribution was the use of Moroccan troops called *Goumiers*, so called because their units were styled *Goums*. They were used in the Aurunci Mountains which lay between the Eighth Army's left boundary and the U.S. Fifth Army's right boundary. "I will flood the mountains with my Goums", said General Juin, the French corps commander. And he did. They moved with stealth and speed, knife-killers rather than users of fire arms. They were said to have terrorized the Germans and also every Italian woman whom their devilish eyes fell upon. For rape was their delight and they would stop off even during battle to refresh themselves with it.

In the middle of the battle, the traffic in the Liri Valley was so dense that the mobile troops could hardly get forward and lost contact for a time with the enemy. They were streaming back to hold delaying positions and also trying to contain the Anzio bridgehead which was a sort of thorn in their right flank. This caused a delay in the use of our Division and while we enjoyed a well-earned rest the Canadian Army Show came up and put on open air concerts. The hit number was the song, *You'll Get Used to It*, sung by a dreary little soldier in a greatcoat several sizes too big and a mournful face under a tin hat.

During this rest period the CO summoned me to his Command Post and said that the battalion had done badly in the matter of officers' decorations since Sicily and that he wanted me to write up some citations. He gave me six names saying he hoped we could get a Military Cross for each of these young officers. I visited their company commanders and got some idea of what each chap had done to personally help Eighth Army break through the Hitler Line. Then the CO and I went over the stories and put the finishing touches to my narratives. Three days later they were returned with the information that the 'Corps allotment' of decorations would mainly go to our 5th Armoured Division, since that formation had not had the same opportunity to win awards as we had. In other words, it hadn't done as much fighting as our Division. We were told to re-submit our recommendations listing them in priority. All were well-deserved, so we decided to list them 1 to 6 as instructed, recalling individual performances during the days spent in those awful vineyards of death along the Arielli, or in the previous bloody fighting along the Ortona Road.

A certain amount of fiction had to be included in these write-ups. The system demanded that specific deeds of heroism be cited and the Staff who vetted the citations always wanted mention made of how many of the enemy were killed by the officer being recommended, or by the subunit he was commanding. This stretched our imaginations as in most cases we had to press six or seven months of consistently brave conduct in previous attacks, or dangerous patrol work, into an imaginary sharp encounter during the Hitler Line action. We did what we were told and reality gave way to colourful tales which were more like a *Boy's Own Annual* story, than a statement of fact. Of course, the germ of truth had to be there. We batted fifty per cent, but were not too happy when the awards came through. Our priorities, 1, 2 *and 6* got their MCs, but 3, 4 and 5 got nothing. Indeed, 3, 4 and 5 all ended the war undecorated, though all three had seen more personal fighting than No. 6 and two of them continued to do so.

Both the QM and I worked day and night during the ten day fighting advance up the Liri. The CO fought the Battalion from what formerly had been called his Command Post, but was now known as Tactical Headquarters, or Tac HQ. The QM and I operated from Main HQ where we had the job of seeing that the fighting troops had ammunition, rations, petrol and other necessities when and where they needed them. We two were not in range of the enemy's small arms fire, which was something, but we were certainly in the battle. One night Main HQ was attacked by enemy aircraft which dropped bombs all around us, as well as flares. Next day we were shelled and an ammunition lorry parked close by was hit and ammunition went off in all directions. Then another truck was hit and immediately burst into flames. The valley was one big dust bowl, churned up by thousands of vehicles, including tanks of the 5th Canadian Armoured Division, pressing forward so they could burst out when the infantry had punched a hole in the Hitler Line.

For me, the most exciting incident was on May 21 when I was hurriedly summoned to Brigade Headquarters and given a new set of orders to supersede those which the CO was carrying out!

The CO, Lt.-Col. Mathers, was off on a foot reconnaissance with his rifle company commanders, Sandy Mitchell, Eric Forgrave, Dick Dillon and Don Rose. They were hiding in a wheatfield looking through their binoculars, preparing to do a left hook on the town of Pontecorvo. Since he could not be contacted, I, as Second-in-Command was sent for and given an entirely new plan for a less spectacular frontal assault to the left of the 48th Highlanders. I returned to Main HQ, which at the time was combined with Tac HQ, just as the four company commanders arrived. The CO had decided he needed a few minutes more to perfect his plan and had sent them back to await his return for formal orders for the attack.

I had been told to move quickly and get the battalion into action. As a result, I was actually commanding the Battalion without the CO knowing it!

This was a most unusual situation, to say the least. The company commanders were much relieved to find out that the 'left hook' plan had been abandoned, as they all said it looked like a complete suicide mission. They scribbled down my orders and were just preparing to leave for their companies, with me in interim command of the Battalion, when the CO arrived. He was astonished at the turn of events. I told him the company commanders had to move quickly and that I would brief him on the new plan, so he could control the battle after the companies had crossed their Start Lines. This I did. Then we both went about our own business. He moved forward to establish Tac HQ where he could command his companies. I relaxed in my farmhouse HQ and waited to carry out my normal duties when the time came.

Pontecorvo was captured by the RCR, as recounted earlier, and after the citation-writing episode the CO suggested that the QM, John Praysner, and I should take 48 hours leave and visit Naples! Off we went in my jeep and that night we went to the opera to see *Aida*. I was so tired I slept through most of it and every time I woke up the thing seemed so hilarious to me that I burst out laughing! The *prima donna* seemed to weigh a ton, for when she swooned in the hero's arms in the tomb scene, he staggered. The spear carriers looked half-starved (and probably were) and the singing was above my cultural appreciation.

When we got back the Battalion had moved two miles forward of Pontecorvo and was in a wooded bivouac with some open glades for sports and the aforementioned Army Show. We also had a band concert and outdoor motion pictures. By this time the *Luftwaffe* had been driven out of Italy's skies during daylight hours, and as the showing of motion pictures proved, were not a high risk factor, even at night.

A tragedy happened just before we entered the second phase of our infantry battle. An entire rifle section, most of whom had arrived as reinforcements only the day before, were killed during a small-scale training exercise when they walked into a hidden German minefield. One of them, Cpl. Gene Hurshman, was a 1939 'old-timer' who had been left behind in the U.K. as an instructor almost a year before. His great happiness at having joined his Regiment on the battlefield was short-lived.

We were twenty-five miles behind our forward troops, 5th Canadian Armoured Division. Now they needed infantry to get them forward. The fleeing enemy, after counterattacking them on the Melfa River, had taken up hilltop defensive positions which tanks could not get at.

After the fall of Agnani, which I have mentioned, all contact with the Germans was lost. Rome was entered on

June 4 — two days before our Canadian comrades-in-arms who were still in England experienced their D-Day on Normandy's beaches. The Germans in Italy were now fleeing north, leaving only their wounded and a few would-be deserters behind in the Eternal City.

A day or two later the adjutant, Birnie Smith, John Sherlock and I took off in my jeep for Rome. Despite Military Police barriers which blocked every road entrance and the presence of huge signs which greeted the eye ten miles outside the city with the words, "ROME OUT OF BOUNDS — TURN BACK NOW", we risked running over any minefields which might lie in our way and drove across the open fields. We entered Rome by some obscure street, ending up much sooner than expected in front of the Coliseum! Rome was in a carnival mood. The girls looked beautiful. Not the filthy slatterns of the war-ridden Italian countryside, but all sun-tanned blondes dressed in the height of fashion. How, we wondered? We drove to St. Peter's Square and had snapshots of ourselves taken in front of the Vatican. We tried the more sophisticated wines of Rome. Six hours later we headed back to Agnani, feeling like schoolboys who had played hookey, when expressly forbidden not to.

When news came over the radio that the Allies had landed on the Normandy coast I said to my clerical staff, busy typing out the ration demands and casualty states under smelly canvas beneath blazing summer skies, "Well, 3rd Canadian Division is fighting on the beaches today."

One clerk, I think it was Cpl. Baker, looked up from his typewriter and said, "It's time those bastards did *something*, Sir."

CHAPTER XIV

A HOLIDAY FOR HEROES

On June 9 we received the unbelievable news that the whole Canadian Corps was to have a holiday from Death. Loaded onto TCVs we retraced our steps through the Liri Valley, past the towns we had captured, past the great pile that is Monte Cassino to our leave paradise, a pleasant area between Caserta and Campobasso called Piedimonte d'Alife.

A week or two later I went on a few days leave in Rome with a chap who, by the standards of the '40s, was an old soldier indeed. He had joined the Permanent Force as a boy in 1922. A war-time major, his previous service in the ranks had brought him the now obsolete Long Service and Good Conduct Medal. His name was Frank Darton.

Outside the Vatican we came upon two babyfaced U.S. privates, both wearing three ribbons. My friend recognized what we had already begun to call their "Before Pearl Harbour Medal", awarded to all those serving in the U.S. forces before the 'Jap' attack, and the ETO medal, given to all U.S. servicemen on leaving American shores for the European Theatre of Operations. But the third ribbon was a mystery.

"Pardon me," said my companion to one Yankee youngster. "What is that third ribbon for?"

"That's the longevity medal," answered the teenaged GI. "It's for long service with good conduct — eighteen months of it."

"Long service!" croaked my friend. Then, pointing to his own single ribbon, he said, "Look sonny. *That's* for long service. For eighteen bloody YEARS service!"

"Jesus, buddy," replied the other young Yank, "in our outfit we just don't live long enough to get a medal like that."

We had an audience with His Holiness the Pope, managing to be included in a large number of *Van Doos*, for whom a special papal audience had been arranged. Most of our time was spent in tourist-type sightseeing, but a Canadian Officers' club had been set up in the *San Georgio* Hotel with a former Canadian hotelier, Major Forbes Thrasher, in charge. The food was doctored-up army rations, but the wine was plentiful and old friends were turning up from other units, so a lot of our time was spent in the clean surroundings of the hotel lounge and our bedrooms, complete with indoor amenities most of us hadn't seen for more than a year.

Two incidents of the lazy days at Piedimonte d'Alife come to mind. One afternoon Lieut. Gordon Potts, the IO, known as 'Benny', and I were sitting in the Officers' Mess — a large marquee in the middle of a field — when in walked the ADMS, a colonel named Sinclair. I got up and introduced myself, and then introduced Benny.

"Potts, eh!" said the medical colonel, "You must be General Potts' son?"

"I'm sorry, Sir," replied down-to-earth Benny, "but there are no Generals in my family. There've been quite a few *privates*, though."

On another occasion Benny and I were again sitting together, just the two of us in the marquee, when to our consternation a jeep drove right in the open door and down between the folding tables. In it was Dan Spry, our former CO and now a brigade commander in our Armoured Division. At the wheel was Dick Dillon, now a captain on Dan's Brigade Staff, but formerly one of our company commanders during the Ortona and Hitler Line fighting. Both were in a jovial mood.

"Guess what!" said Spry, jumping out as Dillon brought the vehicle to a halt, "I'm a General!"

He then proceeded to tell us that he was on his way next day to Normandy to take over command of 3rd

Canadian Infantry Division. Its GOC, Rod Keller, had been badly wounded when his HQ had been hit in error by American bombers.

This was indeed big news and in no time at all the bottles were lined up on the table to celebrate Spry's rise to fame. For fame it really was. At 31 years of age he was the youngest Major-General in the Allied Armies. He had been a Major, and acting Lieutenant-Colonel, eleven months before when he had joined us in Sicily to take over as CO.

Life was easy in the Piedimonte d'Alife area. "B" Company was in a hamlet called San Potito, but the battalion as a whole was in the open air. Some canvas provided shelter, but most of us were bivouacked under trees. The weather was magnificent. The war was forgotten. We were told to expect six weeks or so of respite from battle. We were fortunate to total seven weeks without hearing a shot fired.

Little or no interest was taken in the progress of the Normandy campaign, although it was filling the World's headlines — headlines that we didn't get to see. We did get news sheets from Division, though few of us read them. About all the troops wanted to read were letters from home.

Large leave parties were sent off to Rome and Naples, warned by padre and MO alike to avoid the fleshpots and never to go about except in small groups. Naples was a cesspool of poverty and crime, and because of wartime conditions Rome was almost as dangerous to young soldiers with money in their pockets and hot blood in their veins.

For those who remained in camp there were wine binges, concerts and sports events. We had a regimental sports day and Brigadier 'Drifty' Snow, our CO of United Kingdom days, now a brigade commander in the "Mighty Maroon Machine", as we called our 5th Armoured Division, came over and gave out the prizes.

There was one thing that is sad to relate. Sixteen of our men were court-martialed for absenting themselves during the course of the Liri Valley fighting. Really, they had 'deserted in the face of the enemy', but the charges were made less serious. Just the same, some were awarded up to nine months imprisonment with hard labour and sent off to North Africa. Nobody felt sorry for them, for it was felt that while others died, they had saved their own yellow skins and now they would be safe in prison while many of those who still soldiered on would be in their graves long before their life-saving sentences had been served. Most of the culprits had been sent forward to the RCR as reinforcements early in May and had proved themselves useless fellows indeed. Their crimes and sentences were read out in front of the entire battalion, drawn up in a hollow square and they were ignominiously marched off to their disgraceful destination, bareheaded and badgeless, to the neurotic beating of the *Rogue's March* by four drummers of The Regiment.

"The Drums" had been reactivated as soon as we arrived at Piedimonte. Since October 1943, eight months in all, the drums and bugles of The Regiment had been stored with the municipal authorities in Campobasso.

There is a place for military music in war; if not actually when men are grappling with the enemy, then at least before and after. With this thought in mind The Royal Canadian Regiment managed to smuggle its bugles and drums out to the Mediterranean in June, 1943. It was not until a year later, however, that there was an opportunity to get "The Drums" together as a body.

Under the bright blue skies of our Italian rest area the musical chaps quickly worked their lips and wrists back into shape and soon after claimed to be the first Allied band to play in liberated Rome. Allowed to go on leave as a group, so that practice would not suffer because individuals were away at different times during the rest period, the bandsmen not only took their instruments along in their leave vehicle but managed to march into the Vatican, past the Swiss Guards, playing a rather obnoxious piece usually known by the title, "The Protestant Boys are Marching to War". Hordes of Roman citizens cheered their every brassy note and drum flam. It is doubtful anyone knew that they hadn't any business in Vatican Square — which was probably just as well!

When leave parties were going off to Naples and

Rome the Drum Major, Sgt. Billy Beales, with whom I had soldiered in the militia as a fellow-private some eleven or twelve years before, asked that they go as a group so that they could keep their lips and wrists in shape by practising in the leave camp just outside Rome. This seemed a reasonable request to me. I never suspected they would decide to put on a show on the streets of Rome, so when I read an article in the Divisional newspaper, *The Red Patch*, a week after they returned, I was rather upset and thought I might get a proper rocket from the higher ups. However, there were no complaints.

The news story was headed, "RCR DRUMS PLAY IN ROME", and read:

Claiming to be the first Allied Military Band to play in St. Peter's Square, Rome, the "Drums" of The Royal Canadian Regiment have returned from a forty-eight hour leave to the Eternal City. The "Drums", who were only reorganized ten days ago, after being in abeyance for a year, quickly whipped themselves into shape under the able direction of Sgt. G.H. Mason and Sgt. E.W. Farmer. They appeared for the first time in public six days after their initial practice at an infantry brigade sports meet, and, two days later as a massed band, "went into action" with the Pipe Band of the 48th Highlanders of Canada at a Canadian Divisional sports day. Although drums were not on the War Establishment of an assault battalion in the invasion of Sicily, the instruments were brought along, only to be stored in Campobasso during the long winter campaign on the Adriatic front.

Under Sgt. T.W. Beales, as Drum-major, the "Drums" put on a forty-five minute display of stationary playing and counter-marching before hundreds of Italians who surged around them with shouts of *"Bravo!"* and *"Viva il Canadese!"* Again in the evening the R.C.R. lads put on another impromptu demonstration which was equally well received in the 8th Army car park, where the Romans acclaimed them with such fervour that the

C.M.P.s had a difficult time unravelling a half-hour traffic jam. The drum-major, thirteen buglers and nine drummers comprised the unit, which in khaki drill, white webbing, full dress cords and accoutrements of an infantry bugle corps, sounded the stirring notes of British military pomp.

On occasion, "The Drums" put on their regalia to meet the rifle companies and march them back from a hard fought action. Once while practising in an abandoned factory a few hundred yards behind the line in northern Italy they could be so clearly heard that the enemy shelled their practice area in retaliation.

But their job was not all music and fancy marching. There was no "establishment" for a band. To keep them intact they were used as a protective platoon for battalion headquarters and as an ammunition-carrying detail when battle was joined. Their moment of glory came during the bitter fighting around Rimini in September, 1944. "D" Company had been cut off by aggressive paratroopers of General Heidrich's First Parachute Division. They were running short of ammunition, so "The Drums" set off with the needed .303 and so on. Suddenly they came upon a house which, although "D" Company had captured it twenty minutes before, had been re-entered by eight Jerry paratroopers.

These chaps were preparing to knock out "D" Company from behind and were setting up a machine-gun when the bandsmen came upon them. A short, sharp fight took place. Sgt. G.H. Mason, L/Cpl. W. Halbert, Ptes, J.A. Bennett, W.F. Mack, T.F. Wardman and three others whose names have faded from memory managed to capture five Jerries.

The effort was commendable, but a piece of shrapnel ricocheted off the wall, imbedding itself in Halbert's cheek. He took it out, burning his fingers in the doing. As a result of his wound he was unable to blow a bugle for some time. An equal misfortune was that the lead drummer had his wrist broken!

214

Old friends arrived during this period; Capt. Milt Gregg from the U.K., where he had been commanding a reinforcement training company as an acting Major, and Lieut. Des Egan, who had been a Captain on the training establishment in Canada. A complete company of Other Ranks arrived to undergo field training with us. A month later, when our holiday-for-heroes was over, they had all been absorbed into the various rifle companies to make up for the Liri Valley casualties and the normal wastage from sickness, transfers, and for the first time, personnel leaves for Canada. A point system had been inaugurated which allowed certain married men with long service overseas (it had to be since 1939) to return to Canada as prisoner-of-war escorts.

Certainly, our holiday raised the individual spirits and collective morale of the troops. Life was happy and healthful. Our holiday ended when we embussed in TCVs and took the long road past Rome, Spoleto and Siena, into the heart of the Chianti hills, whose slopes produce the famous *Chianti* wine. Here we remained for several days, part of a deception plan, while we waited to enter the battle zone once more.

Some RCR graves in the Gothic Line, resulting from Abissinia and Misano Ridge fighting, Sept. 3/5, 1944.

CHAPTER XV

"RIMINI BY NOON!"

Bullets were soon to fly around our heads again. This time it was in the city of Florence.

The Regiment occupied one side of the Arno River which splits the city in two, while the Germans held the other side. Some sniping and light shelling took place. The main trouble was that pro-Facist and anti-Facist partisans were continually taking pot shots at one another from the rooftops. Putting the Canadians in Florence was part of a deception plan. We left in three days. Our ultimate destination was the Gothic Line, a new German defensive position which stretched across Italy, protecting the Po Valley and routes into Austria and Southern Germany.

The Florence episode had its interesting moments. When we relieved the 1st Scots Guards we at first concluded that the Buckingham Palace boys didn't know their left from their right. When their IO briefed Jim Ritchie on the battalion's dispositions he put his finger on the map and said, "Our right flank company is over here." He pointed to the *left*! Then he said, "Our left flank company is located in this area." He put his grubby pinky down on the *right*! This confused Ritchie a bit. "Wait one!" he interjected, "I don't get you." Then the chap, Ramsay by name, explained. In the Scots Guards they did not letter their companies "A", "B", "C", and "D", but designated them Right Flank Company, No. 2 Company, No. 3 Company and Left Flank Company. I suppose it was their own business, but it did not simplify matters for the run-of-the-mill infantryman.

"Typically British", growled Ritchie, but the relief took place without mishap, anyway.

Florence had been declared an open city because it housed so much of the world's art and architectural treasure. This was not much help to us, as it was the Germans who occupied the north side of town where these treasures were. We were not allowed to shell their area for fear of damaging the works of Michelangelo, Cellini and such like. But this did not stop them from mortaring us, which resulted in fourteen Royal Canadians getting wounded one afternoon. We had our MMGs trained along the Pontevecchio and our battalion observation post in Galileo's observatory. Through the big telescope we could watch the Jerries walking around across the river, but could do nothing about it. Small arms fire was not prohibited, but the enemy were out of range.

The two nights we were in Florence I slept in a huge four-poster, in a bedroom with an immense wall portrait of a lucious nude reclining with all her ample charms revealed in full, living colour. The bathroom next door was the sunken pool variety in a beautiful marble environment, with erotic artwork to beguile the sensuous mind. There were sixty-four rooms in the mansion. The library had thousands of books, hundreds of them in English. The owners were nowhere to be seen, but apparently had not been gone long, for the place had not been ransacked. Birnie Smith, the adjutant, Frank Darton, OC Headquarter Company, John Praysner the Quartermaster and I, with our four batmen, occupied the place. Our surroundings were indeed palatial, but whose house it was we never found out. It was too good to last, of course, but my bed and bath were indeed a forty-eight hour luxury which I enjoyed. Our several meals were served at a mammoth dining room table with high-backed baronial chairs which gave the necessary post-prandial panache, as we sipped our cheap *vino rosso*, pretending in our minds, though not with our palates, that it was the best of port. The house must have had a wine cellar, but it seems we either did not look for it, or could not find it. Other than acquiring a pair of our absentee host's brown oxfords, I personally did no looting, nor did the others, so far as I know. We left our temporary home unviolated, though God knows what happened to its contents when the next occupants arrived.

The troops were also in edifices of historical significance. "A" Company was established in parts of the Palace of the Medici, which dates from 1430 A.D., whereas "B" Company headquarters was set up in a secluded house belonging to Aldous Huxley, the widely-known English essayist and novelist. Many houses in Florence belonged to wealthy Englishmen, Americans and Canadians. Don Mackenzie, the CO of the 48th Highlanders, was especially interested in what was going on across the river, for his aunt owned a villa on the northern outskirts of the city. A few months later, when Florence became a leave centre, he was able to visit the place. It was in good condition and had been used by German officers as a headquarters or a mess.

On the third night, having removed all our badges and other identification marks, including vehicle markings, we moved out of Florence, handing over to the 1st Royal Fusiliers. We hoped the Germans would not know that we had departed, though with the number of sympathetic Facists still around they probably knew it before we were many miles away. We holed up in the Chianti hills near Perugia for a week's training, then in another secret convoy left for the Adriatic coast. Here we prepared for battle.

On arrival at our new 'conc area' I went out into the surrounding district to look for some exotic footstuffs for the Mess; eggs, green vegetables and the like, which always livened up our regular diet of bully beef or spam and dehydrated potatoes. In one farm cottage I came across a really beautiful blonde, either a patrician or a prostitute — it was always so difficult to tell them apart — lolling about in a yellow silk gown with a magnificent full-length green Chinese dragon embroidered or appliquéd on its back. She spoke pretty good English and when I complimented her on it she demonstrated her French, German and native Italian. I thought afterwards she might have been a spy left behind by the Germans, perhaps with a radio set to tell them what was going on. Certainly I was not sharp enough to think about it at the time. The cottage was remote from anywhere. It was little more than a hovel and certainly a very strange place for a woman of her apparent education and refinement to be living.

* * * *

"I feel as though some bloody Jerry was staring at me through a pair of Zeiss field glasses." The speaker was Lt. Geoff Wright, MC. He was correct!

Wright, Capts. Ted Maxted, Len Courtin, 'Pick' Pickard and Lieut. Ted Shuter were listening to me as I pointed out their company jumping-off areas for the attack across the Metauro River, a dried-up river bed with only ankle-deep streams coursing among the stones that littered its bottom.

Suddenly, a shell hit the house in front of us. We scattered in all directions as two more shells screamed in. I flung myself into a pigsty, thrusting my trembling frame up against the filthy hide of a huge, squealing sow. Nobody was hit. In a few minutes we reassembled and dashed for a less conspicuous observation point.

Just before midnight the attack went in behind a tremendous barrage. Some prisoners were taken, shoddy troops left behind to delay our initial advance. The real enemy was farther back, as we were soon to find out.

That afternoon Ted Shuter was surprised at his post when two visitors arrived to scan the battle line. One was Field Marshal Alexander, the other was Winston Churchill. The two great men drove into the farmyard where Shuter was and asked about the fighting. As Ted explained the tactical situation, a battery of our 25-pounders opened up from gun positions in the rear.

"Ah, cannon!" the Prime Minister exclaimed, lowering the binoculars he had been peering through. The famous pair soon left by jeep. In less than half an hour a heavy concentration of enemy mortar bombs fell on the very ground where they had stood.

In his own memoirs Churchill wrote of this visit, saying it was the closest he ever got to the enemy during the war. He actually watched our "B" Company, commanded by Major Sandy Mitchell, attacking the Convento Beato Sante, which was on a hill known as Point 393. Surely, few infantry company commanders, if any, ever put in an attack under the very eyes of so highly placed a pair as did Sandy Mitchell.

The fighting was not too fierce. The poor quality troops which had been left behind to delay us continued to surrender by the dozens. However, some armoured fighting vehicles made life miserable by running up and down along the roads on hidden high ground ahead of us, shelling our troops and then moving off before our guns could locate them. The tough part was the mountain climbing in the hot, dusty August weather. The scout platoon, moving ahead of the rifle companies, had one sharp encounter, killing and capturing some of the more resolute Germans. This mini-battle resulted in the scout sergeant, a chap named Meadows, winning the Military Medal.

Like so many of those who received decorations for bravery, he was killed at a later date.

For four days we rested after our mountain climbing and skirmishing. Then, on September 2 we assembled in open country near Tomba di Pesaro. Here we remained for a few hours until we moved off in a motorized column, mindful of the remarkable slogan handed down from Divisional Headquarters (possibly they got it from a higher authority!) of "Rimini by noon".

The whole countryside indicated the retreat of the enemy. For miles around burning homesteads and haystacks, glowing like hundreds of cigarette butts in a darkened room, illuminated the otherwise pitch-dark landscape. There was something more ominous in this than just what met the eye. The enemy was not merely being destructive. He was levelling haystacks and crops so as to deprive our advancing army of cover from the view of his artillery O.P.s.

At 3 a.m. on September 3, the battalion debussed and advanced to the line of the Conca River by march route. It was a three mile hike. The scout platoon, ranging in open order ahead of the leading company, picked up ten sleepy prisoners, warning outposts who had failed in their duty. Bridges across the Conca had been destroyed, but the river bed was almost dry. "B" and "C" Companies easily forded the shallow water and as the first grey light of day began to show, battle was joined at a scattering of cottages labelled on the map as Abissinia. Thus began three weeks of fighting which became known as the Battle of the Gothic Line. It was to be the heaviest fighting for the 1st Division since the Ortona battle nine months before. Close, hand-to-hand combat resulted in heavy casualties. "A" Company suffered the worst, losing about half its numbers and being reduced to 54 all ranks by the end of the first day. Prisoners were taken on both sides.

That night we were strafed by an enemy aircraft which flew at what seemed roof-top level down the highway. All the windows of Tac HQ, a small roadside villa, were knocked in, shattered glass flying everywhere. Thinking there might be several sorties following, I made a dash for the cellar steps, closely followed by two or three officers and several Other Ranks. Halfway down the steps I stopped, turned about and stretched my arms across from wall to wall. "Don't panic, men," I said. Most of them were still at the top of the stairs. With me coming up from below, those on the staircase returned to the shattered ops room. It did take a few days for me to live that one down. "Don't panic men, I'm all right", chirped the OC Support Company, Major Morgan John, on more than one subsequent occasion.

The CO was caught in the sights of the same aircraft, as he was at that precise moment on his way back from Brigade. However, the cannon shells were all near misses. It was one of the very few times in either Sicily or Italy that we underwent air attack. The Allies had mastery of the air in these two campaigns, which was far different from what I had experienced in North Africa in the Spring of '43.

At Misano Ridge Lieut. Danny Burns led a bayonet charge and put a small party of the enemy to flight. But on the whole it was confused fighting and this continued for four days, during which period the Regiment lost two officers and 29 men killed, one officer and 15 men missing and five officers and 103 Other Ranks wounded. "A" Company was hit the worst, coming out of the attack under CSM Ian MacDonald with only eighteen men left. Birnie

Smith, who had taken over the company from his adjutant's job, was mortally wounded in an exchange of hand grenades. Just a few hours earlier he had smiled into the lens of my camera at the Battalion "O" Group which sent him to his death.

Some "B" Company men actually fought their way into the church at the little crossroads village of San Lorenzo-in-Strada, which was a German strong-point. Lieut. Dave Fisher led his platoon right into the nave where he was killed. Fighting took place among the pews and Sgt. Roger Duhaime later received the MM for having knocked out a bazooka and its crew somewhere near the altar!

It was next morning, just after dawn, when Birnie Smith took his remaining two platoons of "A" Company into the assault, but they were mowed down in a field just across from the church. Smith was recommended for a posthumous VC, the only such recommendation put up by the Regiment during the war, but he did not get it. One of Smith's platoon commanders, Lance-Sgt. Cecil Sweeney, chased some fleeing Germans with a hand grenade. He threw it at them but kept on running and was killed, as were the Germans, by the explosion. This strange episode was related to me thirty-six years later in Argyllshire, Scotland, by a former British tank officer, who had witnessed it from the highway off to the right flank. His tank had conked out, leaving him an unwilling and helpless spectator to an infantry brawl.

During this fighting the Germans also employed a division of Turcomen, from the Russo-Iranian border. Originally, they had been members of the Soviet Army, but after capture by the Germans on the Eastern Front had been converted, armed and uniformed as Germans and sent to the Italian front. High cheek-boned, swarthy chaps, broad faced and strongly built, they looked more Asiatic than Middle Eastern and may have been the descendants of an invading tribe from a thousand years back.

Scout officer Lieut. Jimmy Quayle and scouts Cpl. Ralph Peters and Pte. Jack Gardner, MM, bumped in to 11 of these fellows while poking around in a brickyard known to be 'enemy' held. But the Turcomen 'joined' the scouts rather than surrender. They offered to go quietly providing they could keep their arms and ammunition. Sitting by the side of the road, I was startled by this strange procession wearing German uniforms and led by one of our scouts. They were prisoners, obviously. But how come they had machine-guns over their shoulders, bandoliers of ammo slung across their bodies and *schmeissers* in their arms?

The scout said he had been nonplussed (and who wouldn't have been?) when they said they wanted to fight on our side. He thought it better to lead them back to headquarters and ask me what to do! That was one of the times when I passed the buck. I returned salutes, nodded my head in feigned understanding, fell in two men and a corporal and told them to march the Turcomen back to brigade HQ and present them to the brigade major with my compliments!

Why they now wanted to fight the Germans remains a mystery. Probably they just wanted to be on the winning side, as they had in Russia when they surrendered to the Germans. Maybe they just thought we ate better.

After two or three days in the open near Gradara Castle, to rest and absorb some eighty reinforcements, we were told that our next battleground was to be Rimini airfield, defended by 1st Parachute Division. Commanding Officers were ordered to be left out of battle. I took over from Ritchie and the advance began, the 48th Highlanders on my left, the Greek Mountain Brigade supposedly on my right. We were beginning one of our most successful, yet most officially unrewarding fights. Our battle casualties totalled ninety all ranks. The fighting was hand-to-hand. The airfield had been criss-crossed with ditches to render it useless. These ditches were covered by machine-guns and were death-traps. Numerous fortified houses dotted the perimeter of the field. Officer losses were particularly heavy and Cpl. N.J. McMahon's DCM and Sgt. T.R. Hardingham's MM were awarded for the splendid leadership they displayed. Dead Germans lay everywhere.

For the attack on the airfield I had selected an

isolated farmhouse, marked on the map as La Brusada, for Battalion Headquarters. On arrival we found a dead German paratrooper sprawled outside the door. In his wallet we found his pay book, which identified him as to age, military qualifications, regiment, previous service and so on, small details which our Intelligence people always wanted to weave into their tapestry of knowledge as to the quality and type of enemy units we were up against.

In his wallet I found three of those little printed death notices so peculiar to Germany. They always contained the deceased's picture, career highlights, dates of birth and death and the like and, finally, religious or patriotic verses. These were for the young soldier's older brothers, all killed in action within the previous two years. All three had been volunteers and all three had been awarded the Iron Cross. Several snapshots showed the happy family together in their hometown of Zweibrueken in the Rhenish-Palatinate, the very same place from where my mother's Pennsylvania-German ancestors had emigrated to America more than two centuries before.

That night, while sitting at the rough table in La Brusada, spread with battle maps and with the wireless set giving reports of my men moving into position, I tore a page out of my message book and scribbled down the following lines, entitling them, "Four Sons".

Frau Hilberath had four strong sons,
  Sent to serve Der Fuehrer's guns.
Now they all have met their death—
  Pity Mother Hilberath.

Franz, Karl, Adolf, paid the price,
  But their lives did not suffice.
War's demands are even sterner,
  Last of all — Lieb' Bruder Werner!

The joke was, the RCR fought *on* the airfield, whereas we were supposed to clear the ground to the airfield's left, swing around its north boundary and then capture Rimini in conjunction with the 48th Highlanders.

On September 18, Lieut. Jimmy Quayle received his

third wound in less than a year, a bullet in the wrist. Next day, awaiting evacuation, a piece of shrapnel gave him his fourth wound!

Language difficulties made cooperation with the Greek Brigade almost impossible. We couldn't speak Greek and they couldn't speak English — at least not well enough to know what was really meant. The Greeks were supposed to fight forward to the north edge of the airfield, thus covering our right flank as we pushed up the open country to the airfield's left. They apparently understood that they had only to reach the *south* edge and there conduct a fire-fight with the Germans. They suffered heavily, but the fact is, they left our right flank open and that was one reason we lost so many men ourselves.

With the Germans watching our every move from the high ridge of San Fortunato, thus being able to shell us heavily, both the 48th Highlanders and our unit actually failed to fully reach our objectives. It was also deadly to have our right flank completely exposed to machine-gun and mortar fire from the airfield. We were literally moving down a corridor of death.

The Greek officers who I saw were pleasant enough fellows, rather British both in dress and in manner. But they were over-polite in the European fashion. More saluting than understanding characterized the few meetings I had with them during the battle. It was their first battle. Both officers and men knew nothing about battlefield procedures, let alone the language of those under whose command they served. One of our officers, Lieut. Jack Davis, was detailed as a liaison officer to their Brigade Headquarters. He later said that he might as well not have been given the job at all. They just smiled at him and saluted. He had no idea what they were doing and figured they didn't know either.

Apparently their entry into battle was a political move to show the world that the Greeks were fighting on the Allied side. They were rushed over to Italy to 'show the Greek flag', so to speak. They paid a heavy price for the privilege. Unfortunately, so did we.

Advance patrols of both the RCR and 48th High-landers finally reached Rimini in the face of only a few departing shots. Capt. Milton Gregg, whose uncle of the same name had won the Victoria Cross with the Regiment in 1918, was in the lead. Suddenly we received orders to withdraw his company back to the airfield. The Greeks were hurried forward and allowed to enter Rimini. Soon the Greek flag flew from the *Municipio* tower. The Greeks paraded ceremonially, the Canadians licking their wounds in the background. Later we read in newspapers from home the annoying headline, HEROIC GREEK BRIGADE TAKES RIMINI. What price glory?

However, Ritchie, who was back in command, received a personal note from the Army Commander. It read: "Your Regiment may well be proud of its part in a great and hard-fought victory. Well done, Canada!"

So much for the "Rimini by noon" nonsense. It was noon *nineteen days later*. Distances seem so short on a one-inch-to-the-mile map, when looked at in a headquarters caravan.

I am reminded of the time, months before at Ortona, when our men were falling like flies and every battalion in the Division seemed to be in contact with the enemy, none in reserve to give freedom of action in the event of a counterattack, or a chance breakthrough on our part which needed to be exploited. The Patricias had been fighting desperately to clear Vino Ridge when their CO, crouched on the earthern floor of a shallow root-house, received a message over the rear link wireless from some pusher in a comfortable caravan at Divisional Headquarters.

"What is stopping you?" came the commanding voice.

The CO, Cammie Ware by name, took a deep breath. "The enemy", he retorted, with no further elaboration, and put the offending voice conveyor down with the unanswerable procedural word, "Out."

The Gothic Line fighting, especially the first two days, and later the actual fighting for the airfield, were costly to the enemy as well as to us. In one short stretch of airfield perimeter, one company commander, Eric Forgrave, counted twenty German bodies while walking back to Tac HQ. The CO had decided to send Forgrave back to "B" Echelon for a forty-eight hour rest. Fate intervened. Stripped to the waist and shaving, so that he could leave the Front in a clean condition, he suffered a piece of metal in the back of his handsome blond head and was dead before he could enjoy his first night out of the Line. The source of the shrapnel was undetermined, possibly a booby trap.

Seventeen days of rest followed. The Regiment had to be rebuilt. From the Metauro crossing to the capture of Rimini, seven officers and 72 other ranks had been killed, 15 officers and 206 other ranks wounded and two officers and 10 other ranks posted as missing. Every third man had been a battle casualty. But, realizing that the assault strength, limited to the rifle companies, was usually less than 400 bayonets, it can be reckoned that by September 22, three out of four men who crossed the Metauro on August 25 had paid for our victory with more than just their sweat and tears.

Farewell to Italy! "Birdie" Quayle with his four wound stripes at Leghorn embarkation camp. Holland next!

CHAPTER XVI

RIVERS OF BLOOD

Fortunato Ridge was finally captured by troops of the 2nd and 3rd Brigades, thus stopping the German artillery fire on us. With the Greeks entering an enemy-deserted Rimini by means of a ceremonial parade, the "corridor of death" had ceased to exist. The RCR rested in its slit trenches and battered farm buildings and absorbed a draft of seventy-five badly-needed reinforcements. On September 22 we embussed in TCVs and went back five miles or so to a large brick orphanage on the seashore. Here we received another thirty-three reinforcements, plus an additional thirty-nine a couple of days later. Three or four officers rejoined, but we were woefully short of both officers and men.

Our summer drill uniforms were shed and the warmer battledress came back into wear. Rest was followed by training our reinforcements for battle. By October 10 we were on our way again, moving up the Rimini-Bologna Highway into the Po Valley. The British brigade which was Eighth Army's leading element had lost contact with the retreating enemy. Our task was to regain it.

Apart from nighly *vino* parties, our main diversion in the rest area was the visit of the Minister of National Defense, the Hon. J.L. Ralston. The CO had been given a week's leave in Cairo and I was in command. When advised that Ralston was coming, I mounted a quarter guard and as he and his party entered the orphanage gate the bugler sounded four G's and the guard commander gave the 'Present Arms!'. I then went up to the Minister and welcomed him. We had been told that a very carefully selected group of twenty-five Other Ranks was to be available to the Minister for questioning. Ralston was in Italy to investigate the allegations that we were short of men and that the reinforcements arriving were not well enough trained to survive in battle. Such was the case, but higher authority instructed us to keep our mouths shut. As a result the Minister got very little from his conversations with the men. Apparently, the day before he had heard an earful from the RSM of the 48th Highlanders. This resulted in instructions to us to say no more than "Yes, Sir. No, Sir, three bags full", or *words to that effect*, as the *Manual of Military Law* used to put it.

As was his custom, the Divisional Commander had visited us almost as soon as we got back into our billets. He congratulated the men on the good job they had done. But, as was usually the case, the ones who should really have received his praise were either dead or in hospital. Certainly, the reinforcements had done nothing. Perhaps he thought it would encourage them for their own blooding! The Corps Commander's written message, printed in the Divisional news sheet as a stop press item, read: ". . . the capture of S. Fortunato and Rimini will rank with the finest Canadian feats of arms. To all ranks *and to yourself in particular* [meaning the Divisional Commander] are my congratulations and thanks. The red patch — the old and bold — has done it again." The same issue of the news sheet announced that the Divisional Commander had been made a Commander of the Most Excellent Order of the British Empire for his "outstanding leadership". Our Division's casualties for the Gothic Line fighting were slightly over two thousand five hundred all ranks. During the same period 5th Canadian Armoured Division lost fifteen hundred, fighting around Coriano on our left flank.

There was much talk these days about the "Zombies" back home. These were the home-service conscripts who refused to volunteer for overseas service. Going into battle about half-strength as we were doing, it could not be otherwise. Some gentler souls were less blasphemous than most against the "Zombies" and put their thoughts into poetry. About this time the Divisional news sheet published a poem signed simply "J.H.P." and entitled *Promise*.

> Though politicians break the faith
> And soulless cowards spurn the call
> Your comrades carry on the fight,
> Nor shall the torch you gave us fall!
> The weary ones still man their Brens,
> The wounded men rejoin the ranks,
> The rationed guns still hunt the foe;
> Some still count honour more than life.
> Your crosses do not stand in vain
> We saw you make the sacrifice!
> The dreams you died for still remain,
> The future must be worth the price.
> Rest not uneasy in your graves,
> Your memories will drive us on!
> And though our history has been stained,
> Beyond the dark we glimpse the dawn.

On October 12 our location was the Villa Gnaldo, a country mansion of the historic Malatesta, or *Badhead* family, as the name translates into English. In the garden we were gratified to see a German cemetery containing 171 graves. The Villa must have been Casualty Clearing Station for the enemy. The dates on the crosses were all between September 10 and 24, the period of the Rimini fighting, which indicated we had done some good.

On the 13 and 14 October the battalion patrolled forward with caution, against considerable hostile shelling but with no sight of the enemy. On the second of these two days the Villa came in for a furious twenty minutes of shelling and the operations room had its windows and doors blown in with those of us occupying it thrown to the floor and covered with dust and flying bits of glass and plaster. When the dust settled after the last shell, we were surprised to find that nobody had even received a scratch. Meantime, our forward company had located an enemy position, overrun it and captured eight of the enemy. It was not until the company had dug in and consolidated their position as a firm base for two more companies to pass through and continue the advance, that they discovered they were sitting in the middle of a minefield. How the entire company crossed the minefield without stepping on a mine is one of the mysteries of the war. But, when the company commander dispatched his outposts they began stepping on the devilish things. Then, more than a dozen had feet, legs and groins shattered or lacerated.

Lieutenant-Colonel, Canadian Guards, in scarlet and gold, 1956.

With former *Luftwaffe* ace, General Adolf Galland, at Bonn, Germany, 1965.

A couple of days later I was placed in command again. Ritchie told me that Brigadier Calder had said that it was time someone in the RCR got a DSO, instructing him to "give Galloway the battalion for a couple of days and see what he can do!" Ritchie told me he had replied to the Brigadier by saying, "We don't get DSOs in the RCR, Sir. We only do our job." Anyway, he remained out of battle and I took over. With me was Benny Potts MC, the IO, whose sense of humour and common sense were always good for my morale, and two signallers and a runner. We moved well forward. I set up Tac HQ about two hundred yards behind "C" Company. About three hours after our arrival a shell shattered the wall of the room we were using as our operations centre. The five of us were thrown to the floor. The wireless set was ruined, thus cutting us off from all communications with Brigade. As a result of this mishap, when communications were re-established in the afternoon, the Brigadier ordered my HQ to locate some 1500 yards to the rear!

And so it was that we reached the Po Valley. But we

had arrived two weeks too late. A rainy, windswept plain was our promised land. The dry, open terrain which our masters had ordered us to provide for them was not there. It was open, but it was far from dry. The autumn rains had won the race. The valley was liquid mud. Rivers and canals crossed our proposed avenue of advance.

The Pisciatello, the Savio, the Ronco, the Montone, the Lamone, the Vecchio Canal and finally the Senio. These were the barriers in full flood behind which our enemies waited to cut us down. It seemed there was always one more river to cross.

Eighth Army, which some of us joined fifteen months before, was no longer the salt of the earth; it had lost its savour. Our rifle companies were always under strength, the reinforcements poorly trained. The eyes of the world were now on the great destructive battles of the Second Front. By October, 1944 we were floundering in a backwater of the war. Only some of us could remember the road to Ortona and our distant walk in Sicily's sunshine.

Life was sour indeed.

In the Po Valley thick stone houses were everywhere, ideal strong-points for enemy machine-gunners. The ground was flat and platoon and section commanders were often more important than colonels and captains.

Lt. Al Ferguson led his platoon onto its objective. He was instantly killed when a stick grenade hit him on the head. Lt. Desmond Egan seized a 2-inch mortar, rushed to the second storey of a house and attempted to wipe out a group of Germans running for cover. Pte. Norman Rauta captured a troublesome machine-gun post single-handedly, at rifle point. He was dead when his award of the Military Medal was announced several weeks later.

Cpl. Jimmy Bain and his section cautiously entered a pink railway building. By the time they had reached the upper floor, the building was assaulted by Germans from slit trenches to its rear. A bazooka bomb blew the upstairs floor away. Bain and one of his men fell ten feet into a heap of debris below. The Germans rushed the interior. As the leader entered the door, another of Bain's men, astride a rafter above, shot the German dead. In a moment the men below were on their feet. They fought off their attackers, killing three and wounding others. One of their own men was killed and four were wounded.

Such were the realities of our "debouchment into the valley of the Po."

One gallant and humorous incident took place. Sgt. E.G. Richardson, who had been wounded when commanding a platoon at Ortona ten months before, distinguished himself under heavy shellfire by chasing a terrified and squealing pig around a barnyard until he caught it. His platoon dined well that night. Richardson ended the war with a well-earned Mention-in-Dispatches and the American Bronze Star medal.

By now the rain was endless. We were pulled out of the Line after seven days of battle. Casualties had not been heavy, but that was because the mud and the bad weather had kept any large-scale attack from developing. Our sanctuary from battle was under leaden skies on the sodden fields of Emilia. Water lay deep on these fields, but they were better than the water-filled slit trenches which others occupied closer to the foe.

Sheltered in scattered stone farmhouses which typified the area, the battle-weary infantrymen were able to enjoy some of the comforts of home. That is, parcels from Canada, NAAFI beer and the blazing hearth fires of their temporary billets.

At this time an eminent Canadian educator and lecturer arrived on a 10-day visit to the 'forgotten front'. He was to see what Canada's fighting men in Italy were doing and then, on his return to Ottawa, give his impressions over the nation's microphones. His name was Leonard Brockington.

We asked him about Canada, which some of us hadn't seen for almost five years. It was wonderful to be able to talk to someone who wasn't clothed in battledress like ourselves, or in the rags of the refugee world. He told us things that were good to hear, even though we couldn't be expected to believe everything he said. We were pretty skeptical people in those days.

In our quarters on the top floor of an Italian farmhouse, over a lower floor which was the stable, we spread our goodies before him and invited him to dinner. Fortunately, the intelligence officer had just received a marvellous food package from his wife in Montreal. It contained all those delicacies that he had dreamed about for months; the kind of things that weren't usually sent, even by the most loving of mothers, wives and sweethearts who thought mostly in terms of nutritious foods rather than gourmet tidbits. He had hidden his fancy foodstuffs for secret indulgence, and none of us blamed him. Then came the breath of the Beast, withering his prospects of personal pleasure.

"Well, Eric," said the colonel. "I guess we eat up your parcel from home tonight. I'm certainly not going to offer Mr. Brockington bully beef, spam or dehydrated potatoes."

"Yes, sir," replied Eric, fully aware that he was living in an extremely monolithic society.

And so the five or six of us, plus our distinguished guest, dined well that rainy night.

"Colonel," said the Great One. "I haven't eaten anything as good as this since I left Canada."

In a barely audible voice, Eric said to the padre, who was sitting next to him, "Neither have I. But I left Canada two years ago."

The next day Eric had his revenge. Not by design, just by the fortunes of war. It happened this way:

As one of the upper floor dwellers, I had husbanded several bottles of NAAFI beer in my room. Because of the continuous rain and the depth of liquid mud outside the farmhouse, I had used an empty beer bottle to relieve myself the night of the Brockington dinner. Having done so, I re-capped it and put it slightly apart from the beer-filled bottles.

Working on some routine returns in the morning the colonel became thirsty and bellowed to his batman that Major Galloway had some beer under his cot, and . . . "go and borrow a bottle for me." The rest of the story is obvious. The batman grabbed the lone bottle and the last laugh was Eric's. Well, not really. The next day the colonel was able to laugh himself.

I suppose that is the way we kept our reason. Wives and sweethearts were far away. Food and drink was rarely a gourmet's delight, or even the way mother cooked it. Warm baths and comfortable beds were few and far between. You had to laugh, even at yourself. Those who couldn't laugh, even at death, had a much worse time of it.

On November 1 we returned again to our orphanage on the seashore south of Rimini. The warmth of September had gone. The beach was no longer an attractive place to lie in the sun. The Adriatic was grey and forbidding. Training was carried out in earnest, most of it devoted to river crossing technique and to firing our weapons out to sea. We remained there for twenty-eight days.

Midway through this period the Officers held a Mess Dinner, attended by the newly arrived Corps Commander, Lieut.-Gen. Charles Foulkes. He was an RCR officer, but had not served with the Regiment since before the war. He was the Captain Foulkes who had taught me more than eleven years before at the Provisional School of Infantry, qualifying me as a sergeant in the militia. This time he appeared in my life straight from Northwest Europe, where he had been commanding 2nd Canadian Infantry Division. He replaced Lieut.-Gen. Burns who had been given the sack because he could not get along with the Eighth Army commander.

Several days later Foulkes addressed all the officers of the Corps from the stage of a deserted opera house. He had a miserable personality and when he started off by telling us that he expected some "spirited leadership" in the next operation, thus giving us the impression that he did not believe we had been giving that type of leadership in the past, he lost any of the personal loyalties he might have hoped to gain — if indeed he ever thought that way.

He had entered operations as a Divisional Commander in France, where he had served less than four months before being sent out to Italy. Those of us who had experienced sixteen months of fighting in Sicily and Italy did not need this high-ranking tyro to tell us how to lead our men. His contempt for the fighting troops was apparent in his very face, and something that would become more evident in the weeks to come.

We were soon to enter battle again. Eighth Army was to keep bashing on, the weather, the flooded rivers notwithstanding. Impossible goals were chosen — the line of the Santerno River was to be reached. As to *why*, nobody at the fighting level was even told. It seems Eisenhower had decided on a winter campaign in Northwest Europe. Allied 'pressure' was to be kept up in Italy so that the Germans would have no respite on any front. The fact that it is always the attackers, rather than the defenders who suffer the most seemed to matter little. As the Bible has it, 'there is a time to die'. For many of the Canadians in Italy that time was to be December, 1944. Not as many as at Ortona or in the Gothic Line, it is true. But this time there seemed no real purpose to the blood-letting.

By December, autumn rains had turned most rivers into raging torrents. Here they flowed between high dykes. Dug into the rear slopes of the far dykes, the Germans were unreachable by artillery fire and completely safe from small arms fire, except from behind. Thus, when our troops managed to cross the double dykes they were not only exposed to counterattack, but were literally between a hammer and an anvil. To attempt such operations was madness.

On the night of December 4th-5th the RCR got two companies across the Lamone, despite mortar fire which caught one platoon and eliminated it. The pioneers then pushed two light footbridges across for the follow-up. A third company crossed.

A heavy barrage had preceded the forward companies. Now the battlefield was strangely quiet. Wireless contact was poor. The exact location of the three companies and their degree of success were uncertain at battalion headquarters. The CO sent me forward to "get the picture". By jeep, the dykes were only ten minutes away, even in the thick fog. We were able to follow the route, marked on both sides with white tape.

Crossing one of the footbridges I saw some shadowy figures. They were Capt. Jimmy Wilkinson and his company headquarters. Wilkinson provided me with a guide to "A" Company. Here I checked with Major Jim Houghton. Then Major Eric Thorne, of "B" Company, appeared out of the fog, to use "A" Company's wireless because his own set was not working. He showed me his company's location on a map.

The two forward companies were to stay put. "C" Company was to exploit fifteen hundred yards forward, consolidate and wait for daylight. My job was to confirm these orders verbally.

Standing in the soggy meadow, Wilkinson received his orders. In a parade ground manner he saluted smartly. His cane was tucked under his left armpit, his right hand properly poised at the rim of his helmet. I returned the compliment, my stick and cap act a duplicate of his. These little frills made the garment of war more wearable.

I returned across the dykes, taking two docile prisoners with me, my pistol drawn and my walking stick tapping them on the shoulder to help them keep direction.

Reaching my jeep I loaded the two prisoners and we headed back. We had hardly gone five hundred yards when the whole area came under heavy shellfire, but back at Battalion headquarters I reported all well in the bridgehead. The CO said rafts were being prepared to ferry Littlejohn anti-tank guns across the river to support the rifle companies. Wireless contact was still unsatisfactory. Suddenly the door burst open. A stretcher bearer, sent by jeep from the RAP, told us that the rifle companies had been counterattacked in force.

"B" Company lost 41 out of its assault strength of 72. This included Thorne and two platoon commanders killed, the CSM captured and the third platoon commander wounded. "C" Company fared worse. Wilkinson and his CSM were captured. One platoon commander was killed, one wounded and the other captured. Out of an assault strength of 69, the company lost 48. They fought well. When the bridgehead was finally ours, some days later, the bodies of the dead were found. Several lay beside heaps of empty cartridge cases showing they had fought till the bitter end. "A" Company was withdrawn with light losses.

The Lamone *débâcle* was not the fault of the fighting troops. It was the result of stupid high level planning by some planners unfamiliar with the Italian terrain and the realities of dykeland warfare. The Hastings and Prince Edward Regiment, which attempted to form a bridgehead on the right of the RCR, failed as well. Many of their casualties were caused by their own supporting artillery. Postwar historians have exonerated the gunners, placing the blame for both failures squarely on staff planners ensconced in comfortable caravans miles behind the lines.

The cardinal error was that a railway embankment on the left flank of the RCR had not been straddled. Thorne had attempted to do this on his own initiative. The platoon detailed to do it, under Capt. Peder Hertzberg, had been mortared, the fire killing Hertzberg and killing or wounding eighteen of his twenty-one men. A prepared track along the far side of the embankment allowed the Germans to hurry self-propelled guns down to the culverts. Machine-gunners in small trucks followed. Setting up on the protected side of the embankment they sprayed the flat ground on the other side. When the RCR tried to escape this fire by occupying stone farmhouses, the SP-guns brought the walls crashing down. The troops in the bridgehead were completely exposed, and the counterattacking Germans completely concealed.

Despite shocking losses the fighting continued all month. Reinforcements arrived in streams, often becoming casualties the same day, or dying before they knew even their corporal's name. On December 18 alone, the battalion suffered 71 more casualties. But it was not all one-sided. In mid-month one "A" Company platoon captured thirty Germans including two officers. Pte. H.G. Otis knocked out an enemy tank singlehandedly, turning back a small infantry counterattack as well. He received the DCM for this act.

Fighting was of the closest possible nature. Two well-known battalion stretcher bearers, Ptes. Bailey and Bean, crossed into the enemy lines with a wounded German in their ambulance jeep. They traded him for a wounded RCR soldier, Pte. Fulford. During negotiations the German medical officer gave them a drink, letting them rest awhile in his RAP. He then sent them back to their own lines with a bottle of wine, as a present from him to their own MO.

The Lamone operation had been a ghastly failure. It was obvious that heads would roll. Ritchie, upon whose shoulders no blame could be laid, was fired in a most callous way. The Acting CO of the Hastings and Prince Edward Regiment was wounded, so escaped being fired. The Brigade Commander, Brig. J.A. Calder, lost his rank which was only 'acting' anyway. He was reduced to lieutenant-colonel and sent back to England. The Acting Divisional Commander, an ambitious brigadier, did not get his anticipated promotion. A new Divisional Commander was hurried out from Northwest Europe. Unfortunately, the Acting Divisional Commander became our Brigadier. We had not deserved that. But such are the fortunes of war.

Although the RCR had only three officers and 26 Other Ranks killed, three officers and 43 Other Ranks wounded and two officers and 29 Other Ranks taken prisoner on the far side of the Lamone, the blow was greater than that. Total strength of the three rifle companies which crossed the river was probably less than 250, so that actually almost fifty per cent became casualties. The Hasty P's lost almost as many men, but in a more demoralizing way, because many of their casualties had been caused by shorts from our own artillery before they even crossed the river. The planning at Brigade, Division or somewhere could not have been worse. Both battalions were in a state of trauma.

Somewhere, to shield the faults of others, the rumour was started that the troops had fought badly.

Five days after the disaster Bunny McWilliams, our battalion liaison officer at Brigade, arrived at our Tac HQ and asked Ritchie if he had an extra RCR cap badge and extra cloth shoulder flashes. He said a senior officer was visiting Brigade and had asked for a set. Ritchie said he was delighted to provide them and sent his batman to his kit bag to get the spare officer's pattern badge and flashes he kept there. When he asked who the officer was who wanted these items, McWilliams managed to avoid giving an answer. Next morning he found out. The new Brigade Commander arrived with Ritchie's replacement in tow. He had belonged to another regiment in the 5th Division. Now he wore Ritchie's badges and flashes and was our new Commanding Officer! Ritchie left by jeep for the rear within the hour.

When Ritchie had gone I wrote a letter to the Brigade Commander asking that I might leave the battalion. I stated my reasons. I was sent on several days' leave to the Officers' Club in Riccione and then summoned to the Corps Commander's caravan in Ravenna.

Here, from Foulkes' own lips I heard the lie that men of the RCR had failed to fight in the Lamone bridgehead. I denied this. I remember one sentence of his conversation.

"Galloway", he said, "are you telling me I don't understand my soldiers?"

"Sir," I replied, "I am not telling you anything, I have only reminded you that I have been in this theatre with them for almost eighteen months and you have been here for less than six weeks."

Why he did not fire me on the spot I will never know. I returned to the Regiment with no option but to soldier on.

CHAPTER XVII

IN THE VALLEY OF THE PO

Christmas night saw the RCR once more advancing into the enemy fire. The companies fought well. At Tac HQ I tried to support the new CO as best I could. He was a nice enough fellow named Bill Reid, who had won the DSO at Coriano Ridge, commanding the Perth Regiment. Unfortunately, we did not see eye to eye on most things and the tension between us was obvious to all.

Most of the fighting involved clearing out small pockets of the enemy nestled between the canals and streamlets that lay across the battlefield. There was no large scale 'punch' behind the operation, but the clearing out of buildings saw many sharp, nerve-wracking fights and rather high casualty rates. After twenty-three days of continuous battle we were lifted back to a miserable little village named San Pancrazio for a rest. Here we were told that since the plan to capture Lugo had failed, we were to merely hold the line of the Senio River for the winter. The December objective, the line of the Santerno River, was a good six miles beyond the Senio.

This was the first time that battle neurosis, known during the Great War as 'shell shock', became a noticeable factor affecting the Regiment's fighting efficiency. Some weeks before, a Medical Officer I had met up with told me that the RCR had fewer cases of battle neurosis than any other Canadian infantry battalion in Italy. This was good to hear. He attributed the situation to the fact that our discipline was of a higher category than that found in most other units. In any event, this malady began to manifest itself during the December fighting. For one thing, climatic conditions were deplorable and for another, the fighting was disorganized and over terrain where the enemy had every advantage. The canals, rivers and ditches made a checkerboard out of our battlefield and provided well-defined lines of fire for the enemy's machine-guns and were most helpful to him in determining where to bring down mortar and artillery fire.

The Lamone *débâcle* had been a bitter episode in the Regiment's history. Even the rear rank privates knew that they had been pushed into a 'killing ground'. They therefore still believed that our newly appointed brigade, divisional and corps commanders either didn't know what they were doing, or didn't care. It certainly looked that way, as there was very little humanity noticeable behind Battalion Headquarters.

On Christmas Eve a company-sergeant-major who had seemed a reasonable sort of chap up until then, arrived at the stone hovel where I was set up, in a state of near hysterics. He wept like a broken-hearted child, saying he could not go on, that we were all being murdered and for no good reason. It was difficult not to agree with him, but of course that could never be. I had him bundled off to "B" Echelon for a 'rest'. Had he not been gotten safely out of the way in this manner he most certainly would have ended up with a court-martial. Also, his effect on the morale of the junior NCOs and men could have caused complete demoralization.

For the most part, the Other Ranks weathered the storm wonderfully well. Looking back, it is hard to believe that ordinary, peaceable men from the cities and the farms of Canada could face the terrors and brutalities of that particular battlefield day after day and night after night. The calibre of the men was quite magnificent. Most were between 20 and 25, quite a few were younger. A man over thirty was a rarity. I think that on the whole we in the RCR had a pretty good Officer-Man rapport. We did try to look after them, and share their hardships while still keeping the distance necessary to maintain discipline. And we did our best to see that they got the rewards they deserved. After the war I counted up the decorations our men had received and on comparing the total was delighted to see that they had been awarded almost double the number of Distinguished Conduct Medals and Military Medals "for bravery in the field" that the men in the other infantry battalions had received.

It often amazed me how so much good service went unrecognized because it was not dramatic enough to please the Staff officers. They always wanted to know: "How many of the enemy did he kill?", as if killing the enemy was the only way to win a war, which it isn't. One of our chaps had 16 months in 'ops' and wore three wound stripes. When we tried to get him a medal for a very brave series of actions, we were told that no one action by itself was worthy of a decoration. Apparently the Staff couldn't add. He never got a decoration, but he did get a fourth wound stripe. I guess you can't have everything.

Once in a while we scored. We had one chap who was the sanitary man. He had the rottenest job in the battalion and he did it well, for months on end. In the line or in rest, he went his weary way with his lime bucket, covering up everything from stinking latrines to dead mules. His contribution to the health of the troops must have been considerable. He was no budding field marshal and didn't even rate one hook. Once he said to me, "I'm only the sanitary man, but I'd rather be a good sanitary man than a poor sergeant." He had the right idea, and his humble services were actually recognized. Of course, a few haughty warriors raised their eyebrows when his Mention-in-Dispatches was announced. But few men in the battalion ever consistently served the cause better. Many a bronze Oak Leaf is worn on a medal ribbon for doing less.

Without the cook, the sanitary man, the clerk in the orderly room, or the storeman in the QM stores, the chaps with the guns couldn't have fought the war.

The regimental stretcher bearers probably had the most dangerous job of all. When everyone else was eating the dirt in the deepest slit trench to be found, or cowering behind stone walls, the stretcher bearers were standing upright amid the flying steel and the whizzing bullets, looking for the wounded to succor and the stricken to carry off the field.

Matching civilian skills with military requirements was never an easy thing to do, apparently. It used to be said that no army cook had ever so much as boiled water before he was put in the cook-house. We all remember that wartime joke of the orderly sergeant bawling out, "Who called the cook a bastard?", followed by the reply, "Who called the bastard a cook?"

Like most accusations there was some truth in it, but there were some good cooks in the army. In our battalion the sergeant cook, a chap named Val Alcock, not only knew how to cook, but he was convinced, like Napoleon, that an army marched on its stomach. He therefore spared no effort to get the food forward during action. When we were in rest, his supervision of the company cooks showed his genuine concern for the taste buds and hungry bellies of his fighting comrades. Twice the battalion was in the line on Christmas Day. On both occasions the bringing up and issuing of the traditional holiday foodstuffs came under the category of gallant and distinguished service in the field. The first year the battalion was in such close contact with the enemy, in fact surrounded, Christmas dinner came up a few days late and was served in a cemetery, in pouring rain with desultory shellfire instead of Christmas music. Our sergeant cook was a sharp-tongued fellow, who unfortunately spent too much time annoying his superiors. He should have received an award, but he didn't.

New Year's Eve was for me a welcome respite. For some reason I was in a small village called Russi, then about three miles from the forward slit trenches. There I ran into Major Lloyd Smith, a 48th Highlander, who was also out of the Line for the moment. He invited me up to his quarters in a deserted village house, produced a bottle of whisky and a piper. The music and the alcohol made us forget the grim side of the war, and thus we two welcomed in what was to prove the year of Victory. For some years now, a long distance phone call has brought our voices together as we recall that evening and salute another New Year in the comfort of our respective homes.

So ended 1944. Our battalion's battle casualties since we had left our summer holiday area five months before were, in round figures, 525, of whom forty were officers. Normal wastage from sickness, non-battle injuries and other causes added many more to this total. On January 6 a draft of 112 Other Ranks beefed us up somewhat. Three days before, we had been shifted by march route to the village of Villanova where our role was that of counterattack force, in case the enemy decided to attack our forward troops.

Frequent visits from the Brigade Commander were designed to keep us on our toes. I remember him touring our rest area to ensure that we were spending our time in vigorous training in battle techniques and not just lolling about. We were training several hours a day, even though the ground was frozen hard and covered with snow.

Coming upon a soldier who was adopting a fire position with a 'projector, infantry, anti-tank' (or PIAT, as it was more often called), the red-tabbed visitor stopped to watch the procedure. He was not pleased with what he saw. "This man would never be able to use his weapon effectively if that's the way he'd go about it," the brigadier fumed. Then, striding over to the chap lying on the frozen, snow-powdered mud he spat out sarcastically, "Do you think you could ever hit an enemy tank from that sort of position?"

"I think so, sir," answered the lad. "I hit two of them this way last month."

It so happened that the young private had been put in for the Distinguished Conduct Medal for breaking up an enemy attack, having ambushed a pair of tanks with accompanying infantry less than three weeks before! He had knocked out the leading tank with his first bomb. He struck a second tank with his second bomb, but it had failed to explode. His third bomb killed a number of infantry following behind the armour. The brigadier was not quite so cocksure of his anti-tank theories from then on. The private got his DCM, which he richly deserved.

Between those who command and those who obey there is always some sort of gap in understanding. On another, earlier battlefield I recall a general criticizing us because we had not kept up to a "creeping" barrage in a recent attack. Because of this, he claimed, we had failed to capture our objective. He was probably right. The facts of life were, however, that keeping up to a barrage by "leaning on it", as the general insisted we should do, was a very unpleasant occupation. Shellfire, especially when a wide "curtain" of it comes screaming and crashing overhead just a few yards in front of an infantryman's plodding pace, can be deadly to our own troops. Besides, the enemy liked to drop his defensive fire just our side of the barrage and our troops knew this. They felt safer by hanging back a bit, taking their chances with enemy machine-guns once the barrage had moved on. Casualties from our own barrage were "acceptable" we were told, providing the attack was a success. Unfortunately, this attitude was not popular with the troops! We just didn't want to become "acceptable" under such circumstances. The general's theories were correct, but they wouldn't work in practice.

As we stood in a semi-circle around the general, a lone shell whined overhead, to burst fully a hundred yards away. Instantly the general's posture changed. He was flat on the ground, "taking cover". The rest of us remained standing. I don't remember any further lectures on "leaning on the barrage". Anyway, "creeping" barrages and the set-piece attack gradually went out of style, which was a good thing.

While we were in the rest area the Battalion was advised that it had been awarded two MBEs, one for an officer and one for a warrant officer. At his daily conference the CO said he intended to award the officer's MBE to the officer who had served longest with the battalion in the Field. "Who is that, Shuter?" he asked the Adjutant. Shuter replied that it was me. "Oh," said the CO, "who has had the next longest service?" He was informed, and the *other one* got the MBE. I had been with the Battalion for more than eighteen months, the MBE recipient for about ten. The warrant officer's MBE went most deservedly to CSM Lloyd Oakley who had been twice recommended for the MM without success.

Later in January we were in the Line again, but things were quiet. The ground was white with snow, and the only disconcerting things were the telltale black marks where mortar bombs had fallen. Going from company to company on my daily visits these sable pockmarks in the snow made me speed my steps, hoping that no bombs would fall on the frozen ground during my afternoon 'walk'. The companies were in sandbagged farmhouses with slit trenches around their perimeters. The ground was absolutely flat and the enemy was hidden behind the Senio dykes. There were tree lines and ditches and these could be followed with the odd dash across open spaces in case an enemy sniper was taking a bead from a loophole in the dyke.

Brigade attempted to unnerve the enemy by pretending that patrols were sneaking up on him. This was done by night patrols who put out loudspeaker equipment behind some clump of bush which later on broadcast the sound of a fairly noisy patrol. It was hoped that this would make the enemy open up, so we could plot his positions for counter-mortar fire. Unhappily, the first night the system was placed between the lines there was a quick thaw and the Germans were not fooled by the sound of heavy footsteps on frozen ground!

One dark night, one of our subalterns, a particular friend of mine named Des Egan, was detailed to take a small contact patrol out into the debatable land over which both German and Allied patrols occasionally roamed. His principal task was, as the name of his patrol indicates, to make contact with the troops on our right to ensure that they were alert and that no enemy penetration between our right flank and their left flank had occurred.

It was a foul night, windy and wet, and even though Des and his comrades moved slowly the exertion of crawling through mud and over rough ground was exhausting. Finally, they came upon what they assumed was the left

248

hand post of the troops on our right flank. These were Italians, soldiers of the *Gruppa Cremona*, a combat formation which had been organized after the Italians had broken with Germany and become our co-belligerents.

Egan gave the password, but there was no answer. He crawled closer to the outline of the post and peered in. Two Italian soldiers dozed peacefully in their slit trench, well below the lip. Obviously, they were observing nothing. Nor were they exposing their cheeks to the biting Adriatic breezes of a February night! But they were maintaining their own form of alert. One had a string attached to the firing mechanism of a machine-gun for quick initial action. The other had a long stick between his legs, sloping over his shoulder. Tied to the end of this stick was a white flag! This, presumably, was ready for secondary action. We were always a bit uncertain after that, when the *Gruppa Cremona* held the line on our flank.

February saw the battalion still holding a static front. The weather was cold, the ground frozen and covered by snow. The Senio dykes separated the opposing sides. By night, standing patrols protected the fortified houses where the majority of the troops sheltered from the cold and from the occasional shelling and mortaring.

Raiding was not often undertaken during WW II since the periods of position warfare were short, but on 16 February a strong German raiding party pulled off a stunt that cost our side 17 prisoners. With a heavy artillery and mortar program, they completely boxed off one rifle company, cut its communication with the battalion and rushed the position with great daring.

This company was in a square formation, with each corner in a farm building. Two platoons were forward; the rear platoon and company HQ completed the square. Between these four was a fifth building in which an artillery OP was protected by a rifle section detached from one of the platoons. On the second floor of this building were a section of MMGs, a couple of wireless operators and a stretcher bearer.

Beginning at 3 a.m. the four corners and middle building were pounded with shells for almost 40 minutes. Meanwhile the enemy raiding party, estimated at 25, overcame the slit trench sentry posts at the front and rear of the middle building from which the bombardment had been suddenly lifted. The Germans rushed in to the ground floor where most of the garrison was cowering. These men were overcome without a chance of fighting back and were frog-marched into the inky blackness across the Senio dykes. They included the NCO in charge, a man who had recently won the Military Medal for his bravery, two signallers and the off-duty members of the rifle and MMG sections.

Upstairs the duty men on the MMGs were helpless. To fire down the stone steps into the ground floor, or to sweep the barnyard with fire as the Germans fled with their captives, would like as not have killed friend as well as foe.

The Brigade Commander was furious. Unfortunately for me, the CO was on a 48-hour leave at an Officers' rest centre and I was acting in command. I was told by the Brigadier that the men upstairs should have fired on the enemy anyway and if some of our chaps had been hit, so what? As it was, I had visited all four company positions just before dusk, and I knew how they were organized. Having ascertained the Germans' clever fire plan from post-raid questioning, I determined that we could not be faulted for the way we were holding our sector. It was just one of those things.

The Senio raid was our Italian *finale*.

By March 5, we were on American Liberty ships in Leghorn harbour. On April 4, we were in the bunkers of the Siegfried Line. It was an unbelievable change of scene. Some of us, though we were very few, had been on Italian soil for twenty months. It had been a long haul from the Pachino beaches up to the Valley of the Po. Since Pachino, one hundred and seventy-two officers had passed through the RCR, of which thirty-five were buried in Italian soil. Some three hundred and sixty Other Ranks had been killed and about twelve hundred wounded. Others were to be killed and wounded in Holland within the next few weeks, but only a few. VE-Day was not far off, although we did not know it, as we sailed for Marseilles. Only four officers had seen both the beginning and end of the Sicilian-Italian campaign. These were myself, John Praysner the QM, Freddie Sims and Abe Pettem. But the latter two had been back in the U.K. for eight months in 1944, and had missed the trench warfare around Ortona, and both the Hitler Line and Gothic Line battles.

As the coast of Italy faded into the misty distance I thought of Billy Pope and his swashbuckling question, "Have you seen much of death in the sun — in the morning?" Some of us had seen a lot of death in the sun — in the morning. We had seen it in the afternoon, in the evening, and in the pitch dark — too much of it. And some of us were to see more. Fortunately, I was not to be one of them.

Pope and Crowe, the first two RCR officers killed. Thirty-four other officers were among the 370 all ranks killed, out of a total of 1,577 RCR battle casualties.

CHAPTER XVIII

FINALLY, THE SIEGFRIED LINE

In the early fall of 1939, when my security guard at the local armoury was pacing its beat, I often joined the off-duty members for a late-night snack at a restaurant across the street. The song we usually sang before we went back home, me to my boarding house and the men to their cots in the armoury, was *We're Going To Hang Out the Washing on the Siegfried Line*.

A year later, in England, with Hitler's invasion barges collecting at the Channel ports the music hall version in London and around the country was,

> I'm going to hang out the washing
>   in my own back yard,
> If my own back yard's still there.

Now, almost five years after Dunkirk, I was to hang out my washing on the Siegfried Line and I did so. Never, while I fought in North Africa, in Sicily, or during the eighteen months' trek up the Italian peninsula did I ever contemplate doing that. But on March 31, 1945, I did.

The Reichwald Forest on the German-Dutch border, through which the heavily fortified northern end of the Siegfried Line ran, was to be our next pre-battle assembly area. For a month we had been refitting and training for another walk into battle, but more or less taking our ease at the Belgian village of Schilde on the outskirts of Antwerp.

During the Schilde rest period I spent some time encouraging our "Drums", taking them to Headquarters First Canadian Army and arranging local Retreat ceremonies both to engender regimental spirit and to amuse the Belgians. There is an old song which goes, "You'd be much better off in the band." But a bandsman's lot is not always a happy one. It is not all marching and counter-marching in Vatican Square to the *huzzahs* of the Roman populace! It is not all exciting fights with infiltrating paratroopers, such as at Rimini. There is a sterner side. Spit and polish, for instance. During the sojourn in Belgium one of the drummers was charged with "conduct to the prejudice of good order and military discipline in that he at Schilde, on such-and-such a date and time, did allow his drag rope to drag in such a manner as to get in a filthy condition and appeared at Retreat with it in such a state as to disgrace the Regiment." At the time buzz bombs were zipping overhead to fall on nearby Antwerp, and our entry into the battle for Holland was just a few days off. But it does go to show that, no matter what sort of excitement is in the offing, if you give some people enough rope they'll hang themselves. At least, that seemed to be the Regimental-Sergeant-Major's belief when he laid the charge.

At the end of March I arrived with an advance party to prepare the Siegfried Line bunkers and dugouts to accommodate the battalion, which was to move in four days later. On April 7, the CO briefed the officers on the next operation — the crossing of the Ijssel River in Holland and the capture of the town of Appeldoorn. Although we were then on German soil we were in a corner of Germany that was flanked on both sides by Dutch territory. The Regiment was to move to a concentration area about twenty miles north, between Zutphen and Deventer and from there launch its attack westward.

By now the tension between the CO and me had reached the stage where one of us had to go. Quite obviously it had to be the subordinate. I was packed off to Ghent where it was anticipated a 'kick upstairs' would see me given my lieutenant-colonelcy. This didn't happen. I ended up as the Second-in-Command of No. 2 Canadian Disciplinary Centre, a huge barbed-wire enclosure out in the Belgian boondocks, full of Canadian deserters, blackmarket operators and other assorted army criminals, both for military and civil offences. The CO, a militia martinet from Toronto, named Medhurst, ran as 'tight a ship' as I have ever seen. Fortunately, I saw it for less than two weeks, for on 2 May I flew back to England. I expected to continue on to Canada to stand in the Ontario provincial elections, having been unanimously nominated to oppose Hon. Mitch Hepburn, the former Premier of Ontario, in the riding of Elgin.

While at the Disciplinary Centre letters from The Regiment revealed to me that the Appeldoorn fighting had been relatively light and successful, with only twelve killed and forty-nine wounded. One of the dead was Freddie Sims. He had been the first officer to land in Sicily, detailed to guide us through the gaps blown in the wire by the gapping party. He was killed at an O-Group when a dud shell came through the window, and hit and fragmented a heating radiator. It was a piece of the radiator metal that killed Freddie. He was the last person of The Regiment, officer or man, killed by enemy action.

Don Mackenzie, CO of the 48th Highlanders had also been killed and this, too, saddened me. The night before I left the Reichwald, Don and some of his officers, had 'dined me out' at their mess in a stable just outside the battered town of Kranenburg. The dinner had been my farewell to the boys of the Old Brigade. Being out of favour with my own CO, nothing could be expected in my own mess.

When Mackenzie had been 2IC of the 48th, during the Hitler Line fighting and before, he and I had often gone off together on Brigade 'scat parties'. This term derived from the codeword 'scat' — the signal for battalion 2ICs and sub-unit representatives to leave immediately for some general billeting or bivouac area, there to subdivide and signpost specific locations. Then, when unit vehicles or the marching troops arrived, they could be quickly and smoothly guided into their new stopping place. If the move were strictly an administrative move the cooks usually came with us so that a hot meal would await the troops on arrival. The doors of buildings would be marked with chalk as to who, or how many, they were to accommodate. Arrows were nailed on trees or hammered into the ground on posts to indicate traffic circles. If it were a night move, shielded lamps with unit and sub-unit designations were set out. Then we set off for the Brigade dispersal point to await the convoy or marching column and guide them in to the proper areas.

Some months before, the CO of the RCR, Dan Spry, had put up signs in the battalion billet area which read "Be Alert!", "Never pass a fault," or, "Are *you* a Royal Canadian?" It so happened that the 48th wore red pompons on their headdress, known in Highland language as 'toories'. They also wore blue half-puttees around their ankles. Mackenzie, who had a sense of humour, had got a bit of a laugh out of our slogans and decided to do something about it. In January or February, 1944, we had been relieved in the Line by the 48th and had taken over their reserve position spread over several little villages behind San Vito. When we marched into the hamlet where our Battalion Headquarters was to be we saw a large, freshly-painted sign hung over the door. It read,

Toories red, puttees blue,
We're alert the same as you!   -

A few months later in the Liri Valley, I was standing beside Mackenzie at the Brigade Dispersal Point waiting for our marching battalions to arrive, so we could guide them to their respective bivouac areas. The Hastings and Prince Edward Regiment had gone by. The 48th had not yet come into view, the RCR were bringing up the rear. All of a sudden, a very scruffy, ragged and unshaven Italian, carrying a big bundle on his shoulders, staggered along the dusty road in front of us.

To annoy me, Mackenzie stepped forward and called out to the dreadful-looking fellow: "Hallo there! Are *you* a Royal Canadian?"

The old chap blinked, shifted his bundle, but still staggering on, simply turned his head toward us and to our astonishment answered in passable English: "No, no, no, Signor. I am only *Italiano refugio*. But I liva for sixa year in Pittsburgh-a P-A."

When I got to England I went to see the Agent-General for Ontario, Jimmy Armstrong, recently 'civilianized' from being a major in the 48th. We dined at the Carleton Club in St. James' and cables were sent off to the Hon. George Drew, leader of the Ontario Tories saying that I was on my way. Alas, the next morning a return cable apologetically explained that a second nomination meeting had to be held since I had not replied to the nomination cables within the required two weeks. Prime Minister Mackenzie King had put the federal election date forward, causing the Ontario elections to be moved forward as well. A new candidate, Fletcher Thomas had been nominated. He beat Hepburn hands down. A teddy bear could have done it, as Mitch was finally in great disfavour, even his staunchest supporters having deserted him.

The whole mess was caused by my having left The Regiment the day the cables — one from the Party Chairman, one from the Constituency, one from Drew and one from my father — had arrived. The Postal Corporal did not try to find out where I had gone but merely sent them to *Post Restante* annotated 'Not at Unit'. It took three weeks for me to get them.

So ended, ingloriously, my first attempt at entering politics.

I left London and went to Aldershot where I looked up Dan Spry, now General Officer Commanding Canadian Reinforcement Units in the U.K. Their formation patch was a bright yellow maple leaf within a bright yellow circle. They called it their 'flaming arsehole'.

Dan got me an appointment as CO of a training battalion which was made up of the rump of the Winnipeg Grenadiers, most of whose officers and men had gone off in drafts to other regiments on the Continent. Promotions were frozen, so I remained a major.

On May 8, I was in London. For me VE-Day was a delirious Piccadilly Circus, a swarming Whitehall. It was Winston Churchill on a balcony giving his famous two-fingered V-sign. It was the sounding of the ceremonial

"Cease Fire" by buglers of the Scots Guards. Next, it was the stentorian tones of Churchill proclaiming his hopes for the Nation he had led so well during five years of war.

"Advance, Britannia!" he said. The thousands in the street below roared their approval, Cec Hollingsworth and I among them. Cec was on leave and our meeting had been a chance one, as I had not seen him since he had left Italy months before.

We were swept down The Mall to the Palace, to see the lights of London shine again, to cheer the King, and to see a slim princess in ATS khaki. That princess was destined to wear the heavy crown of a disintegrating Empire. How little we could see of the years ahead, that VE-Day in London.

It was an especially emotional experience for me. On May 12, 1937 I had stood in the same spot before the Palace and cheered the newly crowned King and Queen on their return from their coronation ceremonies. In 1941 I had driven past in a taxicab and seen the bomb destruction of the east wing of the Palace and the huge crater between the main gate and the Victoria Memorial. Now, on a third historic occasion I again stood before Buckingham Palace.

As dusk fell the lights in front of the Palace, up Constitution Hill and along Buckingham Palace Road came slowly on. It was a magnificent moment in history. For the first time in almost six years the lights of London shone again. The roar of the crowd, stretching from the Palace gates all the way back to Admiralty Arch was like the roar of gigantic breakers rolling in from an angry sea. But this sea of faces was not angry. It was as massive a manifestation of human joy as Man might ever see.

Darkness deepened. I boarded a commuters' train and left for Reigate, our billet area during the almost unremembered days of the Battle of Britain, five years before. Less than an hour later, having detrained at the Redhill Station, I walked past the *Forester's Arms*, the pub which stood in the centre of the old "D" Company billets. The door was wide open, the lights blazing. There was no blackout necessary now. By government order the pubs had been given a late closing time to celebrate the victory in Europe.

I turned back and walked inside. There he was, our former CQMS, who had married the publican's widow after the bomb fell during that amazing summer in 1940. A long-serving Regular, he had taken his pension halfway through the war and settled down as the new landlord of the *Forester's Arms*.

"Hello, Meadows," said I, glad to see a familiar face on this day of days. It had been a long time. Many changes had taken place. On my shoulders I wore a Major's crowns. Sewed on my left breast was the ribbon of the Africa Star with First Army clasp. And on my left sleeve there was a gold wound stripe.

"Why, *Mister* Galloway!" he greeted me. Then taking me by the arm he called his wife, who was busy at the taps. "Look here, it's *Mister* Galloway, the "D" Company salvage officer, remember?" She handed me a beer.

The paths of glory had not led me to the Grave, but back to the corner pub as if nothing had happened in between. The taste of Victory was in my mouth and the taste was mild and bitter. The past five years with its death and destruction, its losses and its disappointments, its hurts and its frustrations had passed like a dream in the night. Scores of my fellow Royal Canadians who had known Reigate as almost a second home were buried in Sicily or Italy, or back in Canada occupying hospital beds, or getting back into civilian life with weakened limbs and infirm bodies. Others, like me, had survived, still strong and well. For us there remained the challenge of Japan.

This day was Victory Day in Europe. And I thought back to the days when all had seemed lost, when invasion had threatened England and I had stood, homesick and wondering what the invasion would really be like and whether we would win the war after all. But now we had. My memories then were of home, not of recently quitted foreign fields. Of school friends and townspeople, not of dead and missing comrades-in-arms. I had written a poem in December, 1940, composing it in my mind as I stood watch on the Palace Pier at Brighton. I had called it *Mirage*, and had subtitled it 'A Canadian Soldier in England, 1940':

I stood, I confess,
With a whimsical stare
At the little street;
For I saw it there,
Filled with the faces
Of Long Ago.
—Now it was sunny,
Now covered with snow;
But the same old street,
The same old scene
As in summer or winter
It always had been.
Old friends passed
By my lonely stand;
In turn to each
I offered my hand

* * *

But it fell untouched —
I could not understand.

Then for an instant
I shifted my glance,
Hearing a bomber flight
Bound for France;
And the reel I imagined
Suddenly snapp'd,
As the screen of my vision
Another view trapped.
My friends?
They had vanished
In vague retreat,
And taken with them
That dear old street.
Then I saw,
(For my eye had played the liar
Till the spell had been broke
By the aerial choir) —

*   *   *

The "dragon's teeth"
And the Dannert wire!

I volunteered to join the Pacific Force for service against Japan and went home in a packed troopship, the *Nieuw Amsterdam*. We sailed out of Liverpool in July. There were thirty-two majors in one cabin, but only sixteen bunks. So we each had to spend half the time on deck. There were four basins, so shaving in the early morning to make the breakfast line-up was a real rush.

Between VE-Day and embarkation I enjoyed a short holiday at Virginia Water, the guest of Brig.-Gen. John Charteris and his wife. Charteris had been Haig's personal intelligence officer in the Great War and has been blamed for a great many of the failures Haig experienced, especially the blood baths on the Somme and at Passchendaele. Charteris was accused of feeding the Commander-in-Chief a lot of imaginative nonsense about the enemy, which resulted in many a battlefield disaster. He and his wife were very kind to me. They had had their own personal tragedy, their only son having been killed in North Africa with the Parachute Regiment.

I had a blazer and flannels with me and spent most of my time walking around the countryside, coming back to the house for meals. The immediate postwar election campaign was on. I helped Charteris, a real Tory, nail up posters on behalf of Churchill and the Conservative Party. It didn't work. Churchill was defeated and Attlee and the Labour Party came in.

Charteris had his World War I medals framed and hanging on the dining room wall. One of them was a Japanese order. One of my friends had told me that his father, a Canadian officer in the first World War, also had a Japanese medal. The day after Pearl Harbour he had thrown it into the river at Saskatoon. I asked Charteris why he hadn't done the same sort of thing. "It looks much too nice in that frame", he replied.

The *Nieuw Amsterdam* docked at Halifax, where I had embarked five years before. Soon trains sped us westward. Halfway to Toronto I found that I could detrain in Toronto and go directly to my parents' home. I had put my destination down as the Regimental Depot at London, Ontario, being of the opinion that I had to report there first. I had no way of warning my parents, so when I got off the train at Union Station in Toronto at about 5 a.m. no one met me. The station was all but deserted and I was the only person to leave the train there.

While I was standing around, wondering what to do, a young civilian idler saw my shoulder flashes. "Royal Canadian Regiment, eh?" he queried. Then added, "Was you at Dieppe?"

Shortly before the war, when a number of regimental amalgamations took place in the militia, the Royal Toronto Grenadiers and the Toronto Regiment were fused under one name — The Royal Regiment of Canada. This confused them with us, or vice versa, depending on how you look at it. Such a similarity of name should never have been allowed. When the Royal Regiment of Canada was shot to pieces at Dieppe, many people thought it was The Royal Canadian Regiment that had suffered so grievously in that shocking raid. We, of course, were quite safe in our English camp, having neither shared in that gory episode nor deserved any part of its glory. Frequently, press stories confused the two regiments, to the annoyance of both and to the bewilderment of friends and families back in Canada.

While in Italy, I received a very nasty letter from the clerk of a municipality in the South of England, blasting The Royal Canadian Regiment's transport for having damaged some brick gateposts by crashing into them and then neglecting to contact the municipality to make amends. The date of the offence was while the RCR was fighting in Sicily. I informed the municipal official of that fact in rather blistering terms. It had been, of course, a vehicle of the Royal Regiment of Canada which had done the damage. No doubt there were other occasions when the Royal Regiment got blamed for the wrongdoings of some of our chaps.

Whoever it was who approved the adoption of a regimental name so similar to one that had been in existence for decades past was very stupid indeed, in my view.

I slept on a bench until 7 a.m., then took a taxi to my parents' house. I roused them from bed as they hadn't expected me until late the next day. Both looked much older. The last five years had been a worry to them, as it was to most parents with sons overseas. My brother had grown from a twelve-year-old to a young man of seventeen. He was a stranger. There was so much to say and no way of saying it. I was glad I had not returned to a wife and kiddies. It must have been difficult to adjust after so long apart. After a week of this unreal life I was ready to leave for the invasion of Japan. I took the train for London, reporting at the Regimental Depot, eager to see where I would be sent.

I had another shock awaiting me.

Ten years before, when I had qualified as a lieutenant at the same Wolseley Barracks, I had been billetted on a bandsman named Pannell. He was a refined sort of chap and played the oboe, one of the most difficult reed instruments. He was a veteran of the Great War in which he served with the British Army. By virtue of my being billetted in his married quarter he automatically became my batman, making my bed, polishing my brass, my belt and my shoes, doing my laundry and pressing my clothes. He brought me my cup of tea every morning and performed his duties perfectly. Five years later, when I was appointed to the Regiment for active service I was delighted to find that Pannell was now a Quartermaster-Sergeant. It was he who issued me my battledress and such other necessaries from QM stores. This was not a 'free' issue, of course. Officers had to pay for everything. I congratulated Pannell on his upward mobility, as they call it in these modern times and he wished me well as an officer, newly-appointed to *his* regiment.

Now, five and a half years later, on arriving at the Depot, I was told to report to the Depot Commander, and was shown to his office. There was a clerk outside and he ushered me into the Depot Commander's presence. I entered the office and saluted the figure seated behind the desk. It was *Major* Frank Pannell!

"Good to see you, Strome", he greeted me. "I must say, you did very well during this war."

On VJ-Day I was in my hometown in Western Ontario. My war actually ended on the same block of pavement where it began in the same month six years before. In August 1939 I had posted my first militia sentries outside the Post Office as security guards for the armoury on the second floor. On VJ-Day I stood beside the Mayor and the local militia company commander and took the Salute as the town's Boy Scouts, Wolf Cubs, Girl Guides, Legion members and various other local organizations marched by, headed by the town band. Everybody wanted to shake my hand. I was the hero of the moment and after the parade most of the fellows headed for the Legion Hall to get 'sloshed'. Several chaps from the Regiment, who had been wounded and already discharged were in the crowd. One of these was my long-time batman, Joe Carroll. He had been invalided out in Belgium with bad feet only five months before.

Shortly afterwards I was dispatched to Vernon, B.C., where the Pacific Force was assembling. The dropping of the Atom Bomb had rendered the Pacific expedition unnecessary. The School of Infantry, commanded by Colonel Eric Snow was also located at Vernon. He had asked for me to fill a lieutenant-colonel's vacancy on his staff. Slim Liddell, my old running-mate of the Pachino landing was already there. He too was scheduled for promotion to lieutenant-colonel. But neither of us was promoted, though for twenty-four hours we were convinced that our new stars were already breaking through the skin on our shoulders.

Snow paraded us to the Senior Officer in the area, a Brigadier Jefferson. He merely signed the promotion documents and congratulated the two of us. The promotions were then wired to Army Headquarters in Ottawa for confirmation. Next day a return wire informed Vernon that the vacancies had been blocked for two Lieutenant-Colonels, Big Jim Stone and Sid Thomson, both of whom everyone knew. They were arriving to fill *our vacancies* in a few days time!

It had been a year of disappointments from a career standpoint, if wartime soldiering for a non-regular can have career implications in the correct sense of the word. But, urged by Colonel Snow, I decided to apply for the postwar Regular Army. I did, and was accepted as a major. This was something. At the time, due to the very small peacetime army proposed, a great many applicants were accepted only if they agreed to drop one or two ranks.

So began my twenty-four years as a Regular soldier.

RCR Officers at the Front, Ortona, January 9, 1944. Wilkes, John, Praysner, Smith, Burdett, Hart (RCAMC), Mitchell, Liddell, Roy, Mathers, Galloway, Littleford.

CHAPTER XIX

SOLDIER NO MORE

As admitted earlier, both sides of my family are singularly lacking in military traditions. As a boy this troubled me greatly. My whole world was a world of soldiers. I had toy soldiers by the dozens. I looked at pictures of soldiers by the hour. Soldiers on parade, or walking singly down the street, always fascinated me. Yet my own family tree was almost devoid of soldiers.

My mother's paternal ancestry traced back to 1690 in the Rhenish Palatinate. Between 1725 and 1765 various of her forbears emigrated to America. They became British subjects and settled down on the rich farmlands of the colony of Pennsylvania, along with others of their kind. These included the Pershings and the Eisenhowers, both of which families, in a future generation, produced a Commander-in-Chief for American armies fighting two successive world wars against their former homeland. These people came from the same district along the Upper Rhine as did my mother's family. They emigrated in the same time-frame, to the same place in America and for the same reason — to get away from European soldiers. They were avowed pacifists! As for the Strome family, apparently the only soldier it ever produced was my mother's brother, the Sapper subaltern of the first World War, whom I referred to in an earlier chapter.

I was much happier about my mother's maternal forbears. They were Scots. Her great-grandfather, John Pirie, had been a Gordon Highlander. He and his father were glovers in Huntly, a small town in the Strathbogie district of Aberdeenshire. When the Napoleonic Wars began to menace Britain's freedom he left the family business and enlisted in the 92nd Gordons as a volunteer private. At Fuentes d'Onor in Spain on May 5, 1811, a cannon ball mangled one of his arms during the furious bombardment of the British infantry which characterized that day's fighting. It had to be amputated. He was discharged with slightly less than five years service and awarded a pension. He received the Peninsular Medal with one clasp, that for Fuentes d'Onor, which indicates it was his only battle.

The Galloways were also Scottish. According to Burke's *Landed Gentry*, they date back for more than fourteen generations to John de Galloway, who was living in 1449. Family tradition takes us back another 250 years to Thomas de Galloway, Earl of Atholl, whose brother Alan de Galloway, Constable of Scotland, was present at Runnymede as one of King John of England's Securities to Magna Carta on June 18, 1215. His name appears in the preamble to the charter and his seal of Arms is affixed with those of the other great men of that day. Alan was the only Scot present. He was there because he also held land in England as a vassal of King John.

The Constable's descendants became extinct in the male line and those of Thomas de Galloway faded into a long line of churchmen, farmers and for a time, petty landowners with the odd contractor, town clerk and banker thrown in. None of them had any money. My own direct line produced for several generations the impoverished Lairds of Lipnoch, a small estate next to that of the Alexanders of Menstrie. One of those, Sir William Alexander of Menstrie, was the founder of Nova Scotia. Strangely enough, the Irish Alexanders from whom Field Marshal Alexander, the Allied C-in-C in Italy sprang, claim descent from the Alexanders of Menstrie, their Irish domicile dating only from Cromwell's time.

One supposed direct ancestor of mine, Robert Galloway, was present at Flodden on September 9, 1513. He escaped the slaughter which saw the complete destruction of the Scottish army by the English. King James IV was himself

266

killed in the fray. Robert was a personal attendant to Sir Alexander Seton, his feudal lord. Seton held the office of Armour Bearer to the slain King. Eleven years after the battle, Robert Galloway was awarded four pounds from the Royal Exchequer in payment for having saved and safeguarded some of the King's personal belongings, which he took with him when he fled from the stricken field.

In the mid-17th Century, a rather distant collateral branch of the family was raised to the peerage by King Charles I. It was probably because of this connection that my branch of the family had the good fortune to obtain its grant of the lands of Lipnoch, becoming minor Perthshire heritors under the *Great Seal Charter* of March 1, 1634. Sir James Galloway, who was later to become Lord Dunkeld, held the office of Master of Requests to the King in Scotland. To have 'friends at Court' is always an advantage. Having a kindly disposed kinsman there is even better.

The third Lord Dunkeld fought under Dundee at Killiecrankie. Fleeing as a Jacobite fugitive he joined Dillon's Regiment in the French service. He was killed as a colonel during the wars of the Spanish Succession. His son, the fourth Lord Dunkeld, led the Irish Brigade at the Battle of Laeffelt in 1747. He gained the Cross of St. Louis and a pension of 3000 *Livres* for his distinguished conduct on that day. He died a Lieutenant-General without children, so this branch of the Galloways became extinct. However, Her Majesty's Lyon Court in Edinburgh has issued Letters Patent allowing our branch of the family to use the armorial bearings of the Lords Dunkeld with certain heraldic differences, one of which indicates our female descent from another extinct family, the Carmichaels. So much for the genealogical side of things.

Despite this lack of direct ancestral response to the military requirements of empire, both my parents were intensely British in sentiment. My mother's family insisted that their forbears were United Empire Loyalists, though it took very little research to discover that Americans who came into Upper Canada as late as 1810 were hardly entitled to be labelled 'U.E.L.' Her paternal ancestors had in fact been Simcoe Settlers, lured to living under the Union Jack again by Governor Simcoe's promises of cheap land and exemption from military service.

Looking at my family tree. Nobody on my branch had any money.

As a child I suffered every winter from bronchial trouble which confined me to bed for several weeks at a time. During these bouts my mother tirelessly read to me about such empire builders as Clive of India, Wolfe the dauntless hero, Wellington the Iron Duke, Drake and Nelson, Cromwell and even such ancient Scottish heroes as Wallace and Bruce. Thus, from my earliest days I was left in no doubt as to my identity. I was British, even though born on one of the remote and foreign-settled rims of that Empire on which the sun never set. Someday I too would fight for England, or Scotland perhaps, or would it be for Saskatchewan? It really didn't matter, since for me they were all one and the same.

My paternal grandfather's loyalty to the Crown manifested itself when my father was born. This was on June 20, 1887, the day of Queen Victoria's Golden Jubilee. He was christened Andrew Scott Jubilee. Indeed, the name Scott had an unusual significance as well. This was to commemorate the fact that the Scott Act, otherwise the Canada Temperance Act, which allowed municipalities to vote as to whether they were to be "wet" or "dry", had been voted upon locally, bringing my grandfather's town into the "wet" category, which was the category he favoured.

Peacetime soldiering has many facets and in many ways is as different from wartime soldiering as chalk is from cheese. My first postwar appointment was to the University of Toronto officers' training corps as Administrative and Training Officer. This looked like a cushy billet and I was pleased with the job. Three weeks after I arrived a Staff officer phoned me to tell me I was to be replaced. It had been determined at District Headquarters that I had neither a university degree nor had I been to Army Staff College, the two requirements for the job. The Staff officer who phoned didn't mention anything about my academic deficiency, but he did say: "You didn't go to Staff College, did you?" When I replied that I hadn't, because I had fought the entire war as a regimental officer at the slit trench level, he put me in my place by saying, "Well, you certainly wasted your time during the war, Galloway, old man."

My next two months were spent on leave until something was found for me to do. Eventually, I was posted to Army Headquarters at Ottawa where I was fitted into a desk in the Directorate of Army Personnel. Here I got some staff training. One job was to draw all the files of infantry soldiers who had been dishonourably discharged during the war and provide them with honourable discharge certificates. This was necessary, as the Department of Labour was complaining that these wretches were swelling the ranks of the unemployed, because nobody would hire them. When they applied for a job and were asked for references, all they could show was a paper which said they had been kicked out of the army for some military or civil crime. The ridiculous sidelight to this was that once they were given honourable discharge papers, we had to research their entitlement to campaign stars and service medals and enter these awards on their discharge certificates. Later, these medals were issued with all the others. That meant that a man who spent all his time in a military prison in Italy, or in France, was able to count this time as qualifying time for the Italy Star or the France-Germany Star and all the other concomitant medals, just as if he had spent his time fighting the enemy.

My spare time during the first six months of 1948 saw me studying for the Staff College entrance exams. I did well. Then I got married and took my bride to Staff College with me. The College was at Fort Frontenac in Kingston, Ontario. Here we underwent a ten-month academic and field exercise grind that ended with the successful candidates being given the qualification symbol *psc* after their name in the Army Gradation List. Of the 49 students on my course, nine were failed at half-term. One was a full colonel and two were lieutenant-colonels. Several had been decorated during the war, but they apparently weren't good enough in the eyes of the DS, as the Directing Staff was called.

Two years later I was back in Kingston at Fort Frontenac as a lieutenant-colonel on the DS myself. The Korean War had broken out and I had promptly asked to be posted to the 2nd Battalion of my Regiment, which was being raised from ex-soldiers for immediate dispatch to Korea. Service in Korea was denied me on the basis that I had seen enough active service already, whereas others needed the experience. I soldiered on at my desk.

My old comrade-in-arms, Major Slim Liddell, was the OC of No. 2 District Depot, which was located at Chorley Park in Toronto. He lived about forty miles from his Depot and the night that the Minister of Defense and the Chief of the General Staff were on the radio issuing a Call to Arms for the Special Force for Korea, he failed to turn his radio on. When he arrived at his Depot at 9 o'clock the next morning, not knowing about the Government's decision, he was astounded to find about 500 would-be recruits lying all over the lawn in front of his office. He usually processed one or two men a day for the Regular Army and this inundation of humanity was quite impossible to handle. For two days a chaotic situation prevailed as the stiff peacetime enlistment tests continued to be administered. Army Headquarters was soon on my phone at local headquarters asking what the hell was going on in Toronto. The *Toronto Daily Star* had reported hundreds of men enlisting for service in Korea, whereas the Depot's daily return showed one recruit! Of course, the 'hundreds' were in various stages of the peacetime enlistment process — doing intelligence tests and the like — while the Minister was screaming for mass enlistments, despite the fact that there was no way that could be accomplished. On the third day the Minister, the Hon. Brooke Claxton, flew to Toronto to put a firecracker up the Depot's rear, so to speak. He did. He bypassed all the procedures and had the men all lined up and sworn in without medicals or character checks, and hustled off to the railway station from where they were shipped up to Petawawa. It was a typical politician's solution. Scores of these enlistees were physically unfit, had been discharged previously as "unlikely to become efficient soldiers", or were found to have bad war records when their wartime files caught up with them. Few ever got to Korea, as most of those in the early rush had to be discharged within a few weeks of their faulty enlistment.

A 3rd Battalion of The Royal Canadian Regiment was also raised and a year later I was warned that I was to be a lieutenant-colonel and take it to Korea to relieve the 1st Battalion, which had succeeded the 2nd on a regimental rotation scheme. This was changed, I am told, because the CO threatened to resign his commission if he were not permitted to take his battalion to Korea. It was he who was to become a DS member at the Staff College, but somehow his threat got him out of it, and as I have already mentioned, I landed the job. To palliate my feelings, I was told that it was a better appointment from a career standpoint. But that was nonsense.

For the next three years I served on the DS. Our teaching method was tutorial in character, with visiting lecturers and demonstrations to liven things up. In the summer most of the time was devoted to outdoor tactical exercises. In these the students took the part of divisional and brigade commanders, or the staff officers of those formations. The DS members were used to create tactical and administrative problems for the play-acting generals and staff officers to solve. It was generally agreed that the DS had a much heavier load to bear than the student body. This was especially true as there was a great deal of written work to be handed in and commented upon. Since most students in the immediate postwar period were officers with service and experience almost parallel to that of the DS, it was not always easy to convince them that the "DS Solution" to any given problem was necessarily the best.

For two years I was a battalion commander in Canada. I had been transferred to the newly-formed Regiment of Canadian Guards in 1955 — then followed General Staff employment at Divisional Headquarters in Petawawa and at Army Headquarters in Ottawa.

When my battalion of Guards was in barracks at Ipperwash, I lived with my family about four miles away in the small town of Forest. Before we obtained our special British style Guards uniform, which included blue caps with a scarlet band and brass-rimmed black leather peaks for the men, I bought several experimental patterns. I had my batman wear one of these. The first day he was thus attired he happened to be out working around my house. A passing veteran, remembering that in his wartime experience red cap bands were worn only by his brigade commander and even higher echelons of command, was flabbergasted at the sight. He went into a local shop and said to the merchant, "This fellow Galloway who has rented the house across from you sure must be a big shot, he's got a brigadier shovelling the snow off his walk this morning."

"Age shall not weary them" — Regimental Dinner, Wolseley Barracks, London, Ontario in October, 1969. Sam Lerner, Don Rose, Rusty Wilkes and the author.

The Regiment of Canadian Guards was the brain-child of Lieut.-General Guy Simonds, then Chief of the General Staff. It was decided that the Regiment should comprise four battalions, one of them French-Canadian. The idea was that, since the Queen had recently been given a change in the Royal styles, designating her Queen of Canada, and no longer listing Canada merely as one of 'her Dominions beyond the Seas', she should have her own regiment of Canadian Guards, just as she had Scots Guards, Irish Guards and Welsh Guards in the United Kingdom. The new regiment was to be a *corps d'élite*. As Guards it would take precedence over all other Canadian infantry regiments. Naturally, this did not sit very well with my own regiment, which had a seventy year history with service in five wars, or with the PPCLI with nearly four decades behind it and service in three wars. Besides, it was all the Royal 22e could do to 'officer' and man its own battalions, so a plan to divert French-Canadians into a unit as British in appearance and character as a Guards regiment was not likely to succeed.

Escorting Their Excellencies, Governor-General and Mrs. Roland Michener.

The Canadian Guards came into being on October 16, 1953, when Her Majesty approved their formation. The four battalions were produced by first re-badging the 3rd Battalions of both the RCR and the PPCLI (at that time serving in Korea). They became the 1st and 2nd Battalions, respectively, of the Canadian Guards. Then the 3rd and 4th Battalions were formed out of two *ad hoc* infantry battalions which had been raised from the militia for NATO duty two years before.

All ranks serving in these four battalions were given the option of transferring to one of the three oldtime regular regiments, or of taking their discharge, or of becoming Guardsmen. A very high proportion, including nearly all the officers, elected to turn themselves into Guardsmen.

There was considerable resentment that this brand-new regiment should be given privileges in matters of precedence, dress and other favours which it automatically adopted from the Brigade of Guards in England. Some nasty remarks were made and the new Guardsmen were given a rough time by the rest of the army. Because the new regiment was unblooded and had no battle honours on its colours it was ridiculed by some tactless people. This was a foolish attitude to take, for the majority of the new Guards' officers and senior NCOs had actually won the battle honours which the RCR and PPCLI carried on their colours. Indeed, many of those by now serving in the RCR and PPCLI had no overseas service to their credit, or if they did their service had been with other wartime units. My own case was a good example. Of the twenty-seven battle honours embroidered on the RCR colours for Second World War fighting, twenty-five had been won while I was with the Regiment, some eight or ten years before. Thus, I did not accept the charge that we of the Guards had no fighting record, especially since those who threw this in our face had merely inherited what I and other newly-made Guardsmen had won on bloody fields they had never seen.

This backbiting went on for some time. Eventually, the war years were forgotten and the Guards built up such an enviable record at home and abroad that they became the smartest and proudest unit in the Canadian Army. What they lacked in history and tradition they made up in performance. The highest infantry standards — Guards' standards — were achieved. We were favoured by receiving the tallest of infantry recruits. We stressed drill, dress and deportment to the extent that soldiers in other units looked positively scruffy when placed alongside the Guards. Or so we thought. Guardsmen took prizes in all sorts of military competitions, both collectively and individually. These included shooting, weapon training and every kind of sports events. Battalions served in Germany and Cyprus with the

NATO and UN forces, where their discipline and decorum were much admired by their allies. A close liaison was established with the British Brigade of Guards and, when considered suitable to Canadian usage, their best customs were adopted.

Alas, the Regiment's history was to be a short one. The 3rd and 4th Battalions were soon disbanded. Then, after seventeen years of existence, the other two battalions, the Regimental Depot and the Band disappeared from the Order of Battle. The regiment was placed in 'suspended animation'. The officers and men were either re-badged collectively into battalions of the RCR or the PPCLI, or dispersed to other units.

A tête-a-tête with His Excellency, Governor-General Jules Léger.

In the meantime, I had been appointed Lieutenant-Colonel of the Regiment, the Colonel of the Regiment being Major-General Roger Rowley, DSO. These may be strange appointments to the uninitiated, mine particularly. Only in Guards regiments are Lieutenant-Colonels of the Regiment

276

to be found. The actual rank is Colonel, but each battalion is commanded by a Lieutenant-Colonel. Both these appointments, somewhat confusing to the civilian perhaps, are administrative, advisory and quasi-honorary in nature. I was the first, and as it happened, the only Lieutenant-Colonel of the Regiment, as the appointment was left vacant for most of the Regiment's history. I considered it a very high honour, as indeed it was, for the appointment was not routine, but conferred on me by the wish of the senior officers of the Regiment.

Much bitterness resulted from the disappearance of the Canadian Guards. We had achieved the highest standards; our morale was superb and our *esprit de corps* second to none. So much so, in fact, that ten years later regular Regimental Birthday reunions and occasional 'get-togethers' continue to be well attended by those ex-Guardsmen now in civilian life as well as those still serving, even after a decade, in other regiments. The decision to do away with the Guards was a political one and with us went the regular battalions of the Black Watch of Canada and the Queen's Own Rifles of Canada. Our crime was that we were 'too British' in uniform and character to pass muster with the Francophone hierarchy which dominated the Defense Department at the time. The Unification program was the official excuse, but the program itself was partly a gimmick to 'Americanize' the Canadian forces and eliminate, as far as possible, the British traditions of the past.

In the summer of 1957, I was one of a group of Canadian Army and RCAF officers specially selected to witness an atomic explosion in the Nevada desert. The device was exploded from a tower some miles from Las Vegas. As atmospheric conditions had to be just so before it could be exploded, we had to remain in the gambling city for nine days before being summoned to the test site. This proved a costly interlude for some. Another attraction was the Broadway cast of the *Pyjama Game* which was staying at the same hotel. By night we dined, wined and watched the extravaganzas for which Vegas is noted. Gambling, for those who took to it, went on all night. The moment for which we waited finally arrived. The desert was cold and we were bundled up and positioned behind a hill. Wearing dark glasses, facing away from the blast and with our hands covering our ears, we crouched down to minimize the shock waves. The explosion, said to be the biggest one touched off up to that date was, of course, terrific. Later, in protective vehicles we drove over the Ground Zero to examine the damage to buildings of various types, to vehicles, mobile equipment and dummy personnel. Except for the inhabitants of Hiroshima and Nagasaki, relatively few people have witnessed such a bang. As a potential destroyer of all human life and of centuries of human endeavour, it seemed rather macabre to me that these tests were being carried out so close to 'sin city' itself. One wondered what God was thinking.

I was back at Fort Frontenac for a year at the National Defense College. This was a higher fount of learning and bestowed on its 'members' — we were considered too senior to be called students — an additional post-nominal symbol of military erudition, the letters *ndc*. At NDC we were concerned with world strategy, not only in the narrow military sense, but in the economic, industrial and every other sense, on a global scale.

While at NDC we travelled far and wide; north of the Arctic Circle, then south almost to the Equator. One month we would visit North American Air Defense Headquarters at Colorado Springs, the next month the United Nations in New York City. During my term our trips included Cairo, where President Abdul Nasser of Egypt was our host; Nairobi, where we met Jomo Kenyatta; and West Berlin, where we conferred with the Lord Mayor, Willy Brandt, soon to become Chancellor of the Federal Republic of Germany. Stops along the way included Rome, Belgrade, Paris, Bonn and London. In these capitals senior defense people and top statesmen spoke to us on problems peculiar to their countries in the tangle of world politics and answered the questions we asked them.

The most dynamic personality we met was Nasser. He was also the friendliest. When he entered the ante-room where we awaited him he did it through double doors, which were thrown open for his entry. Then he stood there momentarily while flood lights played on him. Advancing with a flashing smile he put out his hand to each one of us, greeting us singly. Then he motioned us to be seated in a semi-circle of pre-placed red plush, gilt chairs and our discussion began. He was master of the dialogue that followed and his eyes were piercing.

I remember in Lagos, Nigeria, being conducted around the city in a chauffeured car with a very nice young Nigerian captain as our guide. More British than the British in his military mannerisms, dressed impeccably in British-style uniform with a gleaming Sam Browne, he described to us the sights of his nation's capital city. It was obvious that he was very proud of what had been accomplished in the past decade. Suddenly, he blurted out, "Oh, Yes, Gentlemen, I must now show you the factory where we make the Coca-Cola, the famous Nigerian drink, now, I understand, becoming most popular in the United States of America."

1967: From Her Majesty The Queen — a smile.

In London, Lord Mountbatten proved a charmer. He was full of good humour and joked about the changed conditions under which he had served compared to those under which his father, His Serene Highness Prince Louis of Battenberg had served prior to 1914 — both holding the same appointment. He said that had his father lived to see the day when an admiral actually polished his own shoes he would have had an apoplexy.

On leaving the NDC I was appointed Commander of Fort Churchill, a Tri-Service station on the shores of Hudson Bay in Northern Manitoba. It was the land of *Nanook* the polar bear. And of many other strange things: Dog-teams, igloos, seals, six months of daylight and six months of dark. My wife and children found the life exciting and I enjoyed the independence of my command, eight hundred miles from my next superior in Winnipeg. I was promoted to colonel and had more than 3,500 people under my administrative authority. These included Army, Navy and Air Force units, elements of the U.S. Strategic Air Command (SAC) and of the U.S. Office of Aerospace Research. Canada's winter warfare school was under my command and a constant stream of soldiery came to take the various training courses or to conduct weapon and equipment experiments under near Arctic conditions. We lived some miles above the tree line and for eight months of the year laboured under conditions of snow, blasting winds, 'whiteouts' caused by blowing snow and, sometimes, periods of isolation, when aircraft and even the train could not get through.

Before the NDC course finished the Chief of the General Staff, Lieut.-Gen. Geoffrey Walsh, came down from Ottawa to address us and to be our guest for a luncheon. It so happened that I was sitting directly across from him at a long dining table. During the luncheon I said, "Sir, why is it that I, an infantryman, have been selected to command Fort Churchill when for many years past it has always been an officer from a technical corps?" It was a foolish question.

"I'll tell you why Galloway", the Chief replied, "It is because the commanders from the technical corps have done such a good job and put the place in such good shape, that I decided any damned fool could command it now."

British Army units came to Fort Churchill for cold weather training. Once, two companies of the Royal Scots flew in, forty-eight hours out of Aden on the Persian Gulf where the thermometer hovered at 120° Fahrenheit. At the time we were 40° below zero with a wind chill factor giving an equivalent of 60° below. It was quite a change in temperature for the Scots. It was a dangerous climate in deep winter and death by freezing was not unknown.

While I was commanding Fort Churchill the Cuban crisis occurred. President Kennedy went on the air and stated that the Soviets had missiles in Cuba that could reach Hudson Bay. This put the local community of Churchill, some three miles from the Fort, into a state of nerves. The Mayor phoned me and asked what I was going to do about the vulnerability of the citizenry. I told him there was nothing anyone could do, as constructing atomic shelters in the permafrost and rock of the area was impossible. We were, however, a vital unit in the whole North American defense setup. A squadron of air-to-air refuelling aircraft was on alert on a moment's notice at all times and after Kennedy's speech I was responsible for the security of the SAC airfield. This caused a domestic crisis, as next morning, when my batman did not appear to carry out his daily household tasks, my wife's schedule was put off. I had to tell her that he was out in the snow with a rifle, ensuring that no saboteurs were trying to blow up one of the heavily fuel-laden American aircraft!

After two years as Commander of Fort Churchill I was returned to Ottawa for a course in German, pending my appointment as Military, Naval and Air Attaché to the German *Bundeswehr*.

Again, my family enjoyed a marvellous experience. We lived on the Rhine, and, from our upper windows could see the Petersberg, the Drachenfels and the Siebengebirge. Up and down the river the barges and the pleasure boats plied their ways. We loved the Rhine and enjoyed the opportunity to visit almost every corner of Germany, including isolated West Berlin, which we did several times. My duties took me by chauffeur-driven staff car to various German armed forces units, installations and headquarters and it was exceedingly interesting to hobnob with my enemies of twenty years before. At the American Club in Bad Godesberg, a suburb of Bonn, one ran into people such as General Adolf Galland, Hitler's chief of fighter command during the Battle of Britain, General Westphal, who was Rommel's chief of staff in the Desert and General Hans Spiedal, who was von Rundstedt's chief staff officer on the Westwall. These men were now civilians, in one business or another, but usually with international links. One of my daughter's school fellows at the Nikolaus Cusanus Gymnasium was the grandson of General Hans Guderian, the great Panzer Leader.

Visits to France, Italy and the United Kingdom, as well as to Belgium and the Netherlands were frequent. People of great importance were met on numerous occasions. I spoke with De Gaulle in Paris, was greeted by Adenauer shortly before he died and attended cocktail parties along with such former Nazis as Hitler's financial wizard, Hjalmar Schacht and *Der Fuehrer's* personal aircraft pilot, an undersized female named Hanna Reitsch, one of the last persons to see Hitler alive in his Reichstag bunker.

Adenauer's life had been a strange one. He had been Lord Mayor of Cologne in November 1918 and again in May 1945 when the victorious British had occupied his city, making it the headquarters for their army of occupation on both occasions. By the 1950s he was being hailed as one of the architects of post-World War II Europe. Several months after meeting him, I stood with my family on the banks of the Rhine near our home in Bad Godesberg and watched the old Chancellor's funeral ship, his coffin flag-draped on the open deck, proceed upriver from his funeral service in Cologne Cathedral to his burial place at Rhöndorf. One of my friends, Capt. Eric Brown, of the Royal Navy, stood beside the catafalque as one of the NATO guard of honour. One sometimes wonders what our wars were all about.

My peacetime soldiering had many rewards. Although the excitement of United Nations' tasks in such places as Egypt, Israel and Cyprus were denied me and I missed out on any posting to our NATO Brigade, whereas in the course of thirty years some of my friends had several tours with this force, I did manage many trips to Europe and across the U.S.A. While in the Directorate of Combat Development in the late 1950s we frequently conferred with our 'opposite numbers' in Washington, London or Paris.

I never became a General, but my 47-year career in the Canadian Army was not without compensation. After I retired from the Regular Army the Governor General's Foot Guards honoured me by having me appointed their Honorary Lieutenant-Colonel. The Honorary Colonelcy was always vested in the Governor General himself. I held the post for ten years and it enabled me to visit our affiliated regiment, the Coldstream Guards, for the "Trooping" on Horse Guards Parade, or more private ceremonies in the grounds of Windsor Castle. In fact, every year for nine years I was in England to visit the Guards in London, or at their depot at Pirbright.

One of the nicest compliments I received was an illuminated address from the U.S. Office of Aerospace in Washington, which read in part:

The Officers and men of the Office of Aerospace Research salute your leadership and cooperation, vital to the successful operation of the Churchill Research Range. We admire and appreciate your professional competence and high sense of duty.

I always found my American associates to be generous and grateful for services rendered in a way that seemed beyond the capability of our own people. I often thought that if the Americans were organized on the British military system as the Canadian Army was in my time, their natural enthusiasm and attitude would make them far superior to a force that was either 'straight British' or 'straight American'.

The immediate and even the later postwar years brought me many letters from former comrades of all ranks. Two, in particular, I still treasure. The first, written on February 28, 1947, was from Major Walter Roy, a former fellow-officer who had seen considerable fighting as Battalion Intelligence Officer and then as a Company Commander. He wrote: "In any other Battalion but ours, you would have had a DSO on your handling of the Bn. when we hit the enemy that 'Colossal Crack'." He referred to the Ortona fighting under Montgomery in December 1943. Naturally, I appreciated his assessment, exaggerated or not.

There were others in the RCR who were also short-changed on tokens of appreciation for their efforts. Roy himself was one of these and, had he been awarded the Military Cross, it would have been well deserved. As it was, he died about ten years after the war from lung trouble brought on by a chest wound he received the day we landed at Pachino. Another who could have worn a DSO knowing he deserved it, was Major Sandy Mitchell, a tough fighting officer who did far more than his share in every battle from Pachino to the Gothic Line. He, too, ended the war with nothing to show for it. No officer in the RCR received a DSO during the war, though most infantry battalions and armoured regiments scored six or seven. It was perhaps a perverted form of regimental one-upmanship!

I remember Des Egan relating an incident in Northern Italy, when he and his platoon were crawling down a ditch on the side of a road on their way to assault a house that was occupied by the enemy. Suddenly, a *staghound* from one of our armoured regiments raced up the road and, on seeing the line of tin hats in the ditch, stopped abruptly. The lid opened and out poked an officer's head. "Where's the Hun?" he barked out at Egan. "In those houses", answered the infantry sub, pointing in their direction.

"Christ!" said the man on wheels, who wore a crown on his shoulders. With that the vehicle turned about and raced back from whence it came. Egan claimed that a couple of months later he read that this particular major had been awarded the DSO for conducting on that date "a daring reconnaissance which pinpointed the enemy's hidden positions." Egan, who was recommended for the Military Cross but never received it, had good reason to be peeved.

284

1979: From the Mayor of Rimini, Italy, a silver medal.

My second letter was from an ex-Private, James A. Chalmers, living in Vermilion, Alberta. Writing on September 16, 1954 he said, "It isn't likely that my name will mean anything to you now, or did it ever. But after seeing your photo in the *Edmonton Journal* last night it brought back many pleasant thoughts of days gone by, from the time you joined the RCR until I left to return home. Especially those days when you were acting commander. Most of us had hopes of your being our Colonel in Italy."

Neither was I forgotten in Italy. In 1979, on the 35th Anniversary of the liberation of the City of Rimini, in which The Royal Canadian Regiment played a not inconspicuous part, I was invited to be the official guest of Rimini to take part in several commemorative ceremonies. For me the climax of the visit was when, in the presence of a large concourse in the city's 15th Century *municipio*, the *Sindaco* (or Mayor) presented me with Rimini's *Medaglio d'Argento*. Much handclapping and shouts of '*Viva il colonello!*' humbled me a bit, as my part in the city's liberation, thirty-five years before, had been a minor one indeed. However, the fact that I was the city's official guest, cheered by the populace, accommodated for three days in the Hotel Grande with everything found — even with chit signing privileges in the hotel bar — was something to remember.

And so, the memories remain or return. Some bitter and some humorous. Some are merely just humdrum, about the conditions we lived under, the decisions we made or had made for us, and the experiences we will never have again but which flash in and out of our minds from time to time! The bully beef we ate endlessly; the raw Italian wine we gulped down as an aid to merriment; the laughter and the voices that have been stilled these thirty-five to forty years; the blisters on our feet, the aching shoulders from the packs on our backs; digging for our very lives with picks and shovels; moments of fear and hours of boredom, an entire lifetime compressed into a few unbelievable years or months. For most, there was little chance for personal individuality. We looked so much the same. Hair was clipped short and all the faces had a "Yes, Sir, No Sir" look under the rim of a tin hat. I hated tin hats.

Tin hats always soaked my hair with sweat, marked my forehead with nasty red marks and made my neck tired. I only wore mine when the current colonel happened to be one of those people who was a stickler for regulations. We had several of those. Luckily, none of them was very often in my vicinity.

But tin hats were sometimes useful. You could carry eggs in them. And some chaps I knew, who were particularly sensitive about certain parts of their anatomy, used to sleep with them over their crotches.

Once in Tunisia, during a rather fierce German attack against a Wog farm our company was occupying, a Bren gunner as related earlier was firing his weapon out a window when he was knocked right off the butt of his gun and thrown against the wall behind. He had been hit clear in the middle of his tin hat and the hat had been sent spinning across the room. When he retrieved it there was a dent in the

286

metal — and there was also a bump on his forehead. He replaced it back-to-front, so that dent and bump wouldn't coincide. Grabbing his Bren he went right back to the old business of squeezing the trigger to achieve the recommended bursts of four or five rounds. He kept it up until the enemy withdrew. That is, except for the three or four bodies that lay in rather grotesque, recumbent poses along his erstwhile line of fire. He was a little fellow with beady eyes, a rather long nose and very red cheeks. About 20 years old, I would say. His work that day was good throughout, superior in fact. That is why Rifleman F.E. Janes, of the 2nd London Irish Rifles, was shortly afterwards allowed to add the letters M.M. after his name.

My own experience with a tin hat was catastrophic. I was carrying it slung on my water bottle when I got caught in a barrage outside the Italian village of San Marco on the road to Campobasso. I grabbed the damned thing and jammed it down over my forage cap to save my head from possible damage. I got hit in the small of my back exactly where I would have been protected by the helmet, had I left it where it was! I was carried out on a stretcher several hours later by Cpl. V. Driscoll and another stretcher bearer who placed the helmet on my stomach, so that I looked like a mud turtle that had twisted around in its shell.

Bayonets, like tin hats, are another hallmark of the fighting infantryman. One entry in the Regiment's War Diary for September 1944 reads:

"Great dash was displayed by "D" Company, who went in with bayonets fixed in perfect extended line according to the best infantry traditions."

There's nothing like fixed bayonets to give an infantry attack its finishing touch. But a bayonet charge is a thing of the past, or almost so.

The description in the war diary was by an onlooker, an artillery FOO, so it can probably be believed. Whether the bayonets were 'wetted' or not is another story. After all, it is the threat of the bayonet, rather than its actual use that makes the enemy run.

It is claimed that the Royal 22nd launched a platoon-sized bayonet assault in Sicily. Apart from these two, I have never heard of a Canadian bayonet charge during World War II. Perhaps some took place in France or Holland after D-Day.

There is a reason, of course. In WW II the main infantry tactic was a battle drill movement based on the Bren group applying fire and the rifle group moving around to outflank the enemy. Modern wireless communications made artillery, tank or mortar support quickly obtainable, so the enemy was usually knocked out by heavy weapons before the boys with the bayonets arrived — or else the enemy anticipated the fast response of heavy weapons and quickly evacuated to an alternative position, leaving empty trenches when the Canadian infantry came in from the flank.

My only bayonet experience as I have previously recounted, was in Tunisia where I actually gave the order "Fix bayonets!" and then "Charge!" because there was no other way out. When our ragged line of bayonet men stormed through the farmyard we found no opponents! The supposed defenders were firing from high ground behind the farm, so no bayonets were wetted.

The operations order for our battalion in the Sicily landings contained the remarkable instruction: "Bayonets will NOT be allowed to soak but will be used to kill as many enemy as possible in as short a time as possible." The officer who wrote that line must have had one hell of an imagination. It was either the CO, Ralph Crowe, or the 2IC, Billy Pope.

I have yet to meet a man who actually stuck a bayonet in an enemy. No doubt a lot of bayonet work took place during WW I when the proximity of opposing trenches and the short, sharp trench raids and long lines of frontal attack made the bayonet man as important as the bomber. They were a complementary team in the primitive tactics of hand-to-hand fighting. It was tanks, not bayonets, that got the infantry forward when the enemy stuck to his guns in the second fracas.

Rifles were not used much in WW II. The Bren gun,

the section commander's Tommy gun and later the Sten gun were the personally used killers of the enemy. It might be said that the average Canadian (and British) infantryman did not have too much faith in his rifle. He went into battle with four Bren gun magazines, with his rifle magazine fully loaded and usually with a bandolier of 50 additional rounds in clips of 5. One might assume the 50 rounds were issued primarily for his rifle, but they were mostly used to refill the Bren mags.

The WW II rifle had a screwdriver bayonet, a most unimpressive weapon compared to the old 16¾-inch bayonets used in WW I.

The shiny long bayonet was more threatening than the tiny spike of the second war and more impressive for ceremonial purposes. It was a dramatic moment during drill when the orders "Fix bayonets!" or "Unfix bayonets!" were given. As the flashing blades were drawn from their scabbards and clicked onto the rifle bosses in unison, the front rank bristled like a knightly pageant of old. When they were unfixed the effect was almost as stirring. Not so with the pitiful little screwdriver we used in Hitler's war.

Besides, the oldtime drill pigs loved the complicated movements to tip the rifles with steel: "When I says 'Fix' you don't fix. But when I says 'Bayonets,' you whips 'em out and whops 'em on." Nothing could sound more military.

We speak of two world wars, but it was really one war with a 20-year armistice in the middle. Like a play, it had two acts with an intermission, an unhappy time for me because I had missed Act One. So, when Act Two began I was there — tin hat, webbing and all.

Twenty years meant some changes. Our khaki was now called battledress, and it had no buttons to shine. But we still had to obey orders. A few of my comrades wore medal ribbons from the Kaiser's war. In Western Ontario one volunteer was issued the same rifle he had turned in when he was discharged at the same depot 20 years before! He remembered the serial number.

There was no generation gap. There was a generation

overlap. Old soldiers and young soldiers understood one another. It wasn't much of a singing war because we didn't march in fours. We marched in single file, well spaced, along the ditches. Air attacks were the new menace and troops hobnailing on surfaced roads were easy targets.

Some of our updated weapons dictated new tactics. Movement rather than lack of movement shaped our daily lives. But as men we were almost the same fellows as those of Great War vintage. Not quite as tough, they told us, for the years between had urbanized Canadian youth. And the motorcar era had softened it. But as compensation we had a mobile attitude giving us a new battlefield pattern, a winning one. And one with fewer casualties.

It was when we came home that everything seemed changed.

In 1919 those of us who spoke English were British in outlook. There were few New Canadians. Citizens of foreign origin had yet to enter into the mainstream of national life. There were only about two million isolated French-Canadians. We were a nation undivided, or so we thought.

The only cloud on the 1919 Canadian horizon was the war-enriched U.S.A. pouring its endless all-American propaganda across our border. We were bombarded by their movies, their yellow press and a new gadget — the radio. All three weapons took their toll on the rugged Canadianism that had shaped our Confederation.

After 1945 other things happened. Our population jumped and we found our French-Canadian compatriots had almost doubled their numbers. Next came postwar immigration and the emphasis on multiculturalism. In 1945 things weren't that much different from 1919.

But in the 35 years since VE-Day we have become a new-look nation. Seeds of discontent have blown in with the winds of change.

Today we are a nation divided and our next war could be a civil war. There are 23 million Canadians, almost twice the population since boys from Quebec, Ontario, Manitoba and Saskatchewan died on the beaches of Dieppe together. Almost six million Canadians speak French. There are millions of New Canadians who know and care no more about Canada's sacrifices in two world wars than we know about the circumstances that brought them within our shores.

I remember seeing Lord Byng in 1922, the year that, at a Manitoba war-memorial unveiling, he said:

"There they stood on Vimy Ridge that 9th day of April, 1917; men from Quebec stood shoulder to shoulder with men from Ontario, men from the Maritimes with men from British Columbia, and there was forged a nation tempered by the fires of sacrifice and hammered on the anvil of high adventure."

People believed him.

Forty years later, on Remembrance Day, Gov.-Gen. Georges Vanier said on television: "I have never been so proud of my compatriots as on the battlefield. Having lived with them in the trenches for three years I proclaim their valour." He spoke of his own World War I regiment, which English-speaking Canadians call the *Van Doos*.

No one disputed him.

Later, Vanier said: "Cherish not the digressions which divide us, but the major bonds of shared heritage and common values which unite us."

He uttered a challenge greater than two world wars. It is a challenge Canadians of every origin must be prepared to accept. If not, two generations of our compatriots will have died in vain.

In these days Canadian soldiers are flown back and forth across the Atlantic to their NATO and United Nations duties in aircraft. Such travel was in its infancy during the Second World War. I remember how surprised I was, late in 1944, when an officer who had been back in Canada on a staff course rejoined us as we rested in billets near Rimini. He told me he had flown from Canada to the U.K. and then down to Italy in the course of two or three days. I could hardly believe him. Canada had seemed so far away.

Troopships in anti-submarine convoy usually moved in a zig-zag course across the Atlantic and this took many days.

"Trooping", as was called the dispatching of soldiery to theatres of war or more frequently to Empire garrisons during the days of Britain's imperial might, introduced most Regular soldiers and all those in wartime expeditionary forces to extended travel by sea. For the men, at least, this was not a pleasant experience, as they were always crowded together below decks. During both world wars the German U-boats made the journey dangerous, though relatively few troopships were actually sunk, due to the Royal Navy's magnificent convoy system. In this system the Royal Canadian Navy played a most conspicuous part. The seamen who crewed these merchant ships underwent a dangerous war.

In 1937 I sailed across the Atlantic as a cattleman on the SS *Dakotian* and returned on the SS *Sularia* as a galleyhand. Both these Donaldson Line cargo ships, each of about 4500 tons displacement, were torpedoed and sunk during the war.

The pleasure liner *Oronsay* took me to Britain in 1940, shortly after it was badly damaged by aerial attack in Norwegian waters. Whether *Oronsay* survived the war or not, I don't really know. I was told that it was eventually sunk. In those early days the troopships were not as packed with soldiery as they were later. Steward service was still available to the military on some of them and I recall a white-coated Merchant Navy man asking me one seasick morning if I wished him to draw my bath. "You can paint it in oils if you want to," I replied with immature wit, "but I'm staying in this bunk."

The Dutch ship *Marnix van Sint Aldegonde* took me to Sicily's offshore waters from the Clyde. Later it was sunk off the coast of North Africa. And the RMS *Duchess of York*, in which I went from Liverpool to Algiers and back was not only harmlessly attacked when I was aboard, but on its previous journey had taken bombs down its funnels, causing much damage and some loss of life.

To be a merchant seaman then was to be in the war's front line 24 hours a day, not knowing what danger lurked beneath the waves. And, if you were on an oil tanker, one torpedo or one mine prong could send you out of this world in one huge flash of fire. They were heroes, those mariners, from the moment they weighed anchor until they returned for a short leave before another voyage into danger.

If two of the three ships on which I crossed the Atlantic were sunk and one damaged; if one of the two which took me to the Mediterranean was sunk and the other damaged, then the percentage of Merchant Navy ships sunk by enemy action must have been fantastically high.

Maj.-Gen. Sir George Burns, Colonel of the Coldstream Guards, presents the author, then Honorary Lt.-Colonel of the Governor General's Foot Guards, with a drum major's mace, as a gift from his regiment to the author's, on the occasion of the GGFG 100th anniversary, 1972. Colonel Smyth-Osborne, Regimental Lieutenant-Colonel commanding the Coldstream Guards, looks on.

Sometimes, I wonder what the war did for me. For five years my Regiment was my life. One wise man has said: "Men die, wars end, but the Regiment lives on." I have often thought how true that is. Men, thousands of them, pass through a regiment. Each group or generation in its turn *is* the Regiment. But as that group or generation diminishes and finally passes from the scene altogether, it is discovered that others have taken their places and that the Regiment still exists. A regiment, therefore, is not only a gathering of this day, or that. In its ranks march the ghosts of Yesterday and across its files fall the shadows of those who will march with it Tomorrow. Those who wear its badges one day are but the custodians of its treasured Past, and it is their honour and privilege to add something to it, ere they in turn pass it on to the younger, more vigorous hands of the Future.

No man can soldier forever. Some are dead and buried while still little more than recruits. Others leave the ranks to tend their broken bodies, or nurse their injured minds. The hardy and the lucky soldier on. But the time comes eventually when each and every survivor has to think in terms of a phrase from the old pre-war *Manual of Military Law* . . . "I will soldier no more, or words to that effect."

GLOSSARY OF ABBREVIATIONS

BM — Brigade Major
PPCLI — Princess Patricia's Canadian Light Infantry
MM — Military Medal for Bravery in the Field
REME — Royal Electrical and Mechanical Engineers
ENSA — Entertainments National Service Association
RHLI — Royal Hamilton Light Infantry
RCOC — Royal Canadian Ordnance Corps
Bde — Brigade
Bn — Battalion
TCV — Troop Carrying Vehicle(s)
RTO — Railway Transportation Officer
OC — Officer Commanding (of a Company, Squadron, etc.)
LIR — London Irish Rifles
CQMS — Company-Quartermaster-Sergeant
NAAFI — Navy, Army and Air Force Institute
CSM — Company-Sergeant-Major
MMG — Medium Machine Gun
FDL — Forward Defended Locality
LMG — Light Machine Gun
CIGS — Chief of the Imperial General Staff
GOC — General Officer Commanding
LO — Liaison Officer
IO — Intelligence Officer
PLDG — Princess Louise Dragoon Guards
CO — Commanding Officer (of a Battalion, Regiment, etc.)
ADMS — Assistant Director of Medical Services